Henry Robert Addison

Recollections of an Irish police magistrate and other reminiscenses

of the south of Ireland

Henry Robert Addison

Recollections of an Irish police magistrate and other reminiscenses of the south of Ireland

ISBN/EAN: 9783337114862

Printed in Europe, USA, Canada, Australia, Japan

Cover: Foto ©Andreas Hilbeck / pixelio.de

More available books at **www.hansebooks.com**

RECOLLECTIONS

OF AN

IRISH POLICE MAGISTRATE

AND OTHER REMINISCENCES

OF THE

SOUTH OF IRELAND

BY

HENRY ROBERT ADDISON

(FORMERLY OF THE SECOND DRAGOON GUARDS)

AUTHOR OF

"WHO'S WHO," "STORIES OF INDIAN LIFE," "THE DIARY OF A JUDGE,"

ETC. ETC.

LONDON

WARD AND LOCK, FLEET STREET

MDCCCLXII.

Dedication.

.NOT AS A WORTHY TRIBUTE,

BUT AS A SINCERE TOKEN OF FRIENDSHIP,

THE FOLLOWING SLIGHT SKETCHES

Are Dedicated to

JOHN HENRY LAW, ESQ.
OF URMSTONE HOUSE.

BY HIS ATTACHED FRIEND,

THE AUTHOR.

L'ENVOI.

AT a moment when the horrors of agrarian outrage, and those of base assassination, threaten again to fill the South of Ireland with just terror—when not only has it been found necessary to send down a special commission to inspire terror and promptly bring the bloodthirsty offenders to justice; but, above all, when more than one grand jury have recorded their doubts respecting the efficiency of the present police system, it certainly cannot be an ill chosen opportunity to place before the public some accounts of those misdeeds which at a former period disgraced and paralysed the greater part of the province of Munster, and which were then put down by the effective and strong exertions of the local magistrates, many of whom still live, and still possess the powers of their youth, powers which they would doubtless display, if properly called on to exhibit them. The gentlemen who now honourably hold the commission of the peace in Limerick, Clare, and Tipperary, are men of undoubted courage, energy, and intelligence. An appeal to them would at once arouse them; and though (perhaps from personal attachment) I believe I never saw so clever, so wonderful an officer,

both in the detection of crime and in the punishment
of it, as Thomas Phillips Vokes, yet I have no right
to do otherwise than to believe that there may be
many others now alive capable, if encouraged, of
equalling his, as yet, unrivalled powers.

His Excellency, ever on the spot where the interests
of Ireland call him, has made the opportunity of at-
tending the meeting of the Agricultural Society in the
South a pretext for addressing the landed gentry. He
has told them (and he doubtless believes it) that the
police are efficient, and do all that men can do. But
he does not attempt to disprove the one glaring fact,
that in making them mimic soldiers, they have become the laughingstock of those whom they can now
no longer pursue in secrecy; or that in loading
them with a very heavy rifle and a long bayonet-
sword, they utterly destroy their activity and shackle
their motions; and, above all, that the system of
reporting direct to the Castle in the *first* instance
destroys every hope which would arise in the locality, of
instant aid in the detection of crime. If this be
doubted, let the impartial reader turn to the recent
case of Walsh, who wandered through the county for
several weeks with impunity, and was only brought in
to prison when he thought fit to surrender himself; or
the still more disgraceful fact of the escape of Hayes
from a crowded hotel, and through a crowded town,
in the middle of the day, and in the sight of hundreds
of people.

I am not, however, going to write an essay on this
subject, though volumes might profitably be filled by
it, since the impunity which attends the horrible acts

committed in the South of Ireland is the true and real source whence all the crimes of the ill-disposed portion of the peasantry spring. I am only about to narrate some few of the scenes which came under my personal observation many years ago when Limerick was in its worst state.

I have, as far as possible, given real facts, but have, generally speaking, suppressed all names and circumstances that could tend to wound the most sensitive feelings. That I may have committed some errors it is very possible, for the majority of the events occurred some thirty years ago, and I now write from memory, having never kept a diary. But I believe that on the whole, making a trifling allowance for the necessary embroidery with which every author ornaments his works, these sketches will be found to be "*strictly true.*"

H. R. ADDISON.

September, 1862.

CONTENTS.

RECOLLECTIONS

OF AN

IRISH POLICE MAGISTRATE.

MY HERO.

THE magistrate to whom I allude in the greater number of my sketches, was commonly known as *Major* Vokes; not that he was a military man, but I believe he was entitled, when the post of "police magistrate" was first instituted, to bear this comparative rank in the table of social precedence laid down as between civilians and military men ; and hence almost all the officers at first appointed police magistrates were thus designated. But as Major Vokes became better known and more generally spoken of, his Christian name was quoted, and *Tom* Vokes was the appellation by which the most intelligent magistrate that ever graced the Limerick (or any other) bench, became popularly known. Thomas Phillips Vokes, of whom I now write, boasted his descent from an old French family, spelling their name in the same manner in which a noble family of the present day now write theirs ; and T. P. Vokes always believed that by thus changing the spelling his name his grandfather, Sir Richard Vokes, had lost a chance of obtaining a title, then, and still, extinct.

1

But all this matters little to the reader, who probably only desires to learn the condition of the south of Ireland some thirty or forty years ago, when Limerick, Clare and Tipperary were in a state of decided insurrection—when encounters daily took place between the soldiery and the peasantry—and when the local magistrates, panic-struck by the murder of several of their body, petitioned the Government to grant them official aid.

At this time Vokes was an unpaid magistrate, resident on his small property, which he held under lease from his relative, the Earl of Carberry. But his activity, his fearless energy, had already drawn on him the attention of the higher powers. A ruffian, styling himself Captain Rock, had become the terror of the county of Limerick; and so fearful had been the deeds that he had committed, that the faces of women and children blanched at the mention of his name, and men cared little to risk their lives in an attack on this bold marauder even when supported by soldiers and police. Vokes, however, rather laughed at their fears, and ineffectually endeavoured, on more than one occasion, to meet this terror of the neighbourhood face to face. In some way or another his wish was always baulked, and he failed to encounter him.

One evening in autumn, Mrs. V. having business in the city of Limerick, drove over there in her jaunting car, accompanied by the wife of another magistrate, the two husbands agreeing to accompany them on horseback. At the instant, however, of starting, the gentlemen were detained to transact some pressing business, and as the ladies were unwilling to be overtaken by the shades of night, they at once started, their protectors promising soon to overtake them. So away they went, the distance only being about seven miles.

Vokes, after having discharged his portion of the duty, found that his friend would be probably detained an hour or two. So, mounting his horse, he galloped on to overtake his wife, whom he believed to have nearly reached the end of her journey. On arriving, however, at a short distance beyond Patrick's-well—a village situated some five miles from Limerick—he came up with his wife, who in an agony of fear related to him the fact, that she and her companion had just been stopped by two footpads and robbed of their watches, rings, and purses; and added, that while one tall, fine-looking peasant, armed with a stout cudgel, and a knife conspicuously stuck in his belt, had thus rifled them of their property, the other robber had presented a loaded blunderbuss at the head of the driver, and compelled him to remain quiescent. These facts the coachman (an old retainer) fully bore out.

"Was he tall? Had he very black hair, and a slight cast in his eye?" abruptly demanded the Major.

"Yes, yes; but had we not better hasten on?"

"Can you recollect—had he black stockings, and a frieze coat?" earnestly demanded the husband, inattentive to everything else.

"He had. But——"

"Faith, there's no buts. Here, Tim, take my horse," throwing the bridle to the coachman. "Which way did they take?"

"Over that way. Sure, yer honor! I see one of them,

I do believe, yonder across the bog, going towards the mountains. Faith, I think I could direct the police after them," said the driver. But ere he had well concluded his sentence, the magistrate had loudly exclaimed, " *By Heavens, 'tis he !*" and leaping the dyke beside the road, in the next instant he was seen rushing across the field in the direction pointed out—only turning round once to wave his hand, as an order to his servant to continue his route into Limerick.

It is far beyond the powers of my pen to paint the agony of the lady who thus, as she believed, saw her husband rush recklessly into the jaws of death. It is beyond the graphic delineation of a mere narrator to describe how earnestly she screamed after him. Suffice it to say, that when she found her efforts to call him back ineffectual, she proceeded into the city, and waited on the authorities, who instantly sent out parties of police and military to look after the bold but imprudent magistrate, who had thus pursued the object of his unceasing vigilance, the notorious Captain Rock ; for such the robber, from the description given of him, was now believed to be. But all in vain. The parties, one after another, returned, and that night and the next day passed without any intelligence respecting the missing magistrate. He was already mourned as a fresh victim to the lawless wretches who then held the south of Ireland *in terrorem*. On the second morning after the robbery had taken place, an order was received by the police officer in Limerick, to send four men to Patrick's-well station-house to receive a prisoner of importance. The order was signed T. P. Vokes. All who heard of it expressed their wonder at his escape. Several of the most influential persons in the city accompanied the party out to the village, where they found the worthy magistrate stretched out in a deep sleep; his clothes torn and covered with mud, his face and hands unwashed and his head uncovered, for his hat was gone. But even in his slumbers he grasped tightly in his hand a loaded horse-whip, the only weapon he had carried with him in his perilous pursuit. The first echo of approaching footsteps aroused him. He started up, and with a cheerful smile at the alarmed countenances of his friends, led them into the next room, where, guarded by two policemen and bound by strong cords, sat a prisoner, whom Vokes announced as Captain Rock, the bold, the terror-striking brigand, known by this *soubriquet*, his real name being Fitzmaurice.

Vokes seldom alluded to his deeds of daring, and it was with difficulty the following facts were elicited from him. It appeared that after an hour's severe running, the magistrate came to a cottage where, from certain indications, he found the robbers had partaken of some drink. Convinced of this, he again set out on his arduous pursuit. He came within sight of them, and the lesser peasant, armed with a blunderbuss, turned round and fired, but missed his aim. He then threw away the arm, as it encumbered his flight, and instantly separated from his companion, the latter taking his course towards the mountains. Vokes, on arriving at the spot where they had thus taken opposite directions, took up the blunderbuss and followed Fitzmaurice (for now he was convinced that the robber was no less a personage) towards the hills. It was night, however, before he reached them, and ho well knew there was no chance of overtaking the fellow in the dark; so he fearlessly entered a cottage, where he was hospitably received, and had a comfortable bed of straw afforded to him. Vokes often laughed afterwards at this incident, as he felt fully convinced that he was there sheltered under the impression that he was one of the gang—a belief which his thorough knowledge of Irish strengthened. At daybreak he was again on foot, and ascended the mountain. Here he frequently arrived within a few hundred yards of the man he sought, but each time was disappointed in taking him. He, however, recollected that he had an old and attached follower who had a hut half-way down the mountain. Telling two or three peasants—whom he affected to believe loyal—that he found that the capture was impossible and that consequently he would return to Limerick—he began to descend as night set in, and, as he had well surmised, Rock was soon apprised of his desistance from further pursuit. Vokes, however, had no intention of thus abandoning his prey. So, after thus publicly retracing his steps for about a mile, he suddenly turned aside and entered his tenant's cottage, where he was welcomed, and the doors and windows closely barred, lest his presence might be betrayed. At daybreak he again awoke, and was about to resume his chase, when the farmer's son came in and mentioned that he had just passed Fitzmaurice descending towards Adare—indeed, that most notorious character could scarcely be half a mile off at the moment. Vokes did not hesitate, but rushed out, and being on the higher ground, soon perceived the object of his search. He had turned round, and was now, for some reason or other (known only to himself), re-ascending the brow of the hill. Vokes, as quick as thought, hid himself behind a projecting rock in the path over which Rock must necessarily pass. In a few minutes more he did so, when, suddenly starting out, the bold Major jumped forth, and before the ruffian could look round, had presented the muzzle of the *unloaded* blunderbuss at his head, commanding him to surrender. The other, believing that the next moment would be his last if he ventured to resist, and being wholly unarmed, at once surrendered, and allowed Vokes to pinion him with his horsewhip, which he still retained, and which, bound strongly and tightly with his pocket-handkerchief and another which he had found on the person of the prisoner, completely fettered him. This done, he marched him down to Patrick's-well, taking care to avoid every cottage, every spot, where any of the peasantry were likely to be found, well knowing that they would rescue their captain (as they styled him) if they could. With the blunder-buss—which, being without ammunition, was completely harmless—pointed at him, Vokes marched the boldest brigand that ever infested the south of Ireland nearly three miles, and lodged him in the hands of the police.

Within two months, Fitzmaurice (alias Captain Rock) was tried, convicted, and executed in the city of Limerick—a city whose inhabitants had long trembled at the very mention of his name.

Such being the unexaggerated facts recorded of this wonderful capture—to which others of a minor description might well be added—it is a matter of little astonishment that the then Government of Ireland offered the post of chief magistrate of police to Thomas Phillips Vokes, who subsequently so fully justified their choice, that a considerable income was accorded to him ; that all the powers conferred by Sir Robert Peel's Act were bestowed on him ; that the expenses voted for secret-service money were often left to his discretion and lastly, that when he retired—worn out after thirty years' service—he was allowed a pension for life of 1200*l.* (*Irish*) a year.

He is dead and gone, and a new style of magistracy and police, under the Constabulary Act, have taken the place of his system. That the present mode of repressing crime and detecting offenders is ineffective I think the outrages which now daily occur, even at the moment I am writing, and the mode in which well-known murderers escape their just doom, most plainly show. But the few following sketches are meant merely as a picture of crime in Ireland as she was— not as she is : to portray the state of Munster, rather than give a memoir of my friend.

That T. P. Vokes was estimated, not only in his own country, but throughout the whole British empire, the following paragraph, which appeared in the *London Illustrated News*, most fully certifies, and at the same time bears out the facts given in the preceding sketch :—

"*In our obituary of last month we recorded the death of Thomas Phillips Vokes, for upwards of thirty years the chief magistrate of police in Limerick, a post conferred on him for his daring courage and extraordi-*

nary exertions in putting down the rebellious attempts which threatened the south of Ireland in 1820 to 1822. Mr. Vokes, at that period a country magistrate residing on his paternal estate, single-handed and unarmed, seized the notorious Captain Rock, the terror of the whole district. During three days and nights he pursued him through the mountain fastnesses of Limerick, and at length having captured him, brought him in and lodged him in the county jail. He was soon after tried, convicted, and executed. When Munster was paralysed by the murder of Major Going and others—when magistrates shrunk in natural terror, well knowing the fatal consequences of activity — when harassed authorities, worn-out troops, and ill-organized police held back from a task of no ordinary danger and toil, Thomas Phillips Vokes boldly stepped forward to put down crime, and bring the violators of the law to instant and summary punishment. He claimed descent from the Vauxes, Lords of Gilsland, and in this belief he was borne out by the fact of his grandfather, Sir Richard Vokes, having originally spelt his name Vaux. Three times were the thanks of Government tendered to this officer, accompanied (on two occasions) by substantial pecuniary marks of approval. He was the last surviving magistrate under Peel's Irish Police Act. By his death a pension of 950l. a year reverts to Government."— October, 1852.

THE BIRD'S NEST.

To those only who have long resided in Ireland can be
known the horror inspired by a "process server,"—
the abhorrence with which these poor men are looked
upon by every Patlander. In this quiet and orderly
country, the man placed in "possession" of your property by the formalities of the law is not only considered as the mere tool of a superior power, but is
often, very often, well treated. Nay, courtesy goes so
far, that he is frequently asked, during his forced
sojourn, to join in all the meals and other comforts
which the house affords. Not so in the sister country.
The unhappy man sent in to do this unpleasant duty
is not only ill-treated and abused, but often becomes a
victim of murderous ferocity.

One of the most remarkable illustrations of Irish
feeling occurred some thirty years ago in the county
of Clare, when a gentleman of high standing, good
estate, and old family, was so irritated, that, on his
house being taken possession of, he actually got up in
the middle of the night, and set it on fire, thus periling
the lives of the two poor officials in charge. That which,
however, made the case still worse, was the attempt
on the part of the incendiary to cast the blame on the

"men in possession;" from which charge, however, they perfectly cleared themselves, and Mr. —— was fully committed for setting fire to his *own* house, a somewhat strange occurrence; but several cases of thus destroying the security of creditors having lately occurred, Sir Robert Peel deemed it necessary to make it a felony. Mr. —— was the first party indicted under the new act, and would undoubtedly have escaped, had he not (as we have said) endeavoured to destroy two innocent men, basing his accusation on his own personal observation. This was thought so horrible that the law was allowed to take its course, and Mr. —— was hanged in Ennis, as an example to deter those who would thus savagely avenge their own irregularities on the heads of those who had never injured them.

This striking fact, however, seemed to have little effect on the bloodthirsty nature of the Irish peasantry; for in the journal I was now reading there was a dreadful account of a murder committed (or, rather, discovered the day before) on two keepers, near Kilmallock. The bodies of the unfortunate men were found in a small river, about a mile from the farmhouse they were supposed to be in possession of; and steps had been taken to make it appear as if they had perished by accident; but this belief was at once destroyed by their skulls being found battered in, and their faces so disfigured with blows, that it was a task of great difficulty to identify them.

The account given by the farmer's family was very clear, and the testimony of each member of the circle agreed so consistently, that their evidence was scarcely to be doubted. It appeared from their statement, that the two men had taken up their residence in an adjoining barn, and that one of the daughters had carried them their frugal supper the evening before. They then seemed well primed with whisky, and might be supposed to be in possession of still larger supplies of this intoxicating beverage. The general belief of the family was, therefore, that the two poor fellows, having got drunk, fell asleep, and, on waking, walked across the fields, to bathe themselves, for the purpose of washing away their debauch; but, unfortunately, not being quite sober, they had fallen in, just where the stream was most rapid and deep, and thus fell victims to their intemperance. The wounds on their head they supposed must have been caused by being dashed against some rocks, past which they had been carried by the stream.

The story seemed to the local authorities to be somewhat improbable; but, on strict investigation, they found the footsteps of two men clearly imprinted in several places between the door of the barn and the river, where they again appeared on the muddy and slippery bank. The whole house was examined over and over again; but no weapon, no instrument of death, or cause of suspicion, could be discovered. Forty-eight hours were fruitlessly employed by the local magistrates, the chief constable, and the coroner, in seeking for some evidence; but all in vain. As a last resource, they wrote to Vokes, in Limerick.

Of all this—beyond the paragraph in the newspaper—I heard nothing till the entrance of the chief constable, who arrived, bearing the invitation to my intelligent friend to attend.

" Well, Mac, as they wish it, I'll go ; but you may
depend upon it, it's as the people say. These fellows
got drunk, and slipped into the river. I'll order my
carriage directly, and you and my relative here can
drive over with me."

I began to make excuses.

" Oh, don't be getting out of it ! If you'll come
along we'll touch at ——, and I'll show you the finest
stud of horses in Ireland. Come, don't be fancying
that there's any danger this time ! I'm only going
over to see my brother magistrates. By-the-bye I'd
like to introduce you to some of them. There's no
cause of alarm to any one here, is there, Mac ?" turning
to the police officer.

" None in the world, Major. Sure, if there had been
anything, we would have discovered it without
troubling you."

" You're right ; but as they ask me, we'll just run
over ;" and in half-an-hour more, we were *en route.*

I confess I was not comfortable. Vokes was far too
jovial to please me, and he laughed at the idea of this
murder so loudly, and pooh-poohed it so strongly, that
I felt he was not sincere.

When within three miles of Kilmallock, he, as usual,
got out of his carriage, and mounted on horseback,
making me and his officer do the same. To my
surprise, we found Sergeant M'Grath and six mounted
policemen waiting for him. The chief constable
seemed more surprised than myself. If there really
had been a murder, a larger force ought to have
been called out. If the death arose from accident,
surely no policemen were requisite. The Major,

however, made no remark, and we trotted across the country, followed at a distance by the constables and the carriage. I adhered to my old rule of asking no questions.

Presently we came within sight of the farmhouse where the bodies were lying. It was surrounded by (at least) 5000 persons, many of whom seemed strangely excited. I could not but feel a sensation of terror as I looked upon this lawless body. I believe my countenance must have betokened my alarm, for my relative gave me a reassuring smile. He then directed his sub to join the policemen, with directions to bring them round to the rear of the building, and jumping off his horse, motioned me to do the same. I confess I did so with reluctance, and when I handed the bridle to the boy, who had undertaken to hold the animal, I must needs admit I would have willingly dissuaded Vokes from entering the crowd, who, as he approached, gave three *groans* for him—a welcome they poured forth with all the venom of their souls, for many amongst them had reason to dread his power. The major took off his hat with a smile, and laughingly thanked them, then plunged into the midst of them. Vokes had only a riding-whip with him, and this instrument he did not hesitate to use, when any one attempted to bar his passage, or press too closely on him. Unless I am egregiously mistaken, I read murder and vengeance in the eyes of many. But a secret and unconquerable dread of the chief magistrate, who boldly looked them in the face, seemed to restrain them.

At length we entered the cottage, in which a couple

of magistrates and several policemen loitered. These functionaries assured Vokes that, after a most lengthened and minute inquiry, they could obtain no clue to the perpetrators of the horrid deed.

The Major next interrogated the family—a more intelligent circle I never saw in humble life. They gave their evidence clearly, and one of the poor girls burst into tears as she told her story. She it was who had last seen the poor fellows now lying dead in the adjoining barn. Vokes, after hearing their account, told them he should doubtlessly require their testimony at the approaching assizes in Limerick; to this the whole family, consisting of the father, mother, a son, and two daughters, readily assented.

He next inspected the bodies of the poor men, and when a brother magistrate pointed out to him the probability of its having been a mere accident, the chief magistrate seemed to assent.

I now hoped all was over; but my relative again turned into the house. After examining again and again the rooms upstairs, he returned to the spacious kitchen. Here about a dozen persons were assembled. The room itself bore a look of comfort. There was a good clock. The crockery and saucepans were clean and ranged along the wall. A goose sat hatching her eggs beside the fireplace. A large house-dog, apparently well fed, slept before the hearth. It was one of the cleanest Irish kitchens I ever was in.

Vokes suddenly called to a policeman :—

"Pull that goose out of her nest. That's right. Take out the eggs. Ah! What is the nest made of?"

"Some linen, Major," replied the constable.

" Let us see it, Maloney," and the next instant the
man held up a large linen sheet saturated with blood.
It was now dry, but there was no mistaking it.

"Seize the whole family !   Handcuff them, and off
with them to Limerick.   You may take my carriage,
if you like it.   McGrath, jump upstairs, and, in the
little room on the right, you will find two hocky-sticks.
Take care how you handle them, for there is blood and
clotted brains that must not be rubbed off them ; and
now, Mr. Martin, I think we have you," said he, turning to the farmer.   "No words ! off with him."

"But, Major," interrupted one of the local magistrates, "Martin is a tenant of mine, and a highly respectable man.   Besides, he is —"

" A murderer !"

"You are mistaken—I'll bail him—"

" 'Faith, my dear friend, you can't ; and what's more,
you shan't.   If I'm wrong, I'll take the blame.   Egad,
Harry, I have them," said he, turning to me.   " We'll
be off before the people outside are aware of it," and
out we went.   The people, however, seeing us without
escort or prisoners, believed that Vokes's mission had
failed, and welcomed us cheerfully as we passed through
them.   No time, however, was to be lost, and even
before we were well out of sight of them, their frantic
cries showed they had learned our acts.

On the subsequent trial, one of the sisters having
turned approver (or, as we call it, King's evidence),
declared that she had not only seen, but assisted in the
murder.   Drugged heavily with whisky, the unsus-
pecting men had fallen fast asleep, when the son and
two daughters stole in with the hocky-sticks (produced

in court), and battered out their brains. They then tied their bodies in a large sheet, and the father and son carried them to a spot at least a mile down the river, where they threw them in. A faint picture of this girl—who now without shrinking described the assassination, and by her proved evidence gave her whole family to the scaffold—I have sketched in the next chapter.

About six weeks after the above scene in the farmhouse, I was ordered out with my troop as an execution party (a military duty only, I believe, exercised in Ireland) and as I could get no one to change with me, I was compelled, much against my own will, to see old Martin, his wife, his daughter, and his son, hanged over the gateway of the new prison in Limerick.

OUR COTTAGE NEAR LIMERICK.

My father-in-law had asked me most cordially to pass a few days with him in his suburban residence. So on my arrival from Dublin, I ordered my hired car to drive me out to Rathran; and here I arrived at about eight o'clock, p.m., one fine evening in the month of September. The air was chilly; the light was fast declining; I was tired, and was jolted to death by the bad roads I had traversed. No wonder, then, that I hailed with joy the father of my wife, who, sitting before a blazing fire, was making steady inroads into a cooper of Sneyd's best claret. As I entered, I suddenly imagined I had never seen a more perfect picture of enjoyment. Major Vokes was a good-looking, intelligent fellow, and his countenance—like a frontispiece—bespoke his many good qualities. But there was a *bonhomie* in his smile, as he pronounced the "*Caid mille faltha*" which at once warmed the heart, and guaranteed the welcome he professed.

For about half-an-hour we chatted cosily beside the enlivening flame, and arrived at that stage of perfect contentment, when men least wish to be disturbed. In a word, we sat in that perfect tranquillity and bodily repose which only Englishmen know—and they only when, with their handkerchiefs over their knees, they sip cool claret before a burning fire. At least it used to be so. On a sudden, Vokes started, jumped up, and rang the bell.

"You will excuse me? The fact is, I have an important witness to examine. Will you pardon my leaving you, or shall I have him in here?"

"In here, by all means."

"Send Michy O'Hoolaghan in!" said he to the servant who entered.

The servitor disappeared; and in a few moments one of the most extraordinary men I ever saw, entered. He was short, ill-clothed, and lame. His head was out of proportion, and his face decidedly plain; but he threw out bright glances from eyes—so bright, so intelligent—that it was impossible to doubt his talent, while the sneering leer which often accompanied these looks, made one naturally shrink in terror from him.

He now shuffled into the room, and stood sheepishly awaiting the orders of Major Vokes.

"Well, Michy, my boy, are you ready to sail for America?"

"Sure you know that I am that same."

"There's a fine ship of Spaight's sailing on Monday."

"Oh, sure it's I that know it, and hope your honour 'll send Biddy and I in it. But they tell me young Moore is going in her; and if so, I can't; for sure it was his father I hanged when I turned approver. Sometimes I think I was wrong——?"

"Don't make an omadthawn of yourself. Here, take a glass of potheen. Sure, you're better now! Ay, I thought so. Now, tell me what you've got from the girl?"

"May I spake?" and he leered knowingly at me.

"Go on," said the Major. "It's all right—it's my son-in-law. There, sit down, and tell me all about it, and divil a lie; for, by the cross, if you tell me a lie you'll never see Ameriky."

I closely observed that, as Vokes wished to gain confidence, he increased his Irish accent.

"Is it me—glory be to *her* soul!—is it me would tell your honour a lie? God speed your honour! Do you think that I'd turn upon the man that saved my life, and has fed me ever since? Not I. The Heavens forbid. But, to tell you the truth, I couldn't get spache of Biddy M'Grath to-day. I've not been very well, and I've scarcely left the guard-room."

"Oh, then, you've not been out all day?"

"Not I, fait."

"Michy, Michy," said Vokes, shaking his head and smiling, "you're a bad boy, I fear; you would deceive me?"

"Not I, nor the likes of me. I'll swear on the Book I've never stirred beyont the walls."

"Where did you drop this knife, you roofer? Nay, don't tremble and start. I know all. You met Biddy in the back garden, and she gave you the note which you have in your right-hand pocket. Yes; it's there. Don't shake and lie any further. It comes from Father Anthony, and desires you not to betray the girl. You need tell me nothing."

Down went Michy on his knees, pale with fright. I began to fidget; and I verily do believe I shared, at that moment, the general belief that Vokes obtained his information from some infernal source.

"Oh, your honour's glory, don't be hard on a poor boy."

The fellow was fifty years old; but they all style themselves boys in Ireland.

"Stand up, you bosthoon, and if you don't tell me the whole truth, by my soul—and you know I don't swear false—you shall see the inside of the county gaol before two hours are over. It's not a traitor I'd nurse in my own house. Sergeant Ready (in a moment the Sergeant appeared), take Michy out, and bring Paddy Malone in. He'll tell us the truth. So good evening, Michy O'Hoolaghan."

In a moment the wretch seemed to recover. He sprang to his feet, and roared rather than spoke.

"Is Paddy Malone here? Oh, then it's all up. Oh then Major, it's not Paddy you shall trate with. By the soul of my mother, I'll tell you the truth—I'll tell you all. But don't let Paddy turn approver! Oh now, Major agra, you'll listen to me, won't you? and his voice assumed the tones of supplication.

"Well, we'll see; sit down again. Stand behind him, Sergeant Ready, and if I nod, take him off, and bring Malone. Harry, my boy, take a glass of claret. Now, Michy, begin."

Michy fidgetted for a time, and then slowly spoke.

"Sure, I happened to be strolling down the back garden, and quite by accident I met Biddy M'Grath."

"That's false; you went by appointment." And Vokes nodded to the Sergeant.

"Come along, Michy," said the policeman.

"Arrah, not so; I knew I was lying—your honour's right. Only let me stay, and I'll spake as I would to my clargy. ·(Vokes nodded.) Well, then, you see, I met Biddy in the lower summer-house, and she tould me all. It was her brother—you recollect Jerry, Major? Well, it was Jerry who held the cow-keeper down, while Biddy and her mother finished him with hurley sticks."

" And how could Jerry hold him down so easily?"

"Sure he gave him lashins to drink; and then he took him into the Linnie, and made him a nice straw bed; and when he was fast asleep, Jerry stole in and stunned him with a big stone, afore the women set-to, and they finished him entirely; for when the body was found in the river, it was two days before it could be recognised, the head was so nicely mashed up; and even your honour—great glory to you!—would never have 'dentified him, hadn't you found the process paper in his pocket; and then you knew who it was."

" Well, I knew all you told me before from Malone. So no thanks to you. Malone it was carried the body down to the river. He'll make a good witness."

" Arrah, your honour, then, wouldn't take that thief's word before mine? Sure, I've a right to the reward. Wasn't it I that cajoled Biddy to come here? and isn't it I that tould her you'd do her no harm? and ain't she ready to swear that the Macmahons did it? and ain't she plased with the kind way she's treated? and if I did not tell you at once, wasn't it for fear of Father Anthony? and sure I'd not have tould you now, only as Paddy Malone is here, it's all over; and I claim to be approver."

" Does Biddy know that you communicate with me?"

" Not at all. She believes I'm kept here to keep me from the O'Kellys, against whom I swore."

" That will do."

Vokes nodded, and the witness was led out of the room.

" There goes the greatest villain in Ireland. I'll try a glass of toddy. The fellow makes me sick."

" Who and what is he ?"

" He is what we call an approver. Without such means we could never succeed in obtaining information in Ireland. The history of the fellow is simply this : He and his foster father were taken up for burning an old woman in her cottage, and strangling a poor child that endeavoured to escape. The case was clear, but we had no direct evidence. I sent for Michy; I treated him as an agent, and never pretended to suspect him. I gave him every luxury. One fine day, I committed him to the gaol, and desired him to be rigorously treated. I affected to have heard some details, and accused him direct of the murder. The charge was too startling for him. He believed I had evidence to convict him. He at once turned approver (or King's evidence, as you call it in England), and on his testimony, corroborated by less important witnesses, his foster father was hanged. Since then he has wormed himself into the confidence of several ruffians, and betrayed them. He has joined conspiracies, and enabled me to crush them. Michy is a good tool in his way."

" And can you sleep beneath the roof with such a villain ? I strongly suspect he'd have even thrown you over, if you hadn't got hold of his partner in crime, this Paddy Malone."

"Ha! ha! ha!" roared Vokes; "come, that's good. Why, Paddy is safe in New York. He escaped me."

"He's not here, then?"

"Not a bit; I only wish he was. I merely hinted at it to make Michy let out the truth. But the little rascal is getting so false that I'll send him off, after the assizes, to America. He can't remain safely in this country. If unguarded, his life would not be worth four-and-twenty hours' purchase. So he's bound hand and foot to serve the Government, who will now, probably, give him some twenty pounds and a free passage to New York. I confess he'll be a loss to me. But now you shall see another sort of individual. Sergeant Ready, bring in Biddy M'Grath;" and in a few moments his orders were obeyed.

The girl who now entered was one of the loveliest specimens of Irish beauty. She was neatly, almost coquettishly dressed. Her brown hair flowed down her back, and as she bobbed a curtsey to the Major, I really thought I had never beheld anything so enchanting as her smile—so full of truth and innocence.

"Come in, ma colyeen; come near the fire, and tell us, have you any news of Paddy Malone? (I started.) I've made every inquiry, and I think he may be in Dublin. We'll want his evidence to convict the Macmahons. They'll never be found guilty without more witnesses."

"Sure, Major, I'm here; and I saw them dragging the body across our field as clear as I see you."

"But your evidence must be supported, and Paddy cannot be found. Take a glass of toddy, you look cold! By the bye, have you not a mother? Where is she?"

"It's myself don't know; I think she's gone to England."

"That's a pity; for, you see, it's no use taking up these Macmahons; they'd get off without a second witness. So, Biddy agra, you can go back to-morrow, and I'll institute fresh inquiries myself."

"God be good to us,—you wouldn't think any one else done it?"

"Well, I don't know. I'll go to Rathkeale myself, and inquire into it."

The girl turned deadly pale; the Major listlessly sipped his grog.

"Good night a coushla," and he made a sign to dismiss her. She lingered.

"Stay, Major. Sure, as your honour says, my mother was with me, and so was my brother, when we saw the Macmahons dragging the murdered man across the field."

"Well, but where are they?" suddenly demanded Vokes.

"At the cross-roads in Cratloe Wood?" replied the girl, who the next moment seemed bitterly to repent her candour, and would have withdrawn her statement. She again and again declared she had made a mistake, and the Major apparently believed her. Sergeant Ready rose and conducted her out.

"What a lovely creature!" I involuntarily ejaculated. "How young and innocent! Surely she cannot have offended?"

"Listen! That girl, her brother, and her mother,

committed the most frightful murder, only a few weeks ago, that ever disgraced Munster. This was one of the girls whom Michy told you, just now, battered out the brains of a poor process-server with hurley or (as you call them) hocky sticks. By the bye, I've left the identical sticks in your bed-room; see that they are not touched, for there is a portion of the brains and hair of the victim still sticking to them; they will be produced in evidence. This girl was the most savage of the party, and even struck the face of the corpse, when about to be thrown into the water, to prevent its recognition. She now wants to accuse some neighbours, who have deeply offended her, of the crime, and hopes to see them executed. But she's quite mistaken. After her confession to Michy, there'll be no difficulty in getting her to turn round; so I think now the case is complete. But I see you are tired."

He rang the bell. "Take a light into my son-in-law's room, and send in Corporal Vesey." That functionary arrived.

"Take four mounted men; manage to arrive about two o'clock in the morning at the cottage near the cross-roads in Cratloe Wood. Bring Matty M'Grath and his mother. Don't let 'em speak to each other; and lodge them in jail, with orders to keep them 'solitary' till I see them in the morning. Be off!" and away went the Corporal.

I now sought my bed-room, and found the Major's English valet waiting for me. From him I learned that the " gentle murderess" slept in the next room, and that Michy had a room to himself over the kitchen;

half-a-dozen other witnesses, generally speaking, murderers, slept over the guard-room—for so was the wash-house called—where four policemen sat up all night, as the cottage would probably be some night attacked. There was a recently-mended hole in my shutter, through which a ball had been fired (for I must tell you the whole cottage was on the ground-floor, bungalow fashion), and in the corner I beheld the hocky sticks made use of to destroy a human being.

Shall I say how I slept? and when I slept what dreams I dreamt? No. Suffice it to say, I never spent a less pleasant night, and that I unhesitatingly refused to prolong my stay, though earnestly pressed to do so by the hospitable Major, at breakfast next morning.

After the meal, I drove back to Limerick, while Vokes went to examine his newly-arrived friends in the county gaol.

CARRICKSHOCK;

OR

A PLEASANT EXCURSION.

"HARRY, my boy, you have never been in the county of Waterford?"

"Never!"

"Well, then," rejoined my gallant relative, Major Vokes, "you have now a good opportunity. I have some little business to transact there, so I've ordered my travelling carriage at six in the morning. We shan't be more than two days absent, therefore don't bring much luggage. The weather is remarkably fine, so we shall have a very pleasant trip;" and away went my excellent friend, whistling a cheerful air.

Now, although Vokes took my assent for granted, I felt somewhat doubtful about accepting it. That I had often expressed a wish to see the county into which he was going, I fully admit, and for this single reason, I suppose, he felt certain that I should snap at his proposal. But on the other hand, though I fully intended to see Curraghmore, yet I was by no means desirous of becoming the travelling companion of a man against whom a thousand oaths of assassination had been recorded; and as we were about to traverse Tipperary, a notoriously ill-disposed county, and

going to a spot hardly fifteeen or twenty miles from
tho scene of the most savage butchery that ever disgraced the annals of Ireland, namely, the murder of
nineteen policemen and their officers, which had only
taken place at Carrickshock the week before, I seriously hesitated about accompanying Vokes. So far
from it, I should (in any other case) have not only
given it up myself, but have endeavoured to dissuade
the worthy magistrate from his contemplated journey.
I well knew, however, in his case, that the more
vividly I pourtrayed the danger, the more delighted
he would feel in courting it ; so I held my tongue, and
after dinner allowed myself to be persuaded, partly by
coaxing and partly by the fear of being laughed at,
into joining my friend. We accordingly started the
following morning ; and after traversing the wretched
bog which stretches itself between Limerick and Tipperary, arrived in safety at the latter town without
meeting with any occurrence worth noticing.

Vokes ordered a substantial breakfast, and appeared
in high spirits. He did not, however, tell me the
object of his mission, and I refrained from inquiring.
That it was a pleasing one I drew an inference from
his cheerful manner, and I already began to laugh at
my foolish fears.

The meal over, we descended, and to my utter
surprise I found two horses, ready saddled, standing
at the door. The carriage had returned to Limerick ;
we were to complete our journey on horseback. I
should probably have asked some questions, but Vokes
enforced silence on me by a look, so we mounted
and trotted off on the road to Nenagh, which my

friend readily found, from the directions afforded to him by the ostler of the hotel, a most respectable-looking young man. We had scarcely, however, proceed above three miles, when Vokes turned, without any apparent reason, down a cross-road, and rather increased his speed.

"What are you about? Where are you going?" cried I.

"Why, to Waterford, to be sure!"

"Why, I fancied you had changed your mind, and had intended to go to Nenagh—at least, so you said."

The Major burst out laughing. "Harry, I didn't think you were so soft. Why, couldn't you see, with half an eye, that the ostler was a bad boy—a spy—so I threw him off the scent, by coming round this way. By this time there's more than one carbine loaded to shoot me on that road. Don't be flustered, there's no danger here. Yonder is the main road, and Sergeant Magrath waiting for us."

We were now joined by that active policeman, who was well mounted, and admirably dressed as a groom. He had, however, a pair of holsters, out of which a brace of pistols appeared; but as many country gentlemen in those days carried arms, when riding through the disturbed districts, this fact did not betray the sergeant's calling.

When we came to a certain spot, just beyond the thick woods of Banshea, Vokes paused: "There's Lismackew; just in that corner poor Baker was murdered, in the middle of the day." I confess this little statement, and a subsequent full detail of the assassination, with which my friend favoured me as we rode along, did not add much to my comfort, and I began to wish I had remained within the Barracks at Limerick, where I was at this time quartered.

Presently, a carriage dashed passed us, surrounded by police. These men I recognised as belonging to Vokes's especial force; they, however, took no notice of him, but galloped away in eager haste.

" Bless me, Major ! what does that mean ? "

" Oh, it's Quin, the approver ; they are taking him to Kilkenny, to give evidence against Kennedy, the chief murderer at Carrickshock, who will be tried the day after to-morrow."

" But is this witness so unwilling as to require this guard ? "

" By no means. My men surround the carriage to protect him ; and even to do that they would not be able, if they had not relays of horses to enable them to gallop all the way. They go through no towns, and they travel too fast to be overtaken."

" But why ? "

"Harry, my boy, you're as green as any Englishman I ever met. Don't you see, that if they could be caught, they'd soon be surrounded, and the approver dragged out and torn to pieces."

I shuddered, and rode on to Clonmel without uttering another word. Here we remained for several hours, Vokes evidently wishing to arrive late at Pilltown (the cleanest and prettiest village in Ireland), which he now condescended to tell me was to be our ultimate destination ; and where, according to his settled plan, we alighted at Anthony's snug hotel, about nine o'clock the same evening. We supped, and went to bed. The room in which I slept was, however, unfortunately, near the stable, and I was awakened more than once by hearing the voices of several persons conversing in a foreign language. This, though an annoyance, but did not utterly destroy my slumbers; I was thoroughly tired; and I did not rise till nine o'clock next morning. Vokes was seated at the breakfast-table when I entered. He had evidently received and despatched several letters before I came down. He was sending off a mounted policeman as I opened the door.

After our meal, Vokes proposed a stroll through the village, at the same time expressing his intention to call on some of the cottagers, whom he well knew, as he had resided, for some time after his marriage, at Belline, a very handsome mansion in the neighbourhood, formerly inhabited by the brother of his wife, then acting as agent to the•Earl of Besborough, but who was now abroad. We entered a very pretty cottage, and, to my surprise, I found the interior as clean and neat as any similar establishment in England. It appeared that the noble landlord insisted on this—he might spare a man who could not pay his rent—indeed, he often did so. But he inexorably evicted a dirty or a drunken tenant, and thus made Pilltown the prettiest and best village in the South of Ireland.

The old woman whom we called to see was almost blind, but she instantly recognised Vokes, and to him she related her griefs. Her grandson (a policeman) had been killed at Carrickshock, and she now hoped "the Major" would get her a pension from Government. She evidently believed he was all-powerful;

and I fancy she was not very far wrong in her conjecture.

In the next house we found two handsome girls. They had similarly lost their father, and the magistrate elicited important information from their loquacity. I now began to observe that my friend was anxious to ascertain the details of the affair, for in every cottage we visited he managed artfully to derive some information on the subject. On two occasions the doors, as we approached, were slammed in our faces, and I could not help remarking that we did not meet a single male during the whole time we were out. On these points I questioned the Major; who explained to me that the owners of the two residences, where we had been excluded, had both fallen at Carrickshock; but as they belonged to the murdering party, their relatives refused him admission—looking upon him as a dangerous monster. I expressed my wonder that they should thus be acquainted with his arrival.

"My dear fellow, we had not gone to bed last night, when every soul for ten miles round was aware that we were here, and it's precisely for that reason all the men are out of the way. To-morrow or next day we shall probably see them back."

This was by no means reassuring; and though I said nothing, I felt vexed at the idea of remaining in Pilltown for several days longer, which was evidently Vokes's intention.

During dinner, my friend explained the affair, which he was evidently investigating. It appears that about a week only before the then present time, a party of nineteen policemen, commanded by a chief constable,

3

went out after dark, in order to seize some arms, which they expected to find at a certain farm-house. These men were dressed in uniform, and armed as soldiers, and fine efficient soldiers they were. They each carried a musket, a bayonet, and thirty rounds of ball cartridge; their officer was mounted on horse-back—so of course they anticipated no danger, even in a country where every man's hand is against the law, and where every man (at least it was so in those times) looked upon a policeman as his bitterest enemy.

The party, being disappointed in their search, were returning home towards nightfall, and had arrived at a spot on the mountains called Carrickshock, when they were met by a countryman, who volunteered to tell them where the arms they were in search of lay hid. The chief constable fell into the trap, and ordered his men to turn down a lane, at the end of which the peasant stated the weapons were buried (as is often the case), and to which spot he would guide them. So down they marched, the commander going first, and beside him a civil officer, who had taken advantage of the strength of the party to serve some notices of eviction, under the shield of their protection. The lane did not exceed a couple of hundred yards in length, it was narrow, and had a high bank on either side. It was what is generally styled a "a borheen" in the South of Ireland, and admirably fitted for an ambuscade. Suddenly the guide gave a loud whistle, and disappeared. In an instant the notice-server fell dead ; while on either bank appeared a large party of men and women. Before the policemen had time to come to the "present," a volley had been fired into them, which told with fatal effect. They fired, but it was too late, the crowd had now rushed down, and hemmed them in. The chief constable was one of the first killed, and before five minutes had elapsed, every policeman lay dead or wounded on the ground. The former were mutilated, and dragged about with yells of triumph. The wounded were pierced with innumerable wounds. The arms were seized with avidity, and then the murderers (of whom only three, I believe, were killed) marched off, glorying in the act, and even singing songs of delight. They left behind them the bodies of the civil process-server, the chief constable, and nineteen fine young men, several of whom were natives of this town.

I naturally inquired if the assassins had been seized, as they must be known.

" Known! to be sure they are ; but what's the use of taking them up, when no one will give evidence against them ? O yes, you may be astonished, but such is the state of Ireland. The man's life who identified one of the murderers would not be worth half-an-hour's purchase. So Government has only got hold of one of them, a certain Kennedy ; but although the case is clear against him, although it will be as clear as light, you will see that the jury will not dare to convict him. Even at this instant he is standing before them. But enough of this ; let's go and take a ride. Here, waiter, order our horses out, and request the landlord to come up."

Mr. Anthony appeared.

" Anthony, I am going to take this young Englishman to see Belline, we'll take a gallop through the Park, and be back in two hours. We shall gain appetites by our ride, and would like something nice for supper. It is now eight o'clock, we should like to have it served at ten. Can you get us some trout? and mind there's a cucumber; you know how fond I am of it, and if it's not too late for peas, let us have some."

The landlord (a most respectable man) promised all this should be attended to, and we descended and jumped on horseback. I observed that we had military saddles, and that holsters were attached to each. After the narrative I had just heard, I confess I was not astonished at this; nor was I so, when I subsequently found that Sergeant Magrath had a sword on, under his horseman's cloak.

We rode direct through the grounds at Belline, and then went on to a road which led abruptly up the mountains. There was a wooded angle which hid the onward course of this mountain pass. Vokes walked his horse round it; but no sooner were we out of sight of the main route, than he uttered an exclamation in Irish, and galloped on. The Sergeant did the same, and of course I accompanied them.

" Ride faster, man, ride faster, we shall be missed; keep up, Sergeant!"

" But why this haste?"

"You ride for your life; if they overtake us, we are dead men; and even as it is, there may be parties out looking for us! Ride on, man—don't spare the spur!" And thus we galloped on over six miles of the most hilly road I ever met with. Vokes now pulled up. "Harry, my boy, I think we've distanced them;

so now walk your horse a little, for we have a long ride before us."

" My good and respected relative, are you gone mad, or what does all this mean ?"

" Simply this. I clearly heard the voices in the stables of which you spoke this morning."

" Why, you denied it."

" Yes ; fearful of alarming you. The fact is, they assembled last night for the purpose of destroying me. But as they thought it might prejudice Kennedy's trial, they put it off till to-night. At eleven o'clock they are to shoot us as we sit at supper. The Sergeant is to have his brains knocked out. In fact, every arrangement is made. Let me see, I find by my repeater it is past ten ; they are now beginning to assemble, and will soon miss us ; so we have no time to spare."

" But how is it they were so incautious as thus to proclaim their plans ?"

" They spoke in Irish, a language I happen to understand. So there can be no mistake about it."

" Had we not better hurry on ?"

" No, no. We are going up a terrifically bad road, let us go as easy as we can, till eleven, and then, as they will have discovered our flight, we must ride as fast as our nags can carry us."

At this moment the moon burst forth, and we saw a ragged, barefooted urchin, close to us ; as is usual in Ireland, he at once joined the party, and entered into conversation. Vokes whispered to me to be cautious. This I thought a ridiculous hint, but still I attended

to it, though his "CAVE CANEM" appeared uncalled
for in the present instance.

"What is the name of the town yonder, Pat?" asked
Vokes, who at once assumed an Irish accent.

"Where, yer Honour?"

"Ah, now, can't you answer without making a bosthoon of yourself? Sure I'm a stranger, and want to
know."

"I'm thinking it's Newmarket! Is it through that
town yer'e Honour's about passing?"—At this moment
the Sergeant's sword clanked. The Major uttered an
exclamation of annoyance. The boy, however, did
not appear to notice the sound, and went on talking.

We now came to a wind on the road; round this we
had to pass, in order to arrive at Newmarket, which
made the distance considerably above a mile, though,
by cutting across the valley, the village might be
reached in three hundred yards.

"Where's the boy?" suddenly cried the magistrate.
We looked round—he was gone; but in less than a
minute we heard three distinct notes whistled from
the centre of the valley. "Ride, ride on, now's your
time!" And away we dashed at full gallop. As we
came in sight of the village, we saw a fine fire blazing
in the smithy, and lights in almost every window;
but as we approached, the smith's shop was suddenly
closed, shutters were put up and every light extinguished. It was evident we were betrayed. "Keep
up—keep up, Harry—that's all right!" and we dashed
at racing pace through the town. We had just cleared
it, when a shot was fired. The ball went through the
Sergeant's cloak, but did not injure any of us. When

we had proceeded about a mile, the Major pulled up.

"There, that will do; we're safe now; there is no fear of their following. There are not half-a-dozen men in the village, or they'd not have let us off so easy. Depend upon it they are all gone to Kilkenny, to hear their comrade tried."

Vokes was singularly gifted with perspicuity. He calculated every chance, and drew inferences from apparent trifles. It was thus he sifted evidence, and seemed almost to foresee occurrences which to any other mind appeared unimportant and improbable.

We had not gone far, when Vokes suddenly turned down a lane; as a matter of course, I did the same: the Major, to my surprise, jumped off his horse, and beckoned Magrath to do the like; then leading their horses up to me, he asked me as a favour to hold them for a few minutes; of course I assented. In another moment the magistrate and the policeman were searching about for something which they appeared to have dropped. They examined about, and' seemed occasionally to pick up something out of the mud. At length Vokes suddenly called out to his Sergeant, "I've found it—I've got it here—this will complete the evidence. If it fits his hand, it will at once convict him. Oh, I'm so glad I've discovered it!" At this moment the moon burst through the clouds, and I glanced with horror at the object which Vokes held up with triumph. It was a human finger, or rather half of one, evidently severed from the hand by a sabre cut. "What have you got?" demanded the Major. "I've a portion of skull with human hair attached to it; I've the stock of a broken pistol, and a knife rusted with human blood," said the Sergeant.

"Providence preserve us!" ejaculated I. "Where are we?"

"In the Borheen of Carrickshock. Don't you see the bank all broken where the struggle took place? This dyke ran with human blood only a few days ago."

"Do let us go on; I don't like this place—it makes me shudder," said I.

"Well, as you like; I've got all I want. Here, Mick, take this finger; we'll fit it on Teddy Malony when we return; you may throw away the skull; but bring the knife along with you. Come, we'll warm ourselves with a sharp trot. We are only about eight miles from Kilkenny, where we shall sleep. *Allons!*" and away we rode.

We were within four miles of the city, when we heard loud shouts, mingled with occasional shots; an extraordinary glare of light was apparent in the distance, and we drew our reins, and reduced our pace to a walk, wondering what it could be. Even the Major was puzzled for a few minutes; at length he divined the cause. "I'll stake my head, Kennedy has been acquitted, and they are escorting him home in triumph." Another ten minutes brought us in full view of the party, and, at the first glance, we read the correctness of Vokes's supposition. Shouting, singing, firing, and brandishing lighted torches, we beheld a body of at least five hundred men approaching. Drunk and in-flamed by passion, they were screaming forth alter-nately blessings on Kennedy, and curses on every constituted authority. In the middle sat the released murderer, who (many believed) had escaped his just doom, in consequence of the fears of the jurymen. He was seated on a small mountain pony, and was supported on either side by female friends, being wholly unequal to sit upright, in consequence of the libations he had indulged in; yet his fair partners still kept plying him with liquor. An Irish bagpiper and a wretched fiddler acted as a band, and thus the procession was made up.

On they came, roaring and capering about in maddened ecstatics. By the glare of their torches, they looked like demons; and my heart sank within me, when I considered how small was our chance of escape. If they caught us, we should instantly be sacrificed. If we turned back, our fate was no less certain. What could we do? In my distress, I naturally turned to Vokes, and, to my horror, saw him smile at some incident which had occurred amidst the approaching crowd.

"We are lost!" groaned I.

"Giggy-ma-gow," replied the Major; "be alive, and there's no danger."

"What shall we do?"

"Follow me!" and, in one moment more, he had cleared a low hedge beside the road. We did the same, and, in another, we were all well concealed by a stack of wheat, which served us providentially as a shield.

On came the fearful multitude; they were now close upon us—they were not twenty yards from us—the slightest indiscretion, and we were dead men. It was

a perilous moment. I do believe I trembled. The
infuriated wretches were, however, far too excited to
think of turning their eyes away from their hero ; and
I can now, in cool moments, believe that even had we
not been thus luckily concealed, they would not have
perceived us.

They were fully five minutes filing past us. They
halted a couple of minutes, to raise a drunken man who
had fallen, and seemed in no hurry to proceed. How
I outlived that period, I cannot divine; my every
pulse seemed to stop, and I certainly did not breathe
—at least, such is my impression.

Without a word, the Major stealthily stole out, and,
about a hundred yards in their rear, jumped back into
the road. He and I succeeded in doing so without
attracting any attention ; but, unfortunately, the Sergeant's sword was loose in its scabbard, and, as his
horse sprang over, it gave a loud " clank."

The crowd at once recognised the well-known
sound; for an instant, they shouted, the "ARMY ;"
in the next, they cried out, the "PEELERS." They
turned round, and saw us by the bright moonlight.
Half-a-dozen shots were fired by them in as many
seconds; but they were far too intoxicated to take
good aim, so none of the balls or shot touched us. A
party instantly quitted the main body, and started in
pursuit of us—a fact by no means pleasant, as these
men, when sober, can run for a short distance almost
as quick as a horse can gallop. " On ! on !" roared
the Major ; and again we started at our utmost speed,
and soon left our pursuers behind us.

In half-an-hour more, I sat at supper, in Kilkenny,

with my daring relative, who laughed at my agitation, and endeavoured to assure me that it was "*nothing at all!*"

"It may be," said I, as I drank his health in a glass of old sherry; "it may be! But if ever you catch me on such an excursion again—if ever I accompany you on such a perilous trip—may St. Patrick withdraw his protection from Erin!"

A QUEER JOCKEY.

"I am glad you have returned to dinner," said Vokes, as I entered his mansion, having spent the previous evening at the house of a friend in the county of Clare. "I am glad you have come back, for I wish to introduce you to Mr. K——, chief constable in the police, one of the most intelligent and one of the bravest fellows in that force. So run up-stairs and wash your hands quickly, and join us at table, for dinner has been already announced." This I did, and was in my accustomed seat before the fish and soup had been removed.

"Allow me to introduce you, my dear Harry, to one of my best friends, and decidedly the best officer serving under me; Mr. K——, 'the Jockey!' "added Vokes, with a laugh.

I rose and bowed, and expressed my gratification at making the gentleman's acquaintance, though sadly puzzled to make out the meaning of the soubriquet which my father-in-law had added to his name.

Mr. K——, I should say, rather *stood down* from his chair than otherwise, for his height was barely five feet; his extremely rounded shoulders still further deprived him of his proper proportions, and almost gave him a look of deformity. His large and sinewy hands gave the surest indication of considerable strength. His clear blue eye, however, plainly bespoke an intelligence of no common order—a talented brow—a rich and humorous smile, won friendship at once, in spite of a certain glance which occasionally crossed his countenance, plainly indicating a strong and determined will. When seated, I never saw a man whose intimacy I would rather have cultivated; when upright, I would have chosen him as my defender against any odds. Like the tiger-cat, though small, he was made to be dreaded, and, like the creature in question, capable of overcoming animals superior to itself in size. Such was Mr. K——, a gentleman still well remembered in the counties of Limerick, Cork, and Tipperary.

Dinner over—our usual quantity of wine discussed—the ladies left us, and then, as was the habit in those days, and, indeed, to tell the truth, is still so, whisky-punch was introduced—not *Jameson's* or *Kinahan's* authorized drinks, but real, good, well-smoked *potheen:* the milk which then freely flowed in Cratloe woods. The steaming kettle filled with hot water — *boiling* hot—which was reckoned absolutely necessary for this beverage, was placed on the table. The lemon, the sugar, and the etceteras were all there, and our hearts soon became warmed with the steaming liquor.

"Hand me the jug, my Jockey!" said Vokes, without smiling.

Mr. K—— did so.

My curiosity overcame my good manners, and I could not resist asking our entertainer "why he thus styled his guest."

"Don't you know   Oh, it's a famous story; but

as we are only three of us together, sure K—— had better tell it himself. Sure you'll tell it, won't you ?"

"Ah, then, Major, I'd rather not."

"Just because you're the subject of it; but never mind. If you won't I will, and then, you know, your modest nature will be more shocked with my praise than any self-commendation you can bestow on yourself. So if it's only modesty which ties your tongue, unloose it, and tell it to our friend—just as it happened."

"Well, then, as I must, I must; for it's better to narrate the simple truth than allow a partial friend like the chief magistrate to colour up the sketch till he makes me out a hero, a character I never intended to play, nor one, which, to tell you the truth, do I ever believe nature designed me to enact."

"Well, go on." He did so.

"It is perhaps necessary to tell you, as a stranger to the South of Ireland, that a very few years ago this county, and indeed all Munster, was not only celebrated for its insurrections arising from political and agrarian causes, but it had also won an unhappy celebrity from the cruelty shown in many of its personal attacks on unoffending individuals. These fearful acts were of daily recurrence. Not a night passed without some dreadful occurrence of the kind. Here the military force was of no use; the local magistrates dreaded to act. He who sought to arrest a murderer, or to convict an offender, was marked out for instant immolation. Assassination stalked along our roads and across our fields. Some of the largest and best defended houses were attacked; no wonder, then, that

the local executive shrank from a duty which, earnestly
carried out, would lead to the wife and children of the
active magistrate becoming a widow and orphans on
the morrow. Our friend Vokes, here, braved every
danger, and to a certain extent awed the 'bad boys'
of this county; but, as I have explained to you, he
almost stood alone. Country gentlemen, unaccustomed to danger, unpaid justices, naturally avoided
the dangerous services now required of them. The
Irish bench is filled, and ever has been filled, by a body
of brave and intelligent men—this all the world admits
to be the case—but daily to risk being murdered, your
family attacked, your property injured, was beyond
the fortitude of even an Irish J.P.

"It was at this time that the dreadful murders of
the O'Sheas occurred, one of the most horrible occurrences that ever took place in Munster. On this occasion the house of a well-to-do farmer was attacked by
a numerous band of ruffians, the doors broken in, and
the house set on fire, whilst, as each member of the
family—even to a young child some five years of age
only—endeavoured to make their escape, they were
savagely butchered and thrown back into the flames,
in which they were reduced to cinders, amidst the
cheers and shouts of the savage crowd of assassins. I
merely quote this one instance of the boldness of these
lawless bands who paraded through the county, to
show how fearlessly they made their attacks, and at
the same time I mention it as it was the outrage immediately preceding the one I am about to quote—
the one which made our friend the Major give me the
soubriquet of 'The Jockey.'"

Here we again replenished our tumblers, and after one or two observations our little friend recommenced his narrative.

"One day I was sent for in haste by Mr. ——, the nearest magistrate, and instantly attended the summons. Here I found several of the first gentlemen of the county assembled, debating with closed doors—for there was little doubt that many of the servants and retainers in gentlemen's families were in league with the ruffians—how best to proceed in a case which had just come to the knowledge of Mr. ——. The case was thus explained to me on my arrival. Mr. ——, it appeared, had received that morning an anonymous communication by the post, stating that the farm-house of his most respectable tenant was that night to be attacked by a band of marauders, and " *sarved* (so said the letter) *just as the O'Shays was sarved*" in the neighbouring county. A threat of this kind might have been treated with derision and levity in more settled times. But in those I speak of, it was looked upon with just alarm, and the magistrates had now met to arrange some mode of defence.

" After a lengthened discussion it was agreed that myself and another chief constable should order our men, one by one, to stroll into the farm-house named, that they should go fully armed and provided with thirty rounds of ammunition each, and that myself and my brother officer should follow them in plain clothes, and when assembled with our men (who would make up a party of some twenty well-tried hands) concoct the best mode of defence in case of the information turning out to be correct. The council broke up, and we each returned to our station.

"It was about seven o'clock when, in accordance with my directions, I entered the farm-house in question, where I found that all the men, as well as my brother officer, had already arrived, but no steps had been taken, as the arrangements were left to me, who happened to be the senior in rank.

"We instantly set about barring up the windows and fastening the doors. But after awhile we slightly opened the shutters in order to enable us to fire at any person approaching. We then placed the females of the family in comparative safety, and assigned a post to the father and to each of his sons, locking up in a sort of a cellar all the servants and labourers—being well convinced that one or more of them were in league with the marauders.

"Eight, nine, and even ten o'clock sounded, yet nothing occurred to alarm us, and many of the party began to smile at our apparently useless precautions, when my sergeant, whom I had placed at the top window, came down and told me that an individual had just crossed the lawn in front of the house, and entered an ornamental shrubbery, situated about one hundred yards distant. My next in command derided the information. But I too well knew the intelligence of my sergeant to doubt the accuracy of his statement, so I returned with him up stairs and looked out. The window was beneath a sloping roof, so we could not be seen by any one outside.

"I was a calm moonlight night—not a breeze ruffled

4

the leaves—all was still, and I had already began to
chide my subordinate for allowing himself to be deceived by the dark shadows of the trees, when I
heard a slight rustle in the bushes, and presently the
form of a human being presented itself. I rushed
down quickly, but noiselessly, and ordering all lights
to be extinguished, I ran to the hall there to await
events.

"Presently a loud knock was given, and on my de-
manding what was wanted, a gentle and subdued voice
replied—'Ah, then, Mr. ——' (naming the proprietor
of the farm) 'my wife is suddenly stricken ill, and
will surely die unless I can get some spirit to give her
—only a noggin, and may the blessing of Heaven
reward you.' This was said in such a piteous tone
that had I not been well on my guard I should have
been deceived.

"'I never open the door after dark," replied I, in a
feigned voice. 'My master has gone to bed, and I
don't dare to disobey his orders.'

"'Ah, then, only for a moment—sure you wouldn't
let a poor creature die for the want of a single drop!
Faith you might trust me—ain't I yer auld friend
Paddy Hogan, and no other?'

"Now it so happened I knew this Paddy Hogan well,
so I altered my tactics, and fastening the door with
the chain, I opened it slightly and peered forth. The
robber appeared delighted, and made a rush to enter.

"'Not so fast,' cried I, 'you're not Paddy Hogan,
or any other honest man,' and I slammed the door to.

"'Bad scram to ye, but ye shall suffer for this!'
said the ruffian, and he instantly discharged his blun-

derbuss through the panel of the door, and then called
out loudly (in Irish) to his companions to come on.
Only one bullet had passed through the entrance. So,
unhurt, I ran up to the first floor and prepared to
receive the 'boys.'

"Through the opening of the shutters I could now
see a large body of men—some disguised, some dressed
in white frocks, some with black crape over their faces,
some in their ordinary clothes, but all armed with
weapons of one kind or another. The fellow who had
fired through the door was in front of them, reloading
his gun. He was about six feet six in height, and very
powerful. He was evidently the leader of the band.

" Confident of success—eager to see the blood of their
victims flow—the wretches now set up a shout of
triumph, and, at the signal of their ringleader, advanced
to attack the premises.

"I instantly gave the word, and half the policemen
(as I had previously arranged) discharged their carbines
into the approaching crowd. A yell of fear-stricken
cowardice, of anger and revenge, a cry of astonishment,
instantly arose, and the robbers at once retreated into
the bushes, dragging with them some five or six men
whom our volley had brought down.

" This was looked upon as a victory by my brother
officer, and several of our men advised an instant sortie.
This, however, I felt would be most imprudent, so I
at once negatived the proposition, and ordered those
who had fired to reload. Scarcely had they done so
when again the attacking party emerged—increased in
numbers, and strengthened by a hope of vengeance.
Their numerical force greatly exceeded ours.

" They commenced operations by a well-aimed volley directed at our windows. The broken glass, and the holes made by several of their balls, bore testimony to their accuracy in shooting. One constable was slightly wounded; the party who had not yet fired returned their salute—showing them that the house was well defended.

" The robbers clearly perceived that they had but one of two courses to pursue : at once to retreat, or by a mighty effort to force their way into the house and try a hand-to-hand combat, in which their pikes, swords, and bludgeons might serve to oppose the fire-arms which they now perceived we possessed.

" The latter plan was adopted, and, with the loss of three lives, they succeeded in forcing the front door, which they burst in under cover of a portico, which, unfortunately, was built over it. In they rushed, and now the combat became terrific. Our carbines, comparatively speaking, were of little use. In the dark we did not dare to discharge them, fearing to destroy our friends, whom we could not distinguish from our foes. At this moment our proprietor fortunately appeared with a lantern, and the sergeant threw open the shutters, allowing the bright moonlight to pour in.

" We could now plainly see before us, and hurrying to form a compact body, we discharged into them, another effective volley. Seriously injured by the volley alarmed at seeing the regular police before them, the peasants beat a hasty and disorderly retreat ; they fled, shrieking out, as our people fired after them. We pursued them only through the portico, where, having got fairly rid of them my brother officer very properly rushed forward and shut the front door, which he now thoroughly secured.

"But, oh! who shall paint *my* feelings when I found I was locked out. If I was perceived by those within I should probably be shot as a robber; if seen by the marauders my death was certain. What was I to do? All this flashed across my mind in a single moment; yet what could I do? At this moment the gigantic leader of the wretches passed me; he probably would stumble on me, and as I was wholly unarmed would murder me. Such was my idea. Besides, I felt that if I let him escape I might be hereafter blamed. After an instant's hesitation, the fellow turned round, having evidently determined on joining his comrades, who were now in full flight. He had only made two paces towards them, when I sprang upon his shoulders, and firmly clung round his neck.

"Surprised and terrified by this novel mode of attack, screaming out in Irish that he had the devil on his back, he hurried on his pace; he evidently ran towards the trees for the purpose of crushing me against them, the only mode, and decidedly the surest mode, of dislodging me. If he did so, I felt that I was lost. Yet what could I do? I was too small to combat with him or bear him down; I was too weak to throttle him. What then could I do? I glanced over every chance of escape; the whole train did not occupy ten seconds. I at once determined on my course of action. I gently withdrew my right hand, and dipping it into my pocket I drew forth a penknife, which I opened with my teeth. Thus armed, I began to feel secure. In the meantime, the great savage had endeavoured to shake

me off; but all in vain. My life depended on my
tenacity; I kept my seat, and defied the efforts of the
monster to get rid of me.

" We now approached a grove of trees; my captor
already felt that he had me—he already calculated on
the certainty of my doom. But in this he was grossly
deceived. I threw my right arm round his throat;
in it I grasped my penknife. In less time than I now
tell it I had cut his throat from ear to ear. The man
attempted to cry out; I stabbed him in the throat and
the face, again and again, and as we reached the trees
(where he had hoped to immolate me) he fell a corpse,
bathed in a pool of blood. I now dismounted, and
glanced at the giant to see if he really was without
life. His staring eye, his fallen jaws, convinced me of
the fact; and now I would gladly have returned to
my comrades, but I did not dare to stir or make the
slightest noise. The band, though dispersed, had probably left some member of their gang in the vicinity.
If I attempted to cross the lawn I should probably be
seen and murdered; if I endeavoured to call to my men
I should be overheard and destroyed. So I had only
to await quietly till daylight in my present position.

" To own the truth, I here passed four hours of the
greatest dread (if I may so call it) that I ever endured.
Those only who have passed a night alone with the body
of him whom they have killed, can imagine it. Look
towards the corpse I dared not; his eyes seemed fixed
fiercely on me. His gaping throat seemed to reproach
me as a murderer. In a word, I felt terrified and
panic-struck beyond description.

" Oh, how I blessed the daylight, which seemed tardy

in its arrival. No sooner had the first ray of light illumined the heavens than the door of the farm-house opened, and a body of policemen appeared, with anxious faces. They left the place in search of their chief constable, whom they believed to have fallen a victim to the marauders. On my shouting out to them they suddenly turned round, and recognising me, gave a cheer of delight, to which my heart warmly responded. Their joy could not exceed mine. In a few moments others came out, when we rushed together to the shrubbery where the ruffian I had destroyed lay bathed in his blood. He was at once identified as the chief rebel of the province. By accident I had killed the terror of the neighbourhood. Government sent me a letter of thanks for my conduct on the occasion, and a handsome present in money. Indeed, I was well repaid for my lucky exertions on this memorable occasion."

"Don't call it luck; it was pluck, my fine Jockey, that carried you through," said Vokes.

"And conferred on me, as you see," said he, addressing me, "the title of 'The Jockey.'"

We drank his health, and soon after the party broke up and retired to rest.

THE TWO LOAVES.

As you approach the court-house, where the assizes
are being held, and long before you pass the threshold
of that important fane, you behold, with astonishment,
the different mode in which law is carried out in Ireland, as compared to the sister country. The Englishman, who has been accustomed to see the hall of justice
only marked out by a dozen well-dressed persons, and
a constable or two being about the entrance, naturally
starts with dismay when he sees, as is always the case
in Ireland, the court-house surrounded by thousands
of anxious and brawling countrymen, shouting generally, and all pressing for admission—a mob who would,
indeed, be dangerous, were it not that every avenue
leading to the interior is strictly guarded by a well-
armed body of military police. Hundreds of them
surround the building, while the interior would cease
to be a hall of justice if one half the area, at least,
were not bristling with bayonets. The National Con-
vention never displayed a more strange picture than the
interior of an Hibernian assize court. That the Irish
bar and the Irish bench have displayed before the world
some of the very finest orators and sound lawyers that
ever graced the robe of justice, all must allow. But
in their proceedings there is wanting that calm dignity,

that almost chilling pomposity, that distinguishes a court of assize in England. Petty struggles are carrying-on in every corner; brawlers are continually being forced out of the hall. The lynx-eyed policeman has just struck, with the butt-end of his carbine, a fellow endeavouring to smuggle whisky into the dock. The jury don't look happy; they evidently wish to make a party affair of it. The barrister pleads hurriedly, and apparently in a state of irritation. He is fairly tortured by the assumed ignorance of a principal evidence. He loses his temper and his dignity together. The sheriff looks in; he happens to be popular, and in the middle of a trial for life and death a cheer is raised for that functionary, which explodes through the building before the police have time to suppress it. In fact, there is that want of silent dignity which awes the Englishman as he enters a British tribunal. To the high and everlasting honour of England be it spoken, that no charge has ever been made, for a century past, of political or religious bias; on the other side of the channel such things have been hinted at, even during the present century. Who is that seated on the bench—that little man whose sharp, intelligent look seems to pierce through the very soul of a doubtful witness? See how he grasps the subject; how he draws inferences from every trivial circumstance, and how with a cutting joke he at once sets down a flippant counsellor, or causes a laugh through the courthouse by a *bon-mot* uttered at the expense of the prisoner, who is fain to join in the general hilarity, though he well knows the same lips will, within the hour, charge the jury for a conviction which entails death. Yes, that judge has the most perfect mastery over every jury. How far he always wields his power properly may be a question of doubt. At this moment he is trying a case of sheep-stealing ; but before the trial has proceeded far he has called up the clerk of the Crown from his seat, and asked him in a whisper whose tenant the prisoner is. "He belongs to the lands of ——, my lord," replies the other, and down he sits. Now, the tenantry of —— are those most violently and politically opposed to the family of his lordship ; so he at once becomes, as it were, a prosecutor as well as a judge. The trial proceeds, and the case is strong against the poor boy in the dock. That he had stolen the sheep was clear, and the crime was in those days never overlooked. The punishment was death, and all foresaw that the wretched prisoner had but a few hours to survive. Relentlessly did the judge charge the jury. He minutely pointed out the strength of evidence against the prisoner. He was showing how fearful, in an agricultural country, was the crime of sheep-stealing, when the clerk of the crown handed him a very small strip of paper. The judge read it, and whispered to this functionary (who sits immediately beneath him), "Are you quite sure, Mr. B—— ?" "I am, my lord," replied the other ; and the judge continued his charge. He went on in the same strain for a few minutes. Then, turning round, he said, "Yes, gentlemen of the jury, such is the crime of sheep-stealing, and he who is guilty of it deserves his fate. If the lad who stands yonder is a sheep-stealer, he deserves to die. The evidence is strong and conclusive against him. But, gentlemen of the jury, pause ere you condemn one so young on such bad evidence. Let us examine the characters of the witnesses ; let us examine their motives ; let us clearly refer to their different statements, and we shall find them conflicting and unsatisfactory. There is evidently much bad feeling in the matter, and I cannot but look upon the charge as a conspiracy, hatched by a body of enemies to destroy a very young man's life. Gentlemen, I must tell you I don't believe one word of the evidence for the prosecution, and I consider that you will do well to acquit the prisoner at the bar." The jury instantly acquitted the prisoner, who seemed utterly confounded when he found himself thus suddenly and unexpectedly acquitted. I afterwards read the slip, which had been torn in two. It merely ran, "*I was mistaken ; the prisoner is a tenant of your nephew's ; his family have all votes.*" The picture may perhaps be recognised.

After a short time, and before the cheers of the friends of the acquitted had ceased to rend the air, Sir M. Barrington and Major Vokes entered the court-house, and took their places amongst the counsel.

It was now clear that a serious case was coming on, and the pressure in the hall was great. Every place was filled up ; some ladies occupied the sheriff's box. Silence was at length proclaimed, and the prisoner to be tried appeared at the bar. Never did I see a poor wretch afflicted with a worse countenance. He was duly arraigned, and finally pleaded " not guilty." Sergeant G—— now stated the case, and a more fearful one I think I never heard. The man was accused of having murdered an old woman, who had long supported him, and her two infant grandchildren.

The evidence appeared strong and conclusive; but the prisoner retained that stolid, stupid look, which the most intelligent Irish peasant can assume when determined to baffle the investigations of his superiors; and so the case went on, occasionally eliciting a sigh of horror from those unaccustomed to such fearful details. The prosecution closed; a momentary pause took place. The counsel turned to converse together, and a few persons left the court. At this moment some provisions were brought to the unhappy prisoner, and after due inspection (as is the custom) were handed to him over the thin spikes which are fixed around the dock. This was going on, when suddenly the voice of Major Vokes rang clearly through the hall. " Sergeant Reedy, stop those loaves. Man alive ! What does he want with two loaves? Wouldn't one be enough for him ?" The bread that the prisoner's wife was handing to him was instantly pounced upon by the police sergeant. It consisted of two ordinary loaves stuck together, as we often see in bakers' shops, and therefore, beyond the fact of the meal being expensive, there was nothing to remark upon. The prisoner, however, started and turned pale. The woman disappeared.

"Sergeant Reedy, bring those loaves here." He did so. "As long as you live, Sergeant, never allow such a folly as this. Surely one would be enough for three of them ;" and while thus speaking, the Major broke the loaves in two. " Oh, what is that—something binds them together ?" He tears them apart, and out drops a pistol. Every one starts in terror and amazement, except the magistrate himself, who coolly examines the weapon. Then turning to the astonished judge, he coolly remarks, "Loaded up to the muzzle, my lord;" and hands him the pistol. In a moment the high functionary is struck dumb with surprise, then recovering himself, he turns to the prisoner, and sternly asks for an explanation. In a moment the wretch throws himself upon his knees: "Oh, Yarry! Yarry! The Lord be good to us. He has a charmed life, and it's no use fighting agin him. Oh then, Major, it must have been the divil himself who tould you about the arms; for barring Biddy, by the cross of Athlone, there's not a living soul knows a word about it. Ah, then, it's Heaven or the divil takes care of Tom Vokes. Holy Mary be good to us—he knows all." And the man's face expressed the greatest agony of fear—if not remorse.

The judge pressed for a further explanation.

"Well, then, your honour's glory, it's no use to lie. Bedad, he's too much for us boys. I'm guilty, and don't deny it; and it's to Major Vokes I owe my being found out. The corpse of the old woman being discovered and all that—sure I knew from the first I'd be condemned. So I says to Biddy — Biddy, agrah,—get Tim Haglan's big pistol, and put it in the middle of two loaves, and when I want food hand them to me, and by the holy Michael—great glory to him—at the moment they condemn me, I'll blow Tom Vokes's brains out, for he's the terror of all the county. But oh, my lord, it's no use, he has a charmed life, and it's not steel, or powder and ball, will kill him! and sure that's enough; I'll say no more," and the prisoner relapsed into silence.

The case went on; the man was committed, condemned, and within a few hours executed.

As I walked home with Major Vokes, I asked him most earnestly if he had had any information to induce him to suspect that anything was concealed in the bread ?

"Nothing at all."

"And how came you to do so ?"

"Upon my life, I can't say. I thought it odd to see *two* loaves handed in for a single meal—the prisoner's hands trembled as he held them out to receive them."

"And you had no previous suspicion ?"

"None whatever. But remember Dibdin's song about the 'cherub that sits up aloft.' It is not the first time that the observation of the most minute trifle has saved my life. But come, Henry, don't be so inquisitive. Walk quickly, it's dinner-time, and I'm as hungry as a hunter."

So on I hurried with my strange relative, he whistling as carelessly, and apparently as unmoved, as if no miracle (for as such I shall ever look upon it) had just occurred, to save his life.

DANIEL O'CONNELL'S ELECTION.

In 1828 Daniel O'Connell publicly proclaimed his intention of coming forward as a candidate to represent the borough of Ennis (County Clare) in the House of Commons. The first announcement of this strange intention was received with derisive smiles and a general expression of doubt. But when the great Agitator's measures were seriously commenced for the purpose of carrying out this object, the then Government got naturally alarmed. Aware of the extraordinary influence which this celebrated patriot possessed, well read in the violent and exciting oratory in which the popular hero indulged, nothing less than a rebellion throughout the south of Ireland could be expected to arise for an occasion like the present, when thousands and thousands of the peasantry would be drawn together and addressed in fiery language on those religious topics, those unjust distinctions which then existed between the members of the Roman Catholic Church and the Protestants of Ireland—a subject which had for centuries caused blood to flow and discord to lift her head throughout the sister kingdom.

I was not surprised, then, when I found that we

(who were quartered in Limerick) were ordered over to keep the peace in the county of Clare. Right and left, orders to the same effect flew about ; and long before the day of nomination a force of some 6000 men were collected in and around the town of Ennis. The officers of the regiment to which I belonged were quartered in Clare Castle, our men and horses in the adjoining village—being thus situated within two miles of the polling-booths. As regarded our personal comforts, I cannot say much for them, being forced (as were all others) to share my ˈbedroom with eight or ten brother officers. But as the duty would pro- bably be over in a few days, we laughed at these and other little inconveniences, and enjoyed ourselves as well as we could. Not so was it with our worthy Colonel, who, with the head-quarters of the regiment, was also present. He had been to Sir C. D., who commanded the whole force on this occasion, and remonstrated with him.

"We are wretchedly quartered, General. Could you not manage to improve our position ?"

"Indeed !" replied the other. "I thought your men were remarkably well put up."

"So they are, Sir Charles ; but our horses——"

"Oh, never mind them," replied the chief, who had always been an infantry officer. "If the men are well off, hang the horses."

"Hang my horses, General ?" screamed the old colonel, who had watched them with a father's eye during two-thirds of his life. "Hang my horses ! No, you can't mean that ! Hang my horses !" and suddenly turning round, the old cavalry officer bolted out of the room, still reiterating the obnoxious fate to which his troopers had been consigned. Some vowed that he did so in tears, while others declared that he gave his men an extra foot parade that evening, to show how he undervalued them as compared with his horses. Be the case however as it may, the General had unwittingly wounded the Colonel in his most sensitive part. He ate little that day at mess, and the adjutant, who sat next to him, assured me he heard him utter, more than once, "Hang my horses, indeed! Hang my horses!" in tones of impassioned indignation.

The mess-man of the infantry regiment legitimately quartered in the Castle (I think it was the Fifteenth), with great ingenuity made up a mess for us all, and really spread a very fair dinner before us, to which we did ample justice.

On the day of my arrival, just as we were sitting down, who should come in but O'Gorman Mahon, the *right* arm—at least, so I believe he styled himself— of Daniel O'Connell. He sat down with us and delighted us with his brilliant jokes and truly amusing conversation. He was the very antithesis to the agitator's *left* arm—Tom Steel, who was certainly, though very clever and well-read, one of the dullest and most melancholy companions I ever met at a dinner table. The great Dan, like Garrick, represented in his celebrated portrait, must have struggled thus between tragedy and comedy : for more different but more sincere supporters, I believe no man ever had.

The cloth was however scarcely cleared away, when the O'Gorman started up, and assured us he must be off to look after political matters. In ten minutes more we heard him galloping out of the yard. We were all pleased with his society, but from that day to this I have never learnt who invited him.

The next day I was occupied looking up quarters for freshly arrived troops. In a few instances this was a disagreeable duty, inasmuch as many persons objected to receive soldiers into their houses, and in these cases we were compelled to quarter them on the unwilling recipients *nolens volens.*

I particularly well remember riding at the head of a party of artillery, to seek shelter for these men, into the park of Barntick—the estate of the, then, Sir Nathaniel Peacock. Sir Nathaniel was abroad—he had been so several years, and probably would never return; so the house was closed up and left in charge of a man and his wife. These two faithful guardians eyed our approach with jealous fear, and on our knocking for admittance, appeared at an upstairs window, from which they demanded to know our business at Barntick.

"I have an order," replied I, "to quarter these men and guns on you."

"Divil a man comes in here, without the order of the agent," growled the man.

"It's no use we sha'n't let you in," screamed the woman.

"Come down and open the door directly. I've an order here signed by the proper authority, and at your peril refuse to admit us."

"To blazes with your authority, and yourselves too. You sha'n't pass the door-sill till you've tasted of my blunderbuss—not if you were the Lord-Lieutenant;

so the sooner you're off the sooner ye'll get back to dinner," and with this joke, which he appeared mentally to enjoy, the fellow slammed the window to, and walked off.

Had I been in charge of cavalry or infantry, I scarcely know how I should have acted. But here the course was abundantly clear. I ordered a pole to be affixed to a tumbril and backed upon the door, which in an instant was shivered to pieces, while the worthy. old couple inside fled in alarm, uttering cries of terror, firmly believing that we had thus entered by force with an intention of murdering them. We had considerable difficulty in coaxing them back; but at length we did so, when they proved most useful in cooking and supplying us with vegetables. They were paid for the. latter. Where those vegetables were obtained was a question which rested entirely between Sir Nathaniel. and his care-taker. All I know is that we paid for. them.

On the following day I was sent off with despatches to Sir Edward O'Brien, of Dromoland, and here I was. received with the greatest courtesy by that gentleman, and thus formed an acquaintance which afterwards proved to me most valuable; since I have subsequently largely partaken of the liberal hospitality of that excellent man—now no more—and enjoyed with. his sons many a pleasant day's fishing in the lake which is situated close to this beautiful castle. It was here that I saw for the first time William Smith O'Brien, who, in after years, played so conspicuous a part in the historical drama of Eriu.

On the day of the nomination, I was desired to

carry a communication into Ennis. When I arrived, I was told that the gentleman I sought was near the hustings. Thither then I turned my steps, and as long as I live I shall never forget the sight that met my view. I have since seen many, many elections. I have even stood before them as the principal performer on the occasion, but never have I seen so extraordinary a sight as that which now met my view. At least 20,000 (I speak most moderately in saying this,) were closely packed before me. The great agitator was addressing them in that exciting manner so peculiarly his own. His voice was loud—his theme denunciatory; but still a bright smile lit up his beaming countenance. His neckcloth had been taken off, and tied loosely over his breast. His head was bare, and his waistcoat thrown open. Before him was placed a glass of water, from which he not unfrequently sipped. His principal supporters stood around him in silent admiration. The hustings pourtrayed a group of men—men of first-rate talent—awed into silent adoration by the eloquence of the orator.

But if such was the scene pourtrayed by the booth before me, what shall I say of the crowd who listened in mute attention? Crammed into a small space—jammed *en masse*—squeezed painfully together—not a complaint was heard. Every eye was fixed on the popular speaker. The very ears of his followers seemed to distend themselves to catch the accents which fell from their loved leader. A low sigh might have been heard throughout this large assemblage. Guided by his wishes—even when the topic became inflammatory to this impulsive people—still not a murmur—a murmur even of of admiration—could be elicited. Quietly, silently, and seriously, they drank in the words that were uttered. Not a movement of impatience could be traced; no breath impregnated by liquor disgraced by its redolence this living mass. The priest who had led in his share of voters, had no occasion to watch his flock. He was not more steady or attentive himself, than was his usually wildest parishioner. Never did I see before, mind dominate feeling so effectually.

O'Connell saw a mounted military officer in the distance. He stopped for a moment, pointed towards me, and waving his hand, addressed three or four words to the multitude. In the next instant a clear passage was left for me right through the centre of the crowd. Ten thousand men on either hand squeezed themselves into a still more dense body, to afford me a passage to the hustings, and effected this in orderly silence, and without a murmur, at the single wave of the hand of him who afterwards so powerfully and successfully won their cause.

I freely confess I never felt myself in a more awkward situation; as an officer on duty, I had no right to indulge in personal feelings, but having raised my forage cap in acknowledgment of their courtesy, I rode forward, delivered my mission, and gladly (with a feeling of conscious shame at my utter insignificance on the occasion) rode back as hard as I could to Clare Castle, where I drank a great deal more than my wont, to keep up my stamina and toast my polite friends in Clare, while I related to my brother officers, again and again, my adventures of the morning.

The result of this election, which on being confirmed

in the following year, put Daniel O'Connell into Parliament, had been announced, and as the delight of the Irish people knew no bounds, many foretold serious riots. The breaking up of all concerned—of. all those assembled in Ennis, amounting to at least 20,000 persons, could scarcely be carried out without some excesses. The declaration of the result was to be announced at eleven in the morning, and O'Connell had stated that, this over, his electors might follow him in procession as far as Cahirnarry (I believe it is thus spelt), the residence of Mr. James Black, where he was to lunch and after that address them. Such a movement many persons thought savoured of menace, nor, indeed, could anyone believe that such a large demonstration could proceed and finally break up, without serious rioting; no one doubted this.

It was about nine o'clock on the day in question that I found myself waiting for orders in the quarters of the General, who had certainly on this occasion acted most wisely, not only in the disposition of the troops under his command, but also in the stringent way in which he carried out those measures, which effectually prevented any admixture of the civil and military bodies, between whom, thanks to his precautions, not the most distant shadow of a conflict was reported. The peasantry during the whole election remained sober. Not a soldier was accused of being drunk ; the wildest, the most incorrigible, acted alike with sense and discretion on this important occasion.

A few minutes before ten Captain H. D., the son of the General and also his aide-de-camp, announced the arrival of O'Gorman Mahon. Sir O. D.

seemed puzzled by the visit—the motive for which he declared he could not devise—and seemed irresolute about admitting him. But before he had time to exclude him, in came the dashing Irishman, full of importance.

"General, I called to announce to you the triumph of our great leader — Daniel O'Connell has been unanimously elected."

"I know it, sir," coldly replied the other. "I presume you did not put yourself to the trouble of calling on me to announce a fact of which I could not possibly be ignorant?"

"No, Sir Charles. No; I came for a more important purpose. I came to ask you where, and how, the force under your command are distributed, in order that we may take such steps as may be necessary to prevent a collision between your people and ours." This was said with all the effrontery of a rival general.

Sir C. D. paused a moment, and I trembled lest he might commit himself in his reply; but I confess these feelings were changed into admiration when he thus answered:—

"Mr. Mahon, you have come to ask me a question to which I feel, as the commander of a large military force, I should on ordinary occasions be wrong to reply. You come to make a demand which I feel to be unauthorized, and which, consequently, I should be fully justified in treating with silent disapproval but in the present instance I will fully and truly point out the exact position of my forces."

Captain D. and I exchanged looks of surprise. The General went on:—

"Mr. Mahon, so long as the peasantry—whom you call *your* people—are quiet and well-behaved—so long as they maintain the calm demeanour they have exhibited hitherto during this election, you will never know where my troops are; but should they infringe the law—should they break out in disorder or riot— you will find them exactly *at your elbow*, Mr. Mahon, *wherever you are.* Charles, perhaps you will have the goodness to see this gentleman out."

The great O'Gorman for once appeared abashed. The General resumed his writing; half an hour afterwards every arrangement had been made.

We were drawn up in a boreen, or lane, running parallel with the main road, but hidden by somewhat high enclosures; the end of the lane was barred across by a stone wall between five and six feet high; here we remained, and saw the procession of the Great Agitator file past us within three hundred yards. Never did I see a more grand, a more imposing spectacle, nor do I believe it has ever before or since been equalled. Where so many well-dressed peasants—peasants so orderly, so firm, so quietly determined—could have been found in Ireland, was, and is, a problem far beyond my powers to solve. To describe it would be to do it injustice; I therefore shall not attempt it.

Suddenly, while we were gazing on this imposing spectacle, we heard the clatter of horses' hoofs, and our men, who were temporarily dismounted, stood to their troopers, expecting an order to resume the saddle, when, lo! who should gallop in but the O'Gorman Mahon—his shirt-collar open, a wide green ribbon round his neck; his cap was bedecked with that

colour, and streamers of the same fluttered around
him, as he galloped in front of us, mounted on a chesnut
horse, apparently an Arabian. Taking off his cap, he
cheered as he careered along. But as this was no
breach of the peace we had no right to interfere with
him. Whether he came personally to show himself to
us, or entered the boreen by accident, we knew not,
but were equally aware that he had as much right to
canter down it as we had, so long as he committed no
overt act.

Just as he got to the extremity of our line he
reined up and addressed a party of our men; whether
he was asking his way or addressing them politically
I know not, but our chief instantly called out,
"Stop that man, and bring him here." Away we
dashed at him, not doubting that we must take him,
as his progress was barred by the wall I spoke of.
The O'Gorman, however, had no wish to be seized; so,
putting spurs to his nag, which was not above fifteen
hands high, he boldly charged the wall, and cleared it
in the most gallant manner. We none felt inclined to
follow him—in uniform it would have been impossible
—but we could not refrain from giving him the en-
couraging cheer of old sportsmen when we thus saw
him take a daring and dangerous leap with a smiling
adieu imprinted on his fine countenance.

O'Connell addressed his new constituents. By his
desire they gave three cheers for "the army," (as all
military bodies are designated in Ireland). He besought them and commanded them to break up and
return to their homes without riot or drinking. He
foretold to them that by such a line of conduct their

future freedom would be secured. He thanked them, and blessed them; then, jumping into a carriage and four, he hastened on to Dublin and London, to carry out the first act of that mighty two-act play which ended in the removal of Catholic Disabilities.

The election over, we again returned to our proper quarters. I therefore once more entered Limerick, and returned to my snug quarters in Vokes's house.

INSPECTION OF CONSTABULARY.

"HARRY, my boy, Sir C. D. is to inspect my men to·day ; will you come and see the inspection ?" said Vokes, as we sat together finishing our morning meal. "I don't think you've seen my men paraded."

I readily assented, but at the same time expressed my surprise that a general officer should thus be appointed to inspect a civil force.

"Well, it is strange ; but as the order from Government has come down, I've only to obey. It strikes me very forcibly, that since the appointment of the last two inspectors-general, who are both military men of high standing, that the Executive are trying to turn our constables into soldiers."

"Surely this would be unwise."

"Unwise is a mild expression ; it would be the height of folly. We have plenty of soldiers in Ireland to do soldiers' duty—trained men, who can, not only put down any rebellion, but also add a charm by their martial and smart appearance on any occasion when they may be required."

"Are Government, then, determined to make yours a military force ?"

"Faith, most luckily, they can't do so. I hold my

situation under Peel's original Act, and hence the men under me, appointed by the same Bill, are truly called Peelers. I have one hundred of them under my immediate command, bound especially to obey me, and with them I do all my work. I must confess I wholly rely on them. The new constabulary are too much of the soldier and not enough of the Peeler for me. But come along; they are assembled by this time;" and away we went.

Paraded on the strand, we found some sixty policemen on foot and about thirty on horseback; some rode with long stirrups, some with short. Several of the carbines, or muskets, which the infantry men carried had evidently not been cleaned that morning. Some of their coats seemed dusty, and their general appearance (taking them as soldiers) was decidedly slovenly and ill set up. As an adjutant of cavalry myself, I felt strongly inclined to take them in hand; but I said nothing, and waited patiently for about ten minutes, when General Sir C. D. rode up, and having shaken hands with Vokes, proceeded to inspect the men.

Sir C. D. was one of the best-tempered men in the British service; but his looks, I must confess, bespoke no satisfaction as he rode down the line, followed by a brilliant staff of officers and orderlies, who contrasted strangely with Vokes's policemen. Having taken a hasty glance at these men, he withdrew to a short distance, and beckoned us to speak to him.

"My dear Major," said the General, "your men are far from looking well—they are positively unsoldierlike!"

"My dear General, it is just as they should be; mine is a civil, not a military force."

"But as you knew I was about to inspect them you might have made them brush themselves up a little. Look at their arms, their belts, their boots!"

"By no means. I was ordered to parade them before you, and I do so with great pleasure. But allow, me to tell you, my dear Sir Charles, that the appearance of some of the very men you blame is delightful in my sight. Those men with soiled muskets were engaged in a severe affair all night, and brought in two important prisoners: those two men without belts have used them to pinion a celebrated housebreaker, who awaits my examination at the police-office: those men with dirty boots crossed three miles of dangerous bog this morning in pursuit of a notorious offender. In truth, general, I may tell you, that a policeman who really does his duty has but little time for dressing himself up. The 'rough and ready boys' are the boys I like, though I fear the time will come when military appearance will supersede acute intelligence, and a well-dressed constable be preferred to a sharp thieftaker.*

* It may be as well here to notice the fact that Vokes's prognostications have been fully realized. Sauntering across a field in the county of Limerick, some two months ago, I met a small party of policemen, headed by an old sergeant whom I had known in the good old times. With a respect by no means general in Ireland now, he stopped his men and saluted me, and in a few minutes began to converse with me. 'This was what I desired, as I was anxious to hear some account of the present force from one of themselves. "How is it you have not caught Walsh?" asked I.

"Faith, then, I've done my best; but he's too much for me."

"And why?"

I foresee it all; I regret it. But I have no right to complain, since I have the undivided obedience of one hundred men of my own appointment, and so long as I have, the peace of Limerick shall bo maintained, and those who disturb it bo instantly arrested and punished."

"Sure, how can I get hold of him, cut off as we are from the people?"

"Cut off? What do you mean?"

"Aint we placed in barracks away from all information? Aint we dressed up in soldiers' clothes, and taught the manual and platoon, instead of looking after criminals, as we did in the Major's time? Aint we ordered in the printed regulations to mingle and become intimate with the farmers and the peasantry, and sure how can we do that, when we are always forced to go about in full uniform, armed to the teeth? It's well we'd be looking, mixing with the people at a fair or a pattern. The Lord be good to me! our very presence would spoil the fun, and no one would spake except in whispers before us. It would be grand sport to see us dancing with one of the colyeens."

"Well, I'm sorry to hear this. But how do you employ your time?"

"Oh, then, we've enough to do. We go about patrolling in parties, and walking about the streets with a constable's staff in our hands. We carry out the census and emigration reports; we are writing three or four hours a day; and now it is said we are to inspect the weights and measures. Such are the duties we *now* perform, and thus occupy the time we formerly devoted to the detection of crime."

"But I suppose, Sergeant, you could still catch a runaway? I remember how famed you were, many years ago, for your running."

"Faith, I couldn't overtake a lame donkey now."

"Are your limbs, then, worn out?"

"Far from it; I never was better or more active. But a racer could not run with a ton weight on his back."

"What do you mean?"

"Simply this: feel the weight of the new rifles we are forced to

"Upon my word, Vokes, I believe you are right; but as I'm sent to inspect your men, what am I to do?"

"Whatever you like."

"What shall I report?"

"Anything you think will seem good on paper. You are at full liberty to state your views candidly, and I hope you will do so. But deuce an inch I'll stir from the path I've made up my mind to follow."

"Upon my honour, I scarcely, as I said before, know what to do?"

"Then I'll tell you. Come along and lunch with me, and before we part I think I'll make you a convert to my opinions respecting the efficiency of the police-force you have just looked over."

---

carry about now. Sure, they are only good for show : they are so heavy and so long, we can take no aim, unless we find a rest ; and they are so difficult to load that a thief or murderer might easily get away while a man was reloading his piece. I must confess that we all like the old Brown Bess better."

"Then I suppose you'd prefer *running* after a man?"

"Sure, how could I? I would be blamed if I threw my rifle away. But its weight would entirely spoil my pace. Besides, ain't I buckled up, with a military shako on my head, and a weight of ball-cartridge dangling before me? Sure, how could I jump with a long sword-bayonet dangling behind my leg? Faith, you know, I believe we look well; but I shouldn't say we are of much use."

I confess the picture staggered me ; the truth was practically illustrated by the party before me. Add to this a review of the whole system, which has changed men who ought to be efficient policemen and detectives into grim, stiff soldiers, and the officers commanding them into officers of the army ; the resident magistrates selected rather from Government influence than for deeds of daring and intelligence, and, alas ! we find the prophecy of Major Vokes painfully fulfilled.

The General consented. The Major dismissed his men, and we all returned to our house in George-street, where I've every reason to believe the worthy and excellent General was easily and properly won to adopt the views of the chief magistrate.

81

SIFTING EVIDENCE.

An old couple had been murdered in their beds, and the cottage in which they resided had been burnt to the ground by the murderers. The whole country heard with horror and dismay of the commission of this most flagrant crime; aware that it could alone have been effected by a numerous band, organized, and acting systematically. Some two or three crimes of a similar nature had previously been committed; this being the case, it was deemed wise to strike at the root of the evil. The Government, by the advice of the local magistrates, proclaimed a reward of 300*l*. for any information which might lead to the detection of the parties concerned, at the same time offering a full pardon to any one (not being the actual assassin) who would turn king's evidence, or, as it is styled in Ireland, become an approver. But for several days these salutary measures were of no avail. Though great exertions were now made by every member of the magisterial bench, who began to feel no small alarm, since none of whom could say, whether one of their own body might not be the next victim.

My friend Vokes on this occasion (as usual) said little, and seemed to take the affair extremely coolly. But as

6

I knew that he was hourly in communication with the Government, and continually sending his force about the country, I had little doubt that he was deeply anxious about the case. ·

He had gone for a single day to visit some relatives, and only returned on the following afternoon to a late dinner, which we will suppose I was sharing as this sketch opens.

" Any news, Harry, since I have been absent ? "

"None whatever, except one or two visits from county magistrates, relative to this murder, and a heap of letters which have arrived for you."

" I've seen the letters, and read them. As to the case you speak of, I really think the less fuss made about it the better."

" Do you think you've got any clue to it ? "

" It is impossible to say ; but let us change the subject," and away he went into family gossip and public news—leaving me no opportunity to cross-question him further:

The dinner was over, and our first glass of punch just discussed,—by the bye, Vokes had a strange way of always mixing the best sherry with his grog—when the servant entered and announced that the "Major's" car was at the door. Now, as that worthy had only just arrived, I confess I thought the announcement strange. Vokes saw I was puzzled, and at once explained.

"The fact is I have important business to transact at Rathbane" (his cottage, only one mile from the city). " Will you accompany me ? "

" Not I. You are going to run into some perilous

affair, the danger of which I don't feel inclined to share. I hope I may not shrink when called upon legitimately to risk my life ; but, truly, I see no fun in these reckless exposures."

"Bah! my dear fellow, there is nothing to alarm you here. I only want to examine some witnesses, and if you'll come, I'll promise you a bottle of the old claret you profess to like so well."

"That alters the case; but you must promise not to walk off, and talk to your people, while I'm left to drink my wine without company."

"Oh, as to that, if you don't object, I'll not leave the table. But I have yet to finish my second glass of punch ; I always take one extra when I come in from travelling."

"How far have you been ?"

"Nabochlish avich ? Will you come ?"

"I will."

"Let's be off, for I shall return here to sleep. The family will return from Kilkee within an hour, so let us make haste."

I arose, jumped on the car, and in less than half-an-hour I was seated between a bright fire and a well covered table—as far as wine and dessert went. For some minutes my relative did not allude to the business which had thus brought him out of town. At length he rang the bell twice, and Sergeant Reedy, one of his most favoured policemen, entered, saluted him in military style, and then respectfully awaited to be questioned or directed.

"You came in from Cahirconlish in charge of one individual ?"

"I did, Major."

"At what hour did you arrive ?"

"At a quarter before three, Sir, this morning. I was anxious to get in before daylight."

"And where did you find the individual ?"

"At the house of Captain F——, who said he had written to you."

"He has. Has the man told anything ?"

"According to your usual orders, Major, I forbad him to speak till he saw your honour yourself."

"How were you dressed ?"

"As a labourer, sir."

"That's right. I trust you were kind and friendly with this man, and gave him all he asked for ?"

Yes, Major ; except spirits, which you always forbid."

"Bring him in."

"Yes, sir ;" and away went the Sergeant.

"These will explain to you my present business," said the Major, throwing me over two letters. I opened and read them. The first was dated —— Hall, near Cahirconlish. It ran thus :—

"MY DEAR SIR,—The bearer, Paddy Macauliffe, appeared before me this morning, and gave me such important information relative to the late daring murder, that I have little doubt that his evidence will lead to the capture of the whole gang. I know Macauliffe well, and I am sure he may be relied on. He was present during the whole affair, but did not take an active part. I therefore hope, that on the conviction of these wretches, Government will let him have the reward. I will be with you on Wednesday.

"Yours truly,
"WILLIAM F——."

"P.S. I send him in under the care of Sergeant Reedy."

The second was thus worded :—

"Col. L—— sends in a most important and respectable man, a tenant of his own, who it appears beheld the whole of the late savage butchery from a cupboard in which he was hidden. Being a voluntary witness, and a man of some little station, he trusts that Major Vokes will take his information, which may be relied on, as quietly as he can, as the bearer, Michael Tobin, is easily scared, and already feels alarmed at being sent up by a policeman (William Kennedy) whom Colonel L—— has directed to accompany witness to Limerick.

"Green Hough, Co. Limerick,"

"Well," exclaimed I, as I concluded these epistles, "I suppose you are delighted at thus receiving the information you so much desired."

"Faith, you'll see that in a minute." He again rang twice, and Sergeant Reedy appeared, ushering in a very well-looking countryman, dressed in the usual frieze coat, corduroy breeches, and black stockings, so generally worn throughout the county of Limerick; taking off his hat, and bowing slightly to Vokes, he stood with a smiling face, and a preposessing countenance, awaiting his examination.

"You were at the affair near Rathkeale ?"

"I was, Major,"

"What took you there?"

"Sure I was drinking with my cousin, Mat Carmody, and, by the same token, I owed him for a small garden of potatoes; and says he to me, 'Paddy Doody,' says he——"

"I thought your name was Macauliffe?" interrupted the magistrate, with a significant smile.

"And so it is, your honour," replied the other, without wincing; "but I was just then thinking of this same Pat Doody, who was amongst the company, who guv me a puck on the ear because I called him a bad boy. Sure, my name's well known. Faith, thin, it's odd, that his honour, Mr. F——, did not mintion it in his letter."

"Perhaps he did. But go on."

"Well, yer honour, after drinking for some time, who should come in but Corney Macphail, and thereupon there was a great whispering, and several of them looked savagely at me; and thin they drew aside, and talked, and seemed to differ. Presently Carmody comes up to me, and, says he, 'Aren't you a cousin of mine?' 'I am,' says I. 'Thin, sure, you wouldn't betray us—faith we'll make it worth your while?' and thin they swore me on the cross, and tould me they were going to attack the ould couple anent Rath-keale, and that if I'd join 'em they'd give me five silver shillings, and excuse me the bit of potatoes I owed him; so I consinted, and away we went—there were nine of us—but I only remarked five besides myself, and thim same were Mat Carmody, Michael the Fox, Martin Shea and his lame brother Bill, Pat Hogan, and myself. That's all I recognised."

"I thought you said Paddy Doody was there," intervened Vokes.

"Ah, thin, I forgot it ; sure yer honour's right. But he went off to Americky next day, so I did not heed mentioning him."

"Go on."

"Well, when we comes near the house, Mat Carmody crept in, and made sure they were asleep; and thin returning, says he, ' Come boy's, let's do the work at once. Sure, they're nothing better than heretics—they haven't been in chapel these six months—so we need'nt fear any harm will come of it;' and with that we all rushed on, and with a great, big bludgeon Dan Hogan broke in the door."

"I thought you said it was *Pat* Hogan ?"

"Ah, then, sure I'm confused—I meant Dan Hogan."

"Was Michael Tobin there ? You know him, I believe ?"

"Ah, then, ain't he half brother to my wife's first cousin ? I know him well—he was not there, I remember well. He went that evening into Limerick to bring out a coffin for Tim Sullivan's baby that died of the small-pock, or the likes."

"Well, go on ; you say you attacked the cottage ?"

"Faith we did, but I had no hand or part in it, barring the being there. Mat Carmody rushed to the bed-side of the old man, and when he wouldn't tell where his money was hid, Mat knocked his brains out with a hurley-stick, and took his keys from under the pillow. It was Martin Shea and his brother *I think* finished the old woman ; but I can't swear to it entirely, as there was no light in the room ; but I certainly heard their voices while she was being throttled; and then we came down, and some of the boys got the watch and the money."

"And then they burned the cottage?"

"They did your honour."

"Did you see them do so?"

"Sure I handed them the light, and seed 'em do it."

"They set fire to the thatch first—did they not?"

"That's what they did, Major, and sure the straw was so ould and so dry, and it tuk fire directly."

"You will swear to this?"

"I will. But sure they'll give me the reward they promised, for my life wont be safe after the trial, and all my own people will be against me, because I shall have hanged my cousin Mat. Oh, then, Major, you'll see to this."

"I'll see justice done—don't fear. Take this honest man out, Sergeant, and let him have some supper. I'll see him again presently. Take him out, and send in William Kennedy."

"Yes, Major," replied Reedy, and away went the policeman and the approver.

Vokes laughed heartily, but would not communicate to me the subject of his mirth. Presently Kennedy entered.

"Bring in Michael Tobin."

In a few minutes more, he stood before the redoubtable chief magistrate of police.

"You are Michael Tobin—a tenant of Col. L——, I believe. Do you reside near Green Hough?"

"I live on the demesne, your honour," replied the new comer, who was dressed in a most respectable suit of clothes, and whose manner bespoke a far higher station than that of the last witness.

"You beheld the crime committed, about which Col. L—— writes?" The man appeared puzzled, and in his agitation nearly crushed his hat between his hands.

"You may speak out. Kennedy you know, and this gentleman is my near relative, so you may speak out. Tell me, then, how came you over to the spot."

"Faith, Sir, I'm ashamed to tell the truth. But the fact is—ah, now, sir, don't press me."

"Out with it, Tobin."

"Well, then, if I must tell it, I will, though I wouldn't like it known. Sure I went over to coort the servant girl. But when I got over I found she had gone to Dublin, and so I was about returning to Hough Green, when I heard a noise, and, on looking out, I saw two men forcing the door, and as I had no arms I hid in the cupboard in the servant's room."

"That was in the room upstairs?"

"It was so."

"Was it on the first or the second floor?"

"On the first, your honour."

"You are positive?"

"I am, Major."

"Well, then, go on."

"Presently the old man went down, and there was a great scuffle, and he managed to wound one of the men with a carving knife; but the other fellow came behind him and shot him right through the head, and then the missus rushed down, and they shot her too."

"And what were the names of the men?"

"Bryan Quill and Pat Martin, of Pallaskenry."

"Could you swear to them?"

"I'faith I could. Sure wasn't there a light on the table, besides a great big lump of a blazing fire. I've known the two men these five years."

"You are sure there were only two?"

"Quite sure."

"Was not Paddy Doody of the party?"

"Not he: sure he was out of the way—about the the horse stealing affair in Tipperary."

"Was the house slated or thatched?"

"Slated, your honour."

"That will do. You may go now."

"But the 300*l.*, your honour?"

"Oh, we can't talk of that till after the assizes."

"Faix, that's hard, too."

"Is it?" Then suddenly turning round, in an angry voice Vokes demanded—

"Do you remember the pattern, in May last, at Patrick's Well?"

The man, with a pale face and quivering lip, admitted that he had been there.

"Do you remember knocking down James Murphy as you walked home with him, and taking his watch from him? You called yourself William Dawson then."

"Sure, Major," stammered the man, "it's not me you're speaking of?"

"Bedad, my good man, it is; and as you choose to deny the fact, I'll send out for James Murphy."

"Ah, thin, you wouldn't do that. Sure, even if I did the same, my present important testimony will overbalance that. You wouldn't be shaking, by such an accusation, the truth of a witness who is about to convict for you the two greatest rogues in the county? It was the master (Colonel L——) himself who tould me my past faults (if I had any) would all be wiped out by this good act."

"And so they would be if your tale were true; but it's a tissue of falsehood."

"Oh, then, give me the Book and I'll kiss it."

"Not I. I'll not hear you take a false oath. Have you not sworn that you were concealed in a cupboard upstairs?"

"And so I was."

"You are a perjured villain. The cottage of the poor old couple was all built on the ground-floor. So much for your truth. Kennedy, take him away, and let him be strictly guarded till my secretary has had time to draw up a committal for me to sign. No speaking—off with him;" and away went the false witness.

Major Vokes now rang his bell twice, and Sergeant Reedy entered. "Bring Macauliffe back." He did so.

"And now, Mr. Doody, are you not a precious scoundrel to try and hang five innocent men, merely to get this 300l.?"

"Oh, Major, I swear——"

"Silence, sir! You have already told us enough lies. You begin by calling yourself Macauliffe, when I happen to know that your name is Doody."

"Ah, thin, you see, I thought on account of that little affair at Tipperary you might not have believed me, if I did not call myself by another name—that was my rasin. Divil another had I."

" You said the house was thatched ?"

" Didn't they set fire to it ?   Didn't I see them ?"

" You did not, for you were hiding about at the time.   And there's another little fact you are mistaken in.   The cottage is slated, and not thatched, and so you have committed perjury.   Take him to the county gaol at once, and as you return call on Mr. D——, he's a magistrate of Tipperary, and ask him to send an order to the governor of the prison at once, to send him over to Clonmel.   The assizes open there to-morrow. There—there—no talking.   Prove that I'm wrong, and I'll compensate you.   Tell John to bring round the car ;" and the door closed on this forsworn wretch.

" How horrible !" ejaculated I.

" It is, indeed ; but I'm sorry to say these cases are not unfrequent."

" But do tell me ; how did you know that the cottage was slated and built on one floor."

" Oh, then, don't be bothering yourself.   I'll tell you.   When I said I was going to see my relatives, I at once started for the spot, and examined the ruins of the cottage in question.   I then went on about four miles, and discovered, I believe, the actual murderer of the old people.   He will be in our gaol, if my fellows are sharp, within an hour.   I have taken measures."

At this moment Sergeant Macgrath, the best man of the police, after knocking, put in his head, and merely said, " Dillon is lodged safely, sir," and immediately drew it back, and shut the door.

"I told you so," said Vokes. "But the car is ready; come along :" and away we went.

The last prisoner was hanged on clear evidence, and he confessed his guilt. The other two were transported.

THE TERRY ALTS.

In the year 1830 an agrarian system of aggression arose, bearing the name of "Terry Alt." Whence this strange appellation was taken it is impossible to say, though it was generally asserted at the time that the guilty parties borrowed the name of the most harmless and well-disposed farmer in the county of Clare to confer it on a very extensive and well-organized band of marauders, who, under the plea that sufficient land was not apportioned to the growth of potatoes and grain, amused themselves by digging up and thus destroying thousands of acres of land: By every post Government received notices of fresh outrages of this description. Bodies consisting of several hundred armed men nightly passed through portions of the South of Ireland—more particularly through the county of Clare—and marked their footsteps by fresh outrages. Vokes was, of course, as usual, very active in suppressing these aggressions, and, indeed, the particular district over which he presided he kept comparatively free from stain. But daily and hourly alarmed authorities rushed into Limerick to report fresh agrarian attacks. By his advice, the troop (in which I was then a cornet) was ordered over to Newmarket-on-Fergus, and there took up its quarters. The presence of the military had the desired effect, and for several days no Terry Alts ventured into our immediate neighbourhood. In the meantime the magistrates assembled, and after a solemn discussion agreed to declare to the Government their utter inability to put down the dangerous body who now threatened their property—concluding their report by an earnest appeal to the higher powers to send them further protection.

The reply to this was, perhaps, one of the most extraordinary on record. It simply stated that the Marquis of Anglesey, then Lord Lieutenant of Ireland, would at once visit the disturbed districts himself, and that after personally making the requisite observations, His Excellency would take the best steps at once to put an end to the disgraceful state into which the local magistrates had allowed the county of Clare to fall. In a letter written by himself, he informed Sir Augustine Fitzgerald, an old general officer of high standing in Clare, that he would pay him a personal visit at his hospitable mansion (Cahirgoran*) in the course of three days, and further than that, after addressing the Bench, and enjoying the hospitality of the worthy baronet for one night, he would proceed to Cork the following evening.

All was now confusion. In consequence of the turbulent state of the county, every gentleman had, more or less, sent away his silver plate, and other valuables, to his bankers for safe keeping ; and now began a general application for loans of such articles as

* I am aware that this mode of spelling may be incorrect, but it conveys the word in sound.

might be deemed necessary to place on table before the
impetuous Lord Lieutenant, who, if not received in
first-rate style, might naturally (after his differences
with the magistrates) look upon it as a slight. Sir
Augustine's plate was in Dublin; he would scarcely
have time to obtain it, besides the risk and trouble of
having it down for one day. So messengers on horseback were sent to every neighbour and relative from
Dromoland to Hermitage, to swell out this metallic
pic-nic. The parties called upon responded most hand-
somely, and when the noble Marquis dashed into
Cahirgoran Park, in a post-chaise and four, we were
ready to receive him with military honours, and the
hospitable General equally prepared to do justice to his
exalted guest by a show of first-rate entertainment.

But, alas! the deeply-irritated Viceroy was not thus
easily to be calmed; his "soul was in arms," and,
spurning the proffered luncheon placed before him, he
impatiently waited the coming of the magistrates.
They soon arrived, and after presenting a compli-
mentary address to his Excellency, made their report,
which was little more than an echo of their former communication. The Marquis could scarcely hear them
patiently to the end ; when, bursting out, he addressed
them in a strain of unusual censure. He positively
averred that "he had marked each outrage as it
occurred, and clearly perceived that had the landlords
been more conciliatory, and at the same time more
firm, those outrages would have at once been put a
stop to. He had been received at every station where
he had been delayed with an enthusiasm, a demonstration of joy, which Irishmen alone could display. Yes,

if he could only instil his own ideas into the minds of
his hearers, the South of Ireland would be as tranquil
as the most peaceable district in the habitable globe.
Such were his ideas, and therefore he could not but
regret that his counsel and advice had not been more
generally asked and followed; and he most reluctantly
confessed that he attributed much blame to the justices
of the peace in the county of Clare."

To this tirade no one felt inclined to reply, though
at least one-half of those present determined to retire
from the Bench; parties holding the Commission of
the Peace in Ireland being not, as we have them in
England, selected from the church, the army, or the
ranks of placemen in general, but, *bonâ fide*, the most
wealthy and extensive landholders, the most noble and
independent men in the country, and consequently
unused to be snubbed.

His Excellency now went out on the front balcony,
and addressed the peasantry. He first slightly chided
them for their misdeeds; but soon breaking out in a
strain of exalted praise, he glorified the county; he
magnified the people; he showed that the peasantry
were the sole support of the land; he talked of Irish
bravery and gallantry, of stalwart heroes and lovely
women—in a word, he threw his whole affections
amongst them, without reserving one grain for the indignant gentry who stood around him. Need I add,
that each fresh compliment was applauded to the sky,
that cheer after cheer succeeded each other till they
positively became deafening: the blessings called down
on the "Hero of Waterloo" were so numerous that
the "recording angel" could scarcely have found

7

room to inscribe them; and while "Brave Anglesey's" name was still wafted to heaven on the breaths
of hundreds of the Irish peasantry, that most excellent
but impulsive chief retired, once more restored to
thorough good-humour by the *Cade mille falthah* of
the people he had addressed.

The offended magistrates by no means shared the
joyous or confident feelings of the high functionary;
but as they had promised to partake of the dinner
provided for him, they sat down to it, and almost
in gloomy silence discussed the elegant banquet placed
before them.

The cloth removed, the loyal host arose, and
after toasting "the sovereign," drank as usual, that
of the Lord Lieutenant, dwelling on those bright and
brilliant points of his Excellency's character which
will live through future ages of history. To his
present opinions, he wisely and hospitably refrained
from alluding.

As might be expected, his Excellency rose to reply.
His ill-humour had passed away, and he now endeavoured slightly to make up for his severe animad-
versions of the morning. But as he warmed on the
subject, he became almost enthusiastic; and after
pointing out to them the devotion of the peasantry to
himself, the love they entertained for him, he earnestly
besought them to copy his mode of treating them, and
thus secure their warm affections. "Yes," added his
Lordship, in conclusion, "act as I do, and you will
equally gain the same attachment. You see how they
welcome me. They will then equally welcome you. I

have but to hold up my finger, and they at once obey. me. I will stake my life that I could walk alone through the country unmolested. My presence would bring peace amongst them. I only wish I could stay amongst them a longer period to soothe their irritated feelings. *Yes, gentlemen, you may retire quietly to your houses to-night, for I'll pledge myself, from my thorough knowledge of the country, that no one will harm you. No agrarian outrage will be committed while I remain in the south of Ireland."*

Content with this comparatively gentle address, the Viceroy sat down. He soon after rose, which was a signal for breaking up. It having been predetermined that his Excellency would hold a general levée on the following day, those who were not staying in the house at once took their departure. Few felt pleased at the manner in which they had been spoken to. A very few almost believed Lord Anglesey was right; but as they rode and drove through the splendid park at Cahirgoran, now lit up by a bright moon, they one and all agreed to attend the meeting on the morrow.

Tired by the fatigues of the day, I gladly sought my couch at midnight, and determined to take a compensation sleep, as I had ridden into Limerick and back early on the preceding day, previous to my official duties. Need I then say I was soon sound asleep, and enjoying that delightful slumber so peculiar to early manhood, when suddenly a trumpet loudly sounded under my window, disturbing my then delightful dream. Could I be mistaken? No, there it goes again. "By

George ! It's 'boots and saddle !' " exclaimed I, now
thoroughly awake, and quickly jumping out of bed—
for be it known to my non-military readers, that this
said " boots and saddle " is an instant summons " to
turn out and mount."

What this could mean I was fairly puzzled to guess.
Could any accident have occurred to our illustrious
visitor ? Almost impossible. Could any sudden rising
require our presence to put it down ? Not likely.
Could any of the magistrates have been murdered on
their way home ? No ; they would not have called *us*
out on such an occasion. What then could it be ?

Eager to know, I rushed down to parade, and
there met my commanding officer (Captain D——),
who, far from affording me any information, seemed
still more puzzled than myself. The only clue he
could afford was a written order from Sir Augustine, ordering us at once to proceed to Cahirgoran
House.

"It must then concern the Lord Lieutenant. But
in this case why so early. I clearly understood he was
only to be called at eight. It is now scarcely six
o'clock ? "

" We'll soon see," said D——. So ordering the
trumpeter to sound the trot, we went off at the rate of
some nine miles an hour, and soon entered the gates
of Augustine's residence.

At a single glance we read the cause of our being
thus hastily summoned. The whole of the noble, the
beautiful park—more particularly around the house—
was dug up : the grass that had for centuries been the
ornament of the estate, the pride of the owner, was

now turned most skilfully and effectually into a potatoe bed. Not a sod of green pasture remained. *Four hundred acres* of brown mould now disfigured the approaches to the mansion. Between midnight and five in the morning this leviathan atrocity had been committed under the very nose of their popular ruler. Before or since I have never heard of such a demonstration. I confess I never felt so taken aback.

Truly, Vokes had foreshadowed this. He had not foreseen, or perhaps expected, such a wholesale effort on the part of the peasantry; but he had clearly and invariably pointed out the danger of attempting to humbug the people by blarney, or relying too much on what is called enthusiastic popularity.

A carriage and four stood before the house as we approached. His Excellency, accompanied by a single aid-de-camp, stepped in. I can never forget his mingled look of anger, disappointment, and disgust. He drew down the blinds, and, ordering the postilions to drive quickly, started off towards Cork without even bestowing the usual salutation at parting. We escorted him about half a mile, when his aid-de-camp dismissed us.

Thus, then, did he who flattered himself (as many others have foolishly done) that he thoroughly knew Ireland, go away—leaving behind him not only a practical admission that the local magistrates were in the right, but in his first moment of anger, when called up and shown the devastation which had been committed, he had fully admitted the error he had been guilty of in thus blaming those who were correct after all.

The levée was, of course, adjourned *sine die*, while the Clare authorities, having thus triumphed, doubled their exertions, and, by good management and a proper degree of severity, mingled with strict justice, soon after succeeded in putting down the "Terry Alts" without the assistance of a Waterloo hero!

DARBY DEAR.

One of the most frightful murders which had appalled the county of Limerick for some time had just occurred, and as the victim was a female celebrated for her beauty and her kindness of heart, the case enlisted even more than the usual sympathy elicited on similar occasions.

The murdered woman was the wife of a most respectable baker in Bruff, whose surname at this moment escapes my memory, but will probably be better recollected by those connected with Limerick in 1828, or thereabouts. In Bruff the whole tale is well remembered, and persons of my own age will not be found wanting to confirm the details I now give. The Christian name of the baker was Darby—a common name in the south of Ireland. His surname we will assume to be Hogan, and having thus premised, go on with our sketch.

After discussing the news of the day with Major Vokes, with whom I had been breakfasting—after partaking of a somewhat large portion of fried salmon and eggs—for young dragoons are, or at least were, celebrated for their powers of mastication—I rose, and was about to leave the room, when my father-in-law called across to me, and in a careless manner asked me what I was going to do.

"Nothing very particular."

"Come along, then, with me on the outside car. I am going to take a drive in the country—the fresh air will renew your appetite. Run upstairs and take off your uniform, put on plain clothes, and by that time the car will be round."

I assented, and speedily changed my appearance to that of a civilian.

"Where's the car?" asked I.

"It's in the back lane—come along," said the Major, putting on his hat and taking up the horsewhip he generally carried. "Come along; we shall be back to dinner."

Now the last observation, coupled with the fact of the carriage having been brought to a quiet spot behind our stable, instead of the front door, somewhat startled me; and when, on going out, I found Sergeant Macgrath mounted in full uniform in attendance, I began to think over the many scrapes and dangers I had gone through in Vokes's company, and felt more than half inclined to draw back. He saw this, and with loud laughter assured me that there was no danger whatsoever—that he was only going to see Tom Doolan (his senior chief constable, and a great friend of his), quartered in Bruff.

As Vokes seldom deviated from the truth, I felt quite satisfied, and jumped on the car, and away we went.

In less than two hours we arrived at Doolan's quarters, and here we found the worthy C. C.

I now discovered that my father-in-law's object was to inquire into the details of the late murder.

Mr. Doolan first supplied him with the most ample accounts of it, and added that he had been out two days and a night, accompanied by the wretched husband. But all in vain. The police had taken up several persons on suspicion, more particularly a pedlar from the county of Cork; but after strict examination, the magistrates had felt it their duty to discharge them.

" What further course to take, I scarcely know. Tell me what shall I do?" said Doolan.

" Well, then, faith, do nothing at all. Go and fish in Loch Ghurr, or shoot snipes in the bog—or make love to the ladies, as you're a handsome fellow. Do what you like; but leave this affair alone, till you see me again."

Our friend, who was an active and intelligent officer, scarcely liked being thus thrust aside; but as he well knew his superior, he only laughed, and left us, directing the Major to the house of the bereaved man.

When we entered, the poor fellow was in tears. When called on to relate the circumstances of the case, his grief was painful to witness; and no wonder either —for his wife, quite a young woman, had been a good wife to him, and a more attached couple had never existed.

The circumstances were easily detailed. On the Saturday evening previous, Hogan and his wife had taken a long stroll into the country, determined to enjoy the fine weather. But as they were in their

every-day clothes, they rather avoided the frequented
road, and strolled through the fields. At about three
miles from Bruff, in a solitary spot, about two hundred
yards from the road, they were suddenly pounced upon
by a gang of three robbers, with their faces blackened,
They instantly seized the lovely girl, whose screams
were loud and long, and she struggled so hard that it
required the strength of two men to hold her. The
third had seized Hogan, and held a pistol to his head,
Hogan, however—a man noted for his courage—
watched his opportunity, and knocked his captor
down, and instantly fled along the road, crying for
help. Presently he met some people coming back
from Limerick market, and when he told his tale they
instantly returned with him to the spot. But they
were too late. The unhappy victim lay dead on the
ground, her skull battered to pieces by the blows of a
heavy bludgeon. At this sight Hogan cried out
loudly, and throwing himself on the body, fainted
away. The peasants, terrified and shocked, raised the
two in their arms, and conveyed them both back to
Bruff. Poor Hogan was confined to his bed, occasionally raving during the two days following. A
coroner's inquest sat on the body, and brought in a
verdict of " Wilful Murder." The poor woman had
only been buried the night before we arrived. The
husband seemed eager for vengeance, and suggested
many schemes to Vokes by which the savage assassins
might be discovered.

After a moment's pause, the magistrate turned
round, and looking straight at the poor man, said,
" Hogan, you had better accompany me into Limerick

"Faith, Major, I'd rather not—for I'm still weak, and in grief."

"Yes, I know that; but perhaps your deposition may be necessary to bring these murderers to justice."

"Do you then think you'll catch them? Oh, then, I pray to Heaven you could."

"And yet you hesitate to come! It looks ill."

"Not I, Major; sure I'm ready,"

"Yes, yes, my good fellow; but not in that dress. You must put on your Sunday suit, as we shall have to appear before the Bench: it would appear disrespectful to be seen thus."

"True for ye," rejoined the baker; and he quitted the room to change his clothes.

I saw by Vokes's eye, that he was pleased with some result; what that result could be I could not imagine, but I equally knew it would be no use to question him; so I maintained a strict silence, whilst the magistrate went to the window, and beckoned his sergeant up, to whom he gave some directions (apparently important ones) in Irish, and then dismissed him.

Hogan now came out, dressed in his best. His appearance was that of a quiet, industrious shopkeeper, rather above than beneath the rank of his fellow tradesmen.

To my surprise, however, Vokes was evidently in no hurry to drive away; for although the car stood ready at the door, he asked Hogan to give him a crust of bread-and-cheese and a glass of beer. Now, as I knew that my relative eschewed luncheon, and positively disliked the food he had just asked for, I clearly perceived his object was delay. The refreshments were,

however, brought, and slowly partaken of. Whilst we
were thus employed, I heard a horse gallop away. ' In
a quarter of an hour more, we were all again on the
car, driving towards Limerick.

When we had travelled about two miles, we met
Sergeant Macgrath, walking his horse in the direction
of Bruff. This fairly puzzled me; however, I said
nothing, while Vokes, stopping the car, jumped off and
held a few moments' conversation with the mounted
man. Then jumping up again, on we drove, Sergean
Macgrath, to whose saddle I now perceived a bundle
was strapped, following us.

At length we came to the spot near which the
murder had taken place, when Vokes suddenly ordered
the carriage to stop; then turning round, he looked
straight at Hogan, and in piteous accents cried—
"*Darby, Darby dear, what are you doing ?*"

The affrighted man turned as pale as a sheet, and
leaped from his seat. Vokes now faced to him, con-
tinuing to cry out in a voice bespeaking agony, even
in the high tones of a female—"*Oh Darby, Darby !
surely you would not murder me ! Did I ever wrong
you ? Oh, Darby, have mercy on me !*"

I really thought the Major had gone mad; but
imagine my astonishment when Hogan, throwing himself on his knees, screamed out, "*I confess—I confess
it ! But how did I know you overheard her—Oh, the
Lord be good to me !—them is the very words !*"

"Handcuff him, Tinsbury ! handcuff him ! and bind
him to the car." In an instant our coachman jumped
down, and throwing open his top-coat, displayed under-
neath the green uniform of a policeman : in an instant

more his orders were complied with, and the wretch was safely secured.

Sergeant Macgrath handed his brother constable his loaded carbine, and fastening his horse to a gate, jumped off, and accompanied the major and myself to the spot where the outrage had been committed, carrying in his hand the mysterious bundle.

We soon arrived at the fatal spot, when the sergeant opened his packet and produced a pair of shoes. These were those that Hogan had just changed for his boots, and the several other articles of dress he had taken off in order to don his Sunday suit, by the desire of Major Vokes.

Macgrath knelt down, and having minutely examined the footprints, which still were visible in the soil where the struggle had taken place, carefully fitted them to the shoes he brought—they tallied exactly. Vokes then verified them himself. The coat-sleeve was turned inside out, and a large patch of blood-stain found near the wrist; the trousers had been torn in the struggle, and sewed up again. Vokes now began searching amongst the bushes, but without success. On looking into a dirty dyke which ran by, he perceived a piece of stick lying in it; he desired his sergeant to take it out: he did so. It was a short bludgeon, probably the one with which the murder had been committed. The police magistrate now found himself possessed of enough evidence to commit the prisoner upon, and returned to the carriage.

Here sat the wretched man—pale as death, and sobbing like a child. "Do you know this stick?" asked Vokes, displaying the bludgeon he had found.

"'Take it away!—take it away! Sure if I hadn't had it in my hands, I'd never have done it ;" and he covered his face with his hands, and cried aloud.

We drove straight to Limerick county· gaol, and there lodged the prisoner.

After dinner that day I asked Vokes, most earnestly, whether he had acted on any information, or merely on his own judgment.

"Well, then, I declare to Heaven, my dear fellow, I acted entirely on my personal observation. There was something in the look of this man ; there was something in his overwhelming grief that at once made me think *he* was the murderer. Did you see how he winced when I proposed taking him into Limerick ? But he fell at once into the trap, when I recommended him to change his clothes."

"And why did you do so ?" interrupted I.

"Faith, I knew that if he had committed the crime, he had done so in the dress he had on, for he said he had walked out in his every-day attire : did you not remark him saying so ?"

"Not I."

"Well, then, Harry, my boy, you'll never make a good thief-taker, for it is by these trifles we come at the greater truths. Did not you see me call in Sergeant Macgrath ? Well, it was to tell him to go into Hogan's room, and as he left it to seize the clothes he took off, and gallop on to see if the shoes fitted the marks. Had they not done so, he was quietly to put the whole back again. He met us, however, and told us they did. So I thought myself justified in trying the *ruse* I did, and through which the prisoner was brought to confess.

"But how did you happen to know the exact words ?"

"I *chanced* it. I knew his Christian name was Darby, and calculated pretty accurately what the poor girl would have called out on his assaulting her. Even now I cannot be sure they were the exact words she used, nor probably is Hogan ; but they were so like them —so like the appeal she probably made—that he believed that some passer-by had overheard them, and thus in an agony of terror admitted his guilt. But you'll see more strange scenes than this before you leave the county."

"And what will the other magistrates say?"

"Say! Nabocklish, my boy; haven't they been at me already ? Two of my neighbours have already been at me, to blame me for thus taking up a highly respectable man,—while the principal magistrate, who lives near Bruff, has galloped in and offered to bail this excellent young man, whom he has known from his birth, to any amount. I, of course, refused—murder is not a bailable offence. So my friend has gone down to the club-house, and is now probably engaged in writing a memorial to the Lord Lieutenant, requesting his Excellency to remove me from my situation."

Vokes wound up with a hearty laugh.

"And have you no fear that you may have erred ? Suppose this man is acquitted?"

"Suppose the skies were to fall! Here's your health!" and Vokes changed the subject.

At the following assizes, Darby Hogan was tried for the murder of his wife, and convicted on the clearest evidence (though wholly circumstantial) which could possibly be adduced.

The night before he suffered, he fully confessed the justice of his sentence ; but to the last declared his firm belief that Vokes was gifted with *supernatural vowers*.

AN IRISH ELOPEMENT.

———

I HAPPENED to be dining with an English friend at Moriarty's Hotel, who, in company with another tourist, was *en route* to behold the glories of Killarney, when, after the wine had circulated more than once, I proposed an adjournment to Major Vokes's.

"Vokes!" cried the stranger—"Vokes! Surely you do not mean the chief magistrate of police?"

"Indeed I do."

"Then I shall certainly not accompany you. I detest his very name. He has been the cause of all my misfortunes."

"How so?" asked my friend.

"I don't say that he *purposely* injured me—I don't say that he acted improperly; but he was undoubtedly the cause of my leaving the army, and, to a certain extent, causing my character to be defamed."

"How is that?'

"Ah, do tell us."

"As I have said so much, I will. Call for some claret; for not one inch will I stir towards Vokes's—not I. And I think, when you've heard my story, you will say I am right."

He then commenced thus :—

"I had only joined the regiment about six months,

8

when I applied for, and obtained leave for a fortnight on 'private urgent affairs ;' and having done so, left the barrack-yard in high glee. I was dressed in a new suit of mufti, and my heart was as light as youth, health, and hope could make it. My friend Thompson shouted out a wish that I might succeed, as I drove from the barrack-gate in one of those old tumble-down vehicles which formed the most respectable mode of transit some few years ago—yclept a post-chaise—or, as the driver denominated it, "*a poshay of the right sort*"—a term applied to every article to be admired, from a pretty girl to a poldoody oyster.

"But I forgot to explain, that at the time I speak of I was quartered in this very city and that I was now starting for Bruff, where I had been invited by Sir Phelim O'Dowd—or THE O'Dowd, as some of the people called him—to pass three days with him. Sir Phelim, I must observe, had extended his hospitality to me in the hunting-field, where I had won his heart by leaping a high ditch (a ditch being nothing less than a mud-bank in Ireland), and landing safely over the heads of a man and horse that lay sprawling on the other side in gallant style! Sir Phelim was wholly ignorant that I had met his lovely daughter at a race-ball in Limerick, and fallen over head and ears in love with her. Need I say I accepted his invitation, and now hastened to profit by it.

"Arrived at Castle O'Dowd—a modern square build-ing, covered with white plaster and embowered in dilapidated verandahs,—I jumped out of my rickety vehicle, and at once sought the drawing-room, where the domestic forces were drawn up, evidently expecting

my arrival. Sir Phelim, after a cordial welcome, introduced me to his lovely daughter (little suspecting that
we were already acquainted) and his maiden sister, a
gaudily-dressed old maid of some forty-five years of
age; then turning to his butler (for footmen are
always called butlers in Ireland), ordered in the 'red
round,' invariably offered to mid-day visitors.

"My Louisa looked more lovely than ever; the slight
deception she was playing off, in thus concealing, for
purposes of her own, our former intimacy, caused a
most becoming blush to mantle on her cheek; and I'd
have given half the estates of the Earl of Kingston—
that is, if I had possessed them—to have sent papa and
aunt out of the room, only for five minutes.

"Need I say how happily, yet how swiftly the hours
passed! A stroll through the woods; a noble banquet
with tables groaning beneath enormous joints (as is
always the case in Ireland); a cooper of excellent
claret; and some really good music from *my* Louisa—
I call her *my* Louisa, to distinguish her from her old
maiden aunt, who bore the same Christian name—
seemed all to pass in a few minutes; and I could
scarcely credit it, when Sir Phelim's butler announced
midnight, and told us that our candles awaited us in
the hall. Such were the ways of the house.

"Elated by wine to a certain extent, and filled with
the most romantic ideas of love, I was endeavouring
to discover my room, which I had proudly insisted on
finding without escort—indeed, I believe I had rudely
told the old butler to mind his own business, sensi-
tively believing his polite pilotage was proffered under
an idea that I was not quite steady—I was, as I said

before, vainly trying to find the door of the room that
the worthy domestic had indicated, when a very smart
female servant crossed my path, and bobbed an Irish
curtsey.

"'Come here, my colyeen,' said I, 'and tell me
which is my room?'

"'Faith, it's straight before your honour!'

"'You are Miss Louisa's maid?'

"'That same!' says the pretty chambermaid.

"Now, wine may kill, it may enervate, it may con-
fuse—but still, in its early progress through the mind,
it affords inspiration. At least, so I found it. The
reply of the pretty Abigail at once filled me with a
train of new ideas.

"'Come here, ma cushla' (for I found a little native
Irish would win her heart); 'sure you'd give a note
from me to Miss Louisa?'

"'Is it me would do it?'

"'Faith, then, you will. Look here, darlint! I
don't understand much Irish, but, in plain English,
here's your reward, if you will;' and I held up a
sovereign.

"'Will a duck swim?' inelegantly replied the smiling
Abigail.

"'Wait, then, a moment, and I'll do the thing
respectably.' (This was a sentence I had picked up in
Clare.) 'Wait, and I'll bring you the letter:' and
I rushed into my room.

"I tore out a leaf from my pocket-book—took out
my very best pencil-case (a gold one) and wrote :—

"'DEAREST LOUISA,—Meet me near the front gate,
at eleven to-morrow night—a post-chaise will be in

readiness—to bless the affection of one who means honourably, but who, enchanted on a short acquaintance, sets ordinary rules at defiance, the warm beating of his heart having long banished the cold dictates of his head.

'Your adorer, ———.'

"The note done, I sealed it with a love-seal, and delivered it *prepaid*, to the maid, who, for another sovereign, promised to bring me a reply within half-an-hour.

"My friends, did you ever await the reply to a love-letter? No. Then you can know nothing of my throbbing heart, my beating pulse, my feverish temples, &c. &c. &c., so well described by the poet. Suffice it to say, the maid returned; and, having pocketed another sovereign and accepted a kiss, gave me a note redolent of musk and closely sealed, and ran away laughing. I entered my room to read the precious missive.

" With trembling hands I opened it—

"'MY DEAR SIR,—I really feel that I am acting most imprudently. But love is a maddening passion, which carries us off, even beyond the bounds of prudence. Fie!—I almost blush while I write the words, and comply after an acquaintance so short; but that short acquaintance convinces me you are a man of honour. I WILL be there.

'Yours,
'Alas! too much yours,
'LOUISA O'DOWD.'

"Oh! how rapturously I kissed the dear note. I almost devoured it in my ardour. And yet, again, there was a nasty, selfish, intruding thought which said, 'Is this conduct not too hasty? Should she thus have succumbed on the very first attack?' But no! It was the effect of love! omnipotent love! and I hushed every murmur—every scruple, as I fell asleep blessing my own, my adored Louisa.

"Shall I say how the next day passed? Shall I say how my heart kept jumping up in my throat, and how I longed for the coming night? My Louisa kept her room. She said she had a cold. This was evidently feigned to conceal her agitation; and I amused myself by watching the vain attempts of a Captain O'Haggarty, who sought to win the love of the Baronet's sister. The old lady repulsed him with scorn. She evidently saw he was a fortune-hunter, and as such treated him. She even appealed to me. But as I was busy with my own happy thoughts, and as I was by no means desirous of embroiling myself with the best shot in Tipperary, I declined; to the evident annoyance of the old maid, interfering on her behalf.

"After dinner, Sir Phelim, who had been more than usually cordial throughout the day, stretched out his hand and pressed mine; then, with a wink and a knowing look, he drank—'Success to you, my boy; may you succeed in love and war. I suspect you take ladies like fortresses—by assault, eh, Harry, my boy?' then burst out laughing, and proposed to retire to the drawing-room.

"There was a bantering tone about my host that puzzled me. He seemed what is called 'up' to something; but what that something was I could not divine. Louisa could, surely, not have betrayed me?

The maid-servant might have been indiscreet, it is true; but then my abduction of his only daughter, would surely not have been a subject of merriment to her father. Even old Miss O'Dowd kept smiling; and the only one out of humour—for Louisa still kept her room—was the Hibernian captain.

"At eleven precisely we all gladly retired; and I listened at my door to hear that the house was quiet. In ten minutes all was silent; and as my watch told the half-hour, my bribed Abigail appeared, and with caution led me to the garden-gate, where a post-chaise stood waiting. She insisted on my entering it. I did so; and away went the maid to fetch her dear mistress. Oh, how impatient—how anxious I felt! Presently, a light footstep was heard, and in another moment Louisa was clasped in my arms. Her blushes were concealed by a thick veil; but, as I pressed her to my bosom, I felt her beating heart.

"With a wild hurrah! which I vainly endeavoured to silence, away dashed the postboys—for I had four horses on this occasion,—and away dashed the rickety old chaise. My Louisa sank into my arms, and, for the first time, I imprinted a kiss on her sweet lips; that is to say, making allowance for the envious veil which intervened. She sighed; she murmured; I could just catch my name breathed forth, when a seeming earthquake roused me from my dream of happiness. In the next moment I lay sprawling in the high road. The post-boys had turned the corner too sharply, a high stone had caught the wheel, and the post-chaise, being fairly turned over, at once came to pieces, while the released nags galloped on for several yards, the post-boys having been hurled from their saddles. I jumped up unhurt. I rushed across and raised my adored Louisa, who had become insensible. In vain I strove to arouse her ; all was dark. I raised her veil, but was unable to see her dear face ; I could not really discover whether she was severely injured or not. Fortunately, at this moment, I heard a horse approaching. I shouted with all my might ; and to my great joy Captain O'Haggarty came up, and jumping - from his saddle, instantly lent his aid. My cries had been heard, and a farm-servant approached. I explained in a few words my situation to the Captain and he vowed to assist me. The rustic carried a lantern ; we opened it, and cast the light on the face of my Louisa. Oh, Heavens ! I can never forget the moment ; I actually screamed with annoyance, while the Captain rapped out his most powerful oath. In my arms lay extended Louisa O'Dowd—yes, Louisa O'Dowd—but not MY Louisa O'Dowd, but OLD Louisa O'Dowd, her antiquated and crabbed aunt. In my vexation, I let her fall into the mud, from which she instantly arose, seeming to have suddenly recovered in the most miraculous manner, and began to pour out a thousand maledictions on my now too apparent disgust.

" On the other hand, Captain O'Haggarty made use of the most insulting terms, the mildest being traitor ! seducer ! and abductor ! I could not explain without compromising *my* Louisa, so I attempted no defence ; but hurling defiance at him and his old love, I agreed to meet him at daylight, at the eighth mile-stone on the Limerick road, there to settle our dispute with pistols.

"A few words, and we separated. He carried off his venerable charge in triumph. Disgusted, irritated, and somewhat ashamed, I sought the cottage of Tim Sullivan, the master of the hounds, who, though it was now midnight, I felt assured I should find still up, imbibing his fourteenth or fifteenth glass of toddy.

"The worthy squire—or the Master, as he is styled in Munster—welcomed me with a loud shout, and instantly ordered in a reinforcement of glasses and bottles. Then, turning round, he introduced me to Major Vokes, a handsome-looking man, with a cheerful smile on his face, who sat on the other side of the table sharing his liquor,—seemingly nothing loth to do so.

"I was delighted ; for, truth to tell, I felt a conscientious scruple at asking Tim to be my second in the fast approaching affair. Yet, what could I do ? It was hard thus to call on a man with a wife and half-a-score of children to embroil himself; but, on the other hand, if I did not get a second before daylight, O'Haggarty would probably post me as a coward. I had no alternative—at least, so I had supposed—as I sought Tim Sullivan's residence. But now a very proper person sat before me. He bore a military prefix to his name ; he was doubtless a military man ; the Fates had sent him to my aid.

"For half-an-hour I sat, quietly enjoying my toddy, —studying all the time how I should attack the Major. It was a bold measure ; but I had no alternative. It is true he was a stranger ; but among soldiers there is always a degree of masonic brotherhood. So I now only waited a good opportunity. Here, again, Fortune favoured me : Tim was called away by the sudden illness of a favourite hunter.

"I lost not an instant,—I at once addressed my proposed aid.

"'Major, as a stranger,—I really want words to apologize,—but the urgency of the case must plead for me. Will you second me ?'

"'I really do not understand you !'

"'Simply, then, 'tis this—I am abrupt, that I may make my communication before Sullivan returns—I have agreed to fight a duel at day-break.'

"'And you wish to tell *me* this ?'

"'Yes, Major, in the hope of inducing you to become my second.'

"'Your second !—ha ! ha ! ha !—a capital joke. I understand !'

"Now, for the very life of me, I could not see why the Major should be so very merry. I am sure I did not feel so. He surely could not have misunderstood me. So I chimed in—

"'You understand me ?'

"'Oh, perfectly ! I'll be off now ; but I shall be sure to be there,—at daybreak, I think you said ?'

"'I did.'

"'But I forgot the place and the name of your antagonist. You must tell me both, as I must be in time.'

"'My antagonist is Captain O'Haggarty.'

"'Oh ! No wonder you are frightened ; he's the best shot in Ireland.'

"'I'm not frightened, Major ; but under the peculiar circumstances——'

"'I understand!' replied Vokes; and again he burst out laughing. 'Where is the rendezvous?'

"'The eighth mile-stone on the Limerick road.'

"'That's right.' He then took out a small pocket-book and noted down all the particulars. Again he smiled, and rose, saying, 'We shall be sure to be there,' and left the room.

"That Vokes took notes did not surprise me. Many men with bad memories invariably do so. That his coming responsibility should induce him to leave his grog, I could understand, though it vexed me. But that he should not seek to know the cause of quarrel, or any particulars of the affair, I confess astonished me; while the words 'We will be there' puzzled me. But, perhaps, as an old hand, he intended to bring a surgeon, or—as is often the case in Ireland —a friend, to see the fun.

"I passed three long hours with Tim. I borrowed his pistols, but gave him no hint of my projected *rencontre.* I drank little; but chatted away till four o'clock, when Sullivan proposed to retire. We did so. In half-an-hour more I had slipped out, and was already on my way to the Limerick road.

"Although daylight had scarcely fully lighted up the heavens, yet O'Haggarty and a fierce-looking friend awaited my coming with bloodthirsty impatience. I confess I felt somewhat small in thus approaching him, unaccompanied by a second.

"'Where is your friend, sir? I thought you under-stood the rules of these affairs.'

"'And so I do; he'll be here directly.'

"'May I ask who acts on your side?' demanded the fierce looking man.

"'Major Vokes,' said I.

"'What! is that your game?' shouted he.

"'Coward!—poltroon!' roared the captain.

"At that moment Vokes galloped up, accompanied by four mounted policemen, and away bolted the man with the red whiskers.

"'I arrest you both! Take their arms from them, Sergeant Hennessy,' said the Major. 'Gentlemen, you must accompany me.'

"'Infamous traitor!' roared O'Haggarty, frowning at me and shaking his fist. 'Dirty coward!—whew!' and he gave a contemptuous whistle.

"'Come along, gentlemen; you must instantly accompany me to Sir Phelim O'Dowd, who, as the nearest magistrate, will, on my information, bind you both over to keep the peace.'

"Shall I go on with my tale? No; it is too painful! I soon discovered that Major Vokes was at the head of the police; and, consequently, my application to him was quoted as an unmanly mode of avoiding this duel. O'Haggarty first posted me as a coward; then ran away with the old spinster. Miss Louisa O'Dowd the younger with truth declared that she knew nothing at all of the affair; but cruelly added—'the detestable coward!' My brother officers sent me to Coventry; and, in a fit of despair, I sold out of the army and became a settler in Canada; where I afterwards shot my best friend, because he foolishly, when elated by wine, jeered me about old maids and police inspectors."

THE FARRIER'S SHOP.

DID you ever ride on an Irish Outside Jaunting Car
If you have, you may well feel for me—coming in from
Croom to Limerick on a vehicle of the kind ; not that
the great jeopardy of this conveyance is not greatly
avoided in the country ; for although I admit there is
occasionally a fear of being shaken off over rough
macadam, or thrown into a deep ditch, yet your limbs
are not in momentary fear of being crushed by a passing Jehu.   On the roads of Ireland, there is no crowd
of equipages.   Centralization has done its best, and
all the respectability of the country flock to Dublin.
     This is a long exordium ; but never mind,—better
late than never.   So, *revenons à nos moutons.*
     I was, as I said before, travelling from Croom to
Limerick on an outside car with my friend Major
Vokes, the celebrated chief magistrate of this county—
a functionary about whom as many tales are told in
Munster as are related of Robin Hood in Nottingham-
shire.   We were jogging along, truth to tell, half asleep,
when Corporal Mulreedy—a policeman in livery, who
was driving the carriage—turned round and gave us
the pleasing information that Master Bob (the Major's
favourite horse) had cast a shoe, and that consequently
it would be impossible to reach the city in time for the

Sessions then going on. After a short colloquy in Irish, our driver informed his master that there was a *smithee* some half-a-mile down a borheen, and, by his chief's orders, to that *smithee* we now proceeded.

As we neared the forge we perceived to our astonishment, or I should rather say mine (for the police-major seemed as little subject to surprise as a Red Indian), that several groups were collected around the shed we sought—why or wherefore, of course we could not imagine; nor, indeed, did Vokes seem to notice the circumstance in any marked manner.

Our limping animal, and the shoe in the driver's hand, told our tale and expressed our want. The crowd made way for us; and we were soon ensconced in the farrier's shop, indulging in a pleasant chat.

" You've a large assemblage to-day. Is it a fair or pattern?" asked Vokes.

" By no means," replied the shoer.

" Are you a friend of Tom Vokes?" suddenly demanded the farrier, after a pause.

" Me? by no means. I give you my honour I never saw him in my life; and I've every reason to believe I am his worst enemy."

I was about to interfere—a look from Vokes silenced me.

"God bless you, for that same!" said the farrier. " It's all right then, and I'll tell you the truth. This scoundrel, this blackguard of the world—may the curse of Cromwell be on him!—caused my uncle to be hanged for being concerned in the 'rection when the Blennerhassets were killed. Well, there's myself and Carmody, yonder, and Tom Grady, of Carrickonlish — whose brother he killed because they burned the ganger when he came to take Carmody's cattle,—and two or three other boys, and we've all sworn—by this and by that, on the Holy—that we'll kill Tom Vokes, and it's many a day we've looked out for him. But to-day we'll have him—glory to Ireland!—we'll give him a puck that'll send him to the grave of Going. Sure he's coming in at two o'clock to-day, and we'll tache him a lisson in manners."

I stood and trembled,—I confess I did not like it. Not so Vokes, who seemed to enjoy the joke, and replied, with a smile—

"Do you know his person?"

"Divil a bit; I nivir wish to see him till I take my shot."

"Well, he's about my size. But, as to your vengeance, you must delay it for two or three hours; for just before I left the main road, I saw Major Vokes going into Limerick well guarded."

"Sure that's provoking! What will we do?"

"Well," chimed in the fearless functionary, "I'll tell you how you can manage it: let Carmody, Grady, and yourself, be in waiting for him as he comes out. There's the 'Brian Borholm;' be there at five o'clock, and I'll stake my life he'll come out unattended. See that your guns are well charged, and mind no one but the ringleaders are there. I'll not be far off. But now the horse is shod I'll hasten on; and recollect what I've told you. Good-bye, boys," roared Vokes; and away we drove.

I would have spoken to him—I would have expostulated—I would have asked an explanation—but he was equally deaf to all. He laughed, told anecdotes, sang, talked in Irish with the corporal; but not a word on the subject of our late encounter would he deign to bestow on me.

At three o'clock the Sessions closed; and, after partaking of a hurried luncheon, the car came round to the door, and the Major requested me to mount. It was now past four.

I rather demurred to the proposition, and tried to show the folly of driving unarmed and unattended into a nest of murderers.

" Gighy-ma gow," said Vokes ; and as I well knew this meant an expression of unalterable determination, I foresaw the folly of reasoning with him. To attempt to dissuade him from this perilous journey, I felt was a task beyond my powers—to allow him to dare the dangers alone would be the act of a coward; so I jumped up, and off we went.

Major Vokes was in prime humour ; I cannot say that I shared his hilarity.

At length we came in sight of the public-house styled the " Brian Borholm " and in front of it I saw a large party of persons advancing to meet our carriage.

" Fly for your life !" cried I.

" Don't be making yourself a bosthoon," calmly replied the Major.

The stoical coachman drove steadily on. I could have seized the reins and throttled him with pleasure —but, as a military officer, I felt it might seem a want of courage ; so I silently prepared for my doom.

In ten minutes more we were abreast of the assassins. But how great was my astonishment! There stood the stalwart farrier and Carmody : yes, there they stood, with three or four other desperate-looking ruffians, all handcuffed. Around them were some twenty policemen armed to the teeth.

When Vokes arrived, the prisoners uttered a cry between a groan and a yell of execration.

" I promised that you should see me," said the police chief, " and here I am. Two of you are old offendors, and have hitherto eluded me. Faith ! you were soft to be taken in this trap. Sergeant Macmahon, take them into Limerick. Good-bye, boys ! You've seen, as you wished, Tom Vokes."

" Bedad, we have," replied the farrier; " but it's no use fighting wid fate. Sure we all know you've a charmed life. But if ever I get out, you'll not live long—if I have to buy a silver bullet !"

" You'd better buy something else," said Vokes; " for it's you that murdered the Widow Casey !"

" Who told you that ?"

" Faith ! we wont talk now," said Vokes. " Drive on ;" and away we went.

The farrier was tried at the following Assizes, convicted on clear evidence, admitted his guilt, and was hanged.

THE THUNDERSTORM.

ONE of the most sociable, and at the same time one of the most respectable institutions that ever existed, was the Limerick Club some thirty years ago. Here the first men of this and the neighbouring counties were wont to assemble. Here the wittiest and best convivialists of the province were in the habit of meeting and displaying their powers. Here the billiard room (which I have subsequently often seen graced by the appearance of H. R. H. the Duke of Cambridge, and his popular aide-de-camp, Colonel Macdonald) enlivened the tedious monotony of many a wet day. Here, the cook was celebrated for his artistic powers; while, to crown all, here that claret which was once reckoned amidst the charms of Ireland, still existed—that claret, which was about as superior to the worthy grocer's *vin ordinaire* of the present day as pure Falernian to the washing of port wine bottles : for until about 1830, splendid claret still existed in Ireland. It is now all gone ; and more's the pity.

To resume, however.

I was sitting at table, in the snug dining-room of the Limerick Club, joined in my meal by J. V., a relative of my own, a gentleman more than whom none were respected in this old city, of which he had been twice the mayor, and in which he held still several high situations. We had finished our dinner, and washed it down with a couple of bottles of old sherry. J. V. had ordered a cooper (six bottles) of claret, for the two of us. The fire was stirred up by the busy waiter, the red curtains were drawn closer, our napkins were thrown across our krees. J. V. seemed inclined for a comfortable sitting (which, by the bye, was no joke, as the worthy ex-mayor always assured his friends that in company with a good fellow he was ready to wear out a *lignum vitæ* chair). All but a single pair of wax candles were removed, and everything bespoke a coming jollification, when Vokes suddenly entered the room.

"I have come to say, I can't go over to Ennis to-morrow; so my dear Harry you must frame your plans accordingly. I must go over to Tipperary—a riot is expected there. I wish you could come with me, Major," added he, turning to J. V. (who, by the bye was a major in the militia regiment commanded by his brother), "I wish we had you over there, for I know that you are in the commission of that county, and I have so often experienced the benefit of your services as a magistrate, that I should like to have your aid on this occasion."

"I should be happy to go with you; but the truth is I've a few friends coming to dine with me to-morrow."

"Oh, then, if you stay away for that, we shall never get you; for your hospitality is so notorious that we all know you never sit down alone."

"Well, to tell truth, I do like to see my friends around me. But sit down, man ; don't you hear the rain coming down ? the barometer has betokened a coming storm all day. Here, fill your glass ; there's plenty more claret in the house."

Vokes sat down, filled his glass, and listened eagerly to the rain, which now beat violently against the windows.

"So, I hear," continued J. V., "that you rode out to Adare with a single policeman, yesterday, and seized Mick Rooney. Now, wasn't this foolhardy ? Faith, they'll kill you some day or other, and then both the county and your family will mourn over your temerity."

"Pooh, pooh !" rejoined the police magistrate ; "they'll not injure me. Depend upon it, a bold front awes these fellows."

"By George ! I'm not sure of that. No one, I think, doubts my courage ; but I would not run the risk you run daily, to be made lord-lieutenant of Ireland."

Vokes laughed. But at this moment a loud clap of thunder was heard, and a flash of lightning pierced through the interior of the shutters. Vokes turned deadly pale, and uttered an exclamation—an exclamation of terror.

"Why, then, it's nothing at all ; it's only a thunder clap and a flash of lightning. It must not interrupt our evening."

Vokes turned deadly pale, and covered his face with his hands. I tried in vain to rally him. He was evidently terror-stricken, and at the next roll of heaven's artillery, rose and bolted out of the room.

We were fairly puzzled to know what had become of him; but for a few. moments we continued to keep up our conversation, expressing our deep wonder at the bold magistrate's conduct. J. V. thought that he had recklessly rushed out through the storm to rejoin his family, some of the females of whom might feel alarmed. I rather thought he had been taken ill; but evidently did not wish to be followed. So I waited quietly some ten or fifteen minutes, and then, as he did not reappear, I slipped out and asked the waiter about the Major.

The man could not resist smiling as he replied—

" He is below, sir."

" Where?"

" I'll show you, sir."

This I thought strange, and, somewhat surprised, I followed the servant down the kitchen steps. To my astonishment he walked towards a back cellar, and throwing open the door, and handing me the candle, for it was pitch dark, he exclaimed, "He's in there, sir." I started at the idea, and dreaded some misfortune had happened. I waved the candle aloft, and beheld T. P. V., cowering in the corner, with his silk handkerchief spread over his head. " Good heavens!" thought I, "he's dead!" But the next moment my fears were relieved; he raised the kerchief, and asked in timid tones—

" Is it over?"

" What?"

"The thunder and lightning ?"

"Oh, yes! But what is the matter with you, my dear sir? Are you ill, or hurt ?"

"Neither, my dear fellow. But I've the greatest horror of the war of the elements."

"Surely, you are not alarmed at such trifles ?"

"By the soul of my grandsire, I am. I'd rather meet fifty croppies any day than encounter a thunder-storm. Franklin told me last week that silk was a non-conductor, so I've thrown my handkerchief over my head. Egad! the flash was so vivid it almost curdled my blood with fear. But now I'm all right again, and if the rain ceases I think I'll ride over to Derk to-night, and sleep there, and have a chat with the hospitable owner of that mansion before I go into Tipperary in the morning."

"But you forget the state of the county; recollect the danger you run if you are recognised."

"Bah! they'll not dare touch me, and if they did, I know how to defend myself. Besides, to tell you the truth, I feel that this fright has so chilled my blood I require some exercise to restore my circulation. Yes, I'll ride over to Derk at once;" and, in spite of all my entreaties, my arguments respecting the danger, and a thousand other reasons which I equally urged, away went this dare-devil (for really I can call him by no other name), to gallop across a disaffected country at ten o'clock at night. I returned to my friend, and related to him all the facts of the case.

He was, like myself, puzzled and surprised. Nor could he then, nor can I to this present hour, account for this strange inconsistency in human nature—the boldest and bravest man, a stranger to every ordinary fear, flying and shouting in terror at the sound of a roll of thunder and a flash of lightning !

Yet such was the case. I personally bear testimony to the fact—leaving philosophers better versed than myself in such matters, to account for this physiological anomaly.

THE IDIOT BOY.

" Peter, my boy," said Vokes, one evening, as we were sitting round the fire, at the same time addressing a near relation,—" Peter, my boy, why do you never hunt ? I can mount you right well, if you wish to go out with the hounds to-morrow."

" I never hunt now."

" Not hunt ! Why, you used to be a perfect Nimrod !"

" It is true ; but a circumstance which occurred to me about two years ago, when I was out hunting in a distant part of this country, has so thoroughly disgusted me with the sport, that, truth to tell, I don't think I shall ever go out again."

" It must have been a serious cause. Was it an accident to yourself ?"

" Not at all. I'll relate it to you ; though really, even now, I feel horrified as I narrate it. As an old English sportsman, I came over here, anxious to try hunting in the sister country.

" The fact is, the Leicestershire man who has never visited the sister isle has little idea of Irish sport. A hunter worth 300*l.* at Melton would be dear in Ireland at 50*l.* ; that is, as far as his field qualities in that country go. Instead of hedges, ditches, and fences, we have

earth-banks, small rivers, and stone walls to encounter
and overcome ; and as the first of them (which, by the
bye, are miscalled *ditches*) are often some eight or ten
feet high, it is absolutely necessary that the nag which
bears you should be trained to jump on the top and off
again, or slide down on the other side—by no means an
uncommon occurrence—as the exigency of the moment
may require.   Mounted on a thoroughly well-trained
horse, and possessing some knowledge of the country,
I cannot help awarding the sporting prize to Ireland.
There is a joviality and sociality at cover-side unknown
on this side of the water.   There is a cheering shout
and a reckless pursuit, when the game is running, unequalled in our hunting fields.   It is true that every
now and then you are joined and accompanied by a
ragged, barefooted Paddy, who yells as he runs along
beside your horse, keeping full pace with you, and only
pausing while he stands still to see you take your
' *lape.*'   In no place does Irish hospitality shine more
brilliantly than in the hunting field.   Should a check
occur, should a pause arise during the meridian hours
of the day, the sportsmen gather together, and at once
ride up uninvited to the best mansion in the neighbourhood, where with joy they are received and welcomed.   An impromptu luncheon is instantly served,
and a plentiful supply of ' red round,' washed down
by every imaginable drinkable, is offered to the
hungry hunters.   The highly-spiced meat, the no less
exciting liquor, comes pleasantly before the sportsman ; and in half an hour he again starts—like Antæus
refreshed from sleep—stronger and more energetic than
ever.

"Some years ago, I remember, that we had chopped one fox in cover—a second we had lost, after a run of twenty minutes, and vainly endeavoured to find a third; our hounds were scattering about, a blight had come over the scent, we drew in blank our best cover; all without success. It was now past one o'clock, and there seemed no chance of immediate sport. So we at once drew off the hounds, and rode on to Bally-murphy, the seat of Mr. T——, where, as we expected, we found a right good luncheon laid out—to attack which we did not fail. We *drew* the corks, and the claret quickly *broke cover*.

"T—— was one of those fine old Irish gentlemen who appear to have dwindled away ever since the visit of Father Mathew and the Encumbered Estates Bill —two visitations that have destroyed the wit of the lower ' orders, and much retrenched the substantial hospitality of the upper classes. It is not more unna-tural to put a pig in a warm bath night and morning, than to call upon a *real* Irishman to drink little and to owe less.

"T—— kept open house; like the ancient tourna-ments, it was 'free to all comers.' There were always a hogshead of claret and a puncheon of whisky on the run; beef, mutton, and bread (as T—— expressed it) were grown on the estate. There were about a dozen servants, who not only divided, but occasionally alter-nated, the household duties amongst them; besides these, there was the old nurse, the blind piper, and the idiot boy—three characters ever attached to the old Irish mansions. It is hinted that there were also a *fortune-teller* and a *banshee* on the establishment; but this was only whispered.

"I had given my horse to the idiot boy, to lead round to the stables; for the lad, though soft and silly, perfectly understood what he was about. He could run messages, convey letters; and, by doing odd jobs now and then, assisted to support a poor mother who perfectly adored him. To this boy, then, I gave my nag, and cheerfully sat down to enjoy my luncheon.

"As is usual on such occasions, much chaffing, much boasting took place; and, in some way or other, the young lady of the house was induced to enter into a sporting discussion, in which she of course got the worst; but, determined to be quits, she, on the first opportunity, slily left the room, and carried out her project. The argument had been relative to the great acumen of her sporting adversary, who declared that he was beyond the power of being deceived.

"Miss T——— proceeded to the entrance of the kitchen, and called Micky, the idiot boy, out, who joyfully obeyed her summons. She now hurriedly directed him to take a soldier (a red herring), and having fastened it to a string, to drag it on after him at full trail—over ditch, dyke, and wall—for two miles, in the direction of Roby McArthur's farm. Arrived, how-ever, at that house, he was carefully to hide away; for, if found by the infuriated hunter—thus misled by a *drag*—he would surely receive severe castigation. Micky assured his young mistress that he had done the same once before, and would do it right well, if they only gave him twenty minutes' start. These matters were arranged. The young lady, whose absence had not been noticed, rejoined her father's guests. Her health is drunk in a bumper.

"Luncheon concluded, our horses are brought round; we mount, and, with a warm farewell, again we ride towards the cover. We are lightly talking over our late hospitable reception, when, suddenly, the whimper of a favourite hound is heard—the sound increases—a general cry, and we dash forward. The scent lies strong, and away we go. Now Tom Murphy's celebrated horse strikes a stone wall; Tom is thrown; every one is sorry for him; but, dead or alive, we have no time to stop and assist him. Now a high ditch rises before us; only half the hounds climb over it; I clear the summit, and dash off on the other side. In doing so, I jump over a man and horse lying sprawling at the foot; the man is Jem Trollope, who is trying an English hunter in the county of Limerick. But never mind—we dash onward; we arrive at a farmhouse; the hounds jump over the wall with eager yell, and rush into a pigstye, where Reynard has doubtless sought refuge. But, stay—what piercing cry is that? Another, and another! Surely those screams are human! 'Whip off the hounds! Body and soul! whip 'em off! Don't you hear it is a human scream?' cries the master of the hounds.

"In a moment we are all out of our saddles, when an agonizing shout is heard in the opposite direction, and a woman, in apparent frenzy, dashes through us, and leaps into the stye. 'Allanah! Allanah! It's Micky —my boy Micky!' The hounds draw forth an object. But no!—it is too horrible to dwell upon—it is too horrible to describe. Suffice it to say, the wretched parent's fears were too fearfully verified. The poor idiot boy, having completed his task, had crept into the stye, dragging in with him the red herring, on which he had begun to feast, as the pack, led by the strong scent, dashed in on their prey. The mangled remains, still palpitating, were those of poor Micky. In his anger, the Squire killed one of his very best hounds, whose jaws still reeked with human blood. Insensibility sheltered the poor mother for a moment, who never lifted up her head again—was never known to smile. The hounds were sent off to Galway ; and for a long time no attempt was made to hunt the county.

" The circumstances are so indelibly engraved on my memory, that I verily believe, if I found any one 'running a drag,' I'd then and there sacrifice him to the manes of the poor Idiot Boy."

THE COLLEEN BAWN.

THE powerful novel entitled "The Collegians"—the
work of Gerald Griffin—not only made a great impression at the time when it was written, but has since
been revived by its having been dramatized by
more than one author, and in its every shape become
a popular play—the most successful edition or adap-
tation being that of Dion Boucicault, who, with Mr.
Webster, produced it and played in it, at the New
Adelphi Theatre, above 300 nights consecutively, and
thus made the unhappy story, under the title of the
"Colleen Bawn" a household word in the mouth of
every Londoner. This unequalled popularity naturally
introduced it throughout the provinces, and so general
was its production, that I feel certain there are but
few—very few—who have not seen or heard of this
most charming and successful drama. The plot of the
stage version is, however, very, very far from a correct
one, as regards facts. The poor girl whom Boucicault
styles the Colleen Bawn was too surely destroyed, and
happily the hero of the melodrama, as well as his
servant, were brought to condign punishment. Nor
can the correct tale be even gathered from the original
tale by Griffin. The work in question, written by him,
was brought out within ten or fifteen years after the

murder, and consequently the author was compelled ingeniously to alter the true facts, the less to wound the feelings of the culprit's family, who were then alive, bearing a high position in the city and county of Limerick.

Lest some who still bear the name may yet survive, and feel annoyed at a fresh reiteration of facts—naturally distressing to their feelings—I will pass over the early facts of the case, and maintain a strict silence touching those motives which led to the act of horror. A true revelation of them might involve the names of two noble families, who, though of course in no way implicated in the crime, or cognizant of the unhappy circumstances which led to the immolation of a good and most innocent girl, might yet feel wounded in seeing their names once more appear connected with the fearful story. As, however, I look upon the capture and punishment of the criminals as one of Vokes's most talented acts, I quote the story—omitting the names (as I said before) of those who might feel annoyed at being thus once more dragged forward, and only commence the sketch where the general editions of this tale end, namely, *some six weeks after* the murder had been committed.

We will therefore open the present narrative at this period, laying the scene in the beautiful and picturesque village of Glynn, where the unhappy girl had resided ever since her elopement with Mr. S——, who had now, however, almost quite forsaken that place—being deeply engaged (as it was said) in endeavouring to obtain the hand of one of the noblest and most virtuous maidens that graced the British peerage. Eily O'Connor had quietly quitted S——, who however still retained, I believe, his cottage at Glynn, and left his confidential servant, a certain Sullivan, in charge of it, who however, only remained there a few hours and abruptly left. The proprietor of the finest estate in the neighbourhood, and the master of all the soil around, was the then Mr. Fitzgerald, who boasted the honour of bearing the style of "Knight of Glynn,"—one of the *two* oldest titles in Ireland. The knight was, of course, a magistrate for the county, much respected and liked. But to return to my sketch.

The servant man, in that sort of confidence which is ever affected to spread a tale, informed the gossips that Eily had never *really* been the wife of Mr. S——, but that he had been deeply attached to her, and lest he might legally marry her, his family had insisted on his sending her off to America ; and that she had gone there some ten days before with one hundred pounds in her pocket. The man graphically described the parting, and as the possibility of such an emigration had before been hinted at, the statement was readily received and believed.

Some six weeks later the inhabitants of a few cottages near Glynn were horrified by seeing a female body washed on shore by the rough waves of the Shannon — which is here above a mile in width. To recognise it was impossible, and its identity appeared lost, since it was a mere *torso*, or trunk : the head had fallen off and all the limbs were gone—the outer dress had disappeared, and the present remnant of humanity was only preserved and held together by a pair of strong though old brown jean stays. The trunk was at once conveyed to the dead-house of the village, in order that every one might see it—but not with the slightest hope of its being recognised. Of course all the females and the male idlers in Glynn went to see it. All looked at it, shook their heads, and turned away from it in horror. Though, truth to tell, no one suspected foul play, the general belief was that some unfortunate female had fallen overboard, and that the length of time she had lain in the water had thus destroyed her form.

Amongst others who visited the dead-house was an old crone who only occasionally visited Glynn. The instant she beheld the remains she exclaimed "God be good to us! By the Virgin, that is the body of Eily ——— !" The persons around her jeered at her, and reminded her tauntingly that the young girl she mentioned had gone to America. But no power could shake the opinion she had formed, and she went straight before the nearest magistrate (the late knight of Glynn), one of the most upright men that ever lived and reiterated her tale.

" Upon what grounds do you base your assertion ?"

" Sure it's no assertion, but positive truth."

" Why do you say so ? The trunk of one individual closely resembles that of another; then why say that this is the body of Eily ——— ?"

" I'll tell yer honour. About two months ago I got a piece of printed chintz, and I'm ready to swear that the likes of it did not exist in Ireland. It was not only peculiar in its pattern but in its colours."

" But what has all this to do with the matter ?"

" Faix, then, I'm coming to that. May the saints

10

never look down on me, but the stays in the dead-
house are patched with that same chintz which I sold
to poor Eily. Your honor, I'll take my oath to its
being the truth."

Now this was a trivial circumstance; but the
knight thought it worth while instantly to ride into
Limerick, and into that city he caused the old woman
to be marched between two policemen, then and there
to be examined by the chief magistrate of police,
Thomas Phillips Vokes, who cross-examined the woman in every way; but she was firm to her evidence.
Lest, however, she might be tampered with, the
worthy magistrate caused her to be detained and
carefully watched.

Vokes, as I said before, once on a track, sifted
everything. The vessel in which poor Eily had been
said to have sailed, had now returned. No such individual had gone out in her.

About seven weeks before, and about the last time she
had been noticed, she had been seen going out in a row-
boat with Mr. S—— and his servant Sullivan; further
inquiries elicited the fact that cries for help had been
heard in the direction of a neighbouring island; while
one party distinctly swore that he saw the boat return
with the two men but no woman, and had even asked
about the circumstance from Sullivan, who told him
in reply, that he and his master had taken the girl on
board one of Spaight's ships, and left her. Nothing
could be more plausible, more probable, and until the
discovery had been made that she had never been on
board that vessel, the fact did not appear suspicious.

Under these circumstances, warrants against Mr.

S—— and his servant Sullivan were issued. But the first was not to be found, and the second had gone to America. Of this there was no doubt.

The chief magistrate of police and the knight tried every means to apprehend the accused gentleman, but without effect. It is true he was known to be lurking in the county; but secreted and protected by his powerful relations, the task of seizing him seemed to be impossible. Several well-planned attempts at capture signally failed, and months rolled on before anything could be done.

It was a dark evening when Fitzgerald, the knight, walked into the residence of Major Vokes, and in private made him a communication on the subject; the latter at once called out a troop of dragoons, and took with him a dozen mounted policemen. At their head rode the two magistrates.

They proceeded at a brisk trot towards the residence of Mr. M—— of S——, one of the most independent and influential men in the county of Limerick. As Major Vokes rode through the park he spread the dragoons round the house, and communicated his directions to the officers.

He then gave a loud knock, the door was opened, and the functionaries instantly ran into the dining-room. There some ten or twelve gentlemen were assembled, and on the left of the host sat Mr. S——. In a moment they rose and would have fallen on their intruders. S—— already prepared for flight, when, drawing out a double-barrelled pistol, the chief magistrate pointed it at the head of the accused. Fitzgerald did the same. "There is no use in violence, gentlemen," said the former, "opposition is out of the question. I arrest Mr. S—— on a charge of murder, and whoever resists the capture does so at his peril. It is no use looking towards the door or the window; the hall is filled with police, the whole house is surrounded by dragoons. I arrest the prisoner, and shall instantly take him off too Limerick."

"And do you think this conduct gentlemanlike? —to enter a person's house and drag off his guest?"

"When that house becomes the refuge of a murderer, courtesies cease; there is no use in bandying words. Were he in the Pope's dormitory or the sanctuary of Westminster, I would equally drag him forth. Come, sir. Sergeant Reedy put on the handcuffs. In these cases there is no respect to persons. Captain, have the goodness to let your troop mount at once; we must not lose a moment in reaching Limerick. Be good enough to order your men to load their pistols and keep close to the policemen. Gentlemen," said he, turning to the murmuring party around him, "you see there is no hope of a rescue. Let the law, I beseech you, for once be executed without the shedding of blood."

By this time all was ready, and in two hours more Mr. S—— was a prisoner in the old gaol. Many of his friends had followed him at a distance; but the force which Vokes's foresight had caused him to take with him was too imposing to be lightly attacked.

A few days later Mr. S—— was brought to trial; an overwhelming mass of evidence brought forward clearly proved him to have been the actual perpetrator, or immediate participator, in this brutal murder.

As we shall have again to recur to these details, it is unneccessary to give them here; suffice it to say that the jury unhesitatingly pronounced him *guilty*.

At the same moment a post-chaise and four galloped from behind the court-house, in which was seated a county magistrate. The carriage took the road to Dublin; simultaneously another similar equipage started from Moriarty's Hotel, also bound for the capital. They reached it in the morning. The one traveller sought out the Lord-Lieutenant, the other the Lord Chancellor. Each of these functionaries was earnestly appealed to—"the honour of a noble family," "the improbability of the case," "only supported by circumstantial evidence," and a thousand other reasons were urged for extending mercy to the prisoner. But the prayer of each was firmly refused, and the disappointed petitioners returned to their hotel, where they wrote for further influence. Twenty-four hours later the carriage of a most popular nobleman—bearing an Earl's coronet—sought the high authorities; but no audience could be granted. "*The law must take its course.*"

In the meantime the prisoner went on laughing and joking, apparently amused at the preposterous idea of his having committed such a crime. He seemed wholly unconscious of his dreadful situation, and in this line of conduct he was, in all probability, supported by his proud relations, as well as by a thorough belief that he would receive a reprieve.

On the morning of the day appointed for his execution, the sub-Sheriff and the Chaplain visited him, and showed him there was "no hope." He must die!

S—— appeared somewhat terror-stricken, and begged
to be left for a few moments to pray alone. This was
accorded him. But on the return of the functionaries
they found his eyes starting out of his head, and his
cheeks flushed. He had swallowed laudanum ; but in
such a large quantity as to stupify, not kill him. The
usual modes were exercised to empty his stomach, and
in a short time he was out of danger. Who gave him
this poison he never divulged.

In consideration of his connexions, he was allowed
to proceed to the gallows (about a mile and a-half off,)
in a post-chaise drawn by two black horses, the
property of Mr. Denmeade, an undertaker. These
horses were usually accustomed to draw a hearse ; they
were extremely quiet and gentle creatures.

The crowd was immense, and as S—— stepped into
the chaise a shout of execration rent the air ; but
Major Vokes had so guarded the vehicle with police
and troops, that there was no fear of a Lynch law
attack on the part of the people, or a rescue on the
part of his friends.

The horses walked on steadily till they came to the
foot of Baal's Bridge, which spans a fast-running
branch of the Shannon. Here they came to a dead
halt, and neither whip, spur, nor stick could induce
them to move farther. That "*no horse will draw a
murderer across a running stream*" is a strong belief
among the Irish peasantry, so here they believed that
they had a proof vouchsafed by Providence, which
none could doubt, of Mr. S——'s guilt ; so now they
would have torn him to pieces if they could have got
at him. In the meanwhile every means (not omitting

the burning brand, often used to start horses in Ireland) were employed. One horse, however, kicked himself out of his traces, while the other deliberately lay down and refused to move.

Mr. S—— was requested to descend from the carriage, and with a pale face and faltering step he did so. But on the whole it must be admitted he walked with tolerable calmness to the place of execution. ·

Here no news of a reprieve met him, and as he ascended the fatal ladder he seemed to have resigned himself to his fate. He looked earnestly into the crowd and there saw many of his family. Their presence appeared to strengthen his resolution.

The chaplain then came up, and besought him on the eve of eternity to confess the truth. S——, however, again declared his innocence. All but the sub-sheriff (John Cuthbert) and the executioner had withdrawn, and the cap was drawn over his face; the former stepped forward, and, seizing his arm, said, "In another minute you will be before the Judge who reads all hearts. Are you guilty?" "No!" replied the other, firmly, "I die innocent;" and with this falsehood on his lips he was launched into eternity. The world will probably never again see such an example of family pride !

For several months after the execution the most fearful denunciations were fulminated against those who had thus (as they said) sacrificed an innocent man. Major Vokes and the Knight of Glynn were tabooed by half the respectable society in Limerick. But the former was not a man to let anything drop, and while all supposed he had forgotten the case, he had sent out a confidential agent to New York, and found that Sullivan (the servant) had returned from thence to England. This was enough for him. He despatched four of his sharpest policemen to London, and in a few weeks Sullivan was safely lodged in Limerick gaol. He was tried on the same evidence as his master, was found guilty, and condemned to die.

Now Sullivan was a Roman Catholic, and very properly believd that his best chance of heavenly forgiveness was to make an ample earthly confession; besides which he had no pride of family; so he sent for his priest and the sub-Sheriff, and in their presence made the following statement, which may be wrong in some minor particulars, as I have not heard of, or read of, this terrible murder for the last twenty years. But I give the details as I recollect :—

" My master and I," began the servant, " had agreed for several days to put Eily out of the way, and we only waited an opportunity. I was then and there to get 100l. and a free passage to America. Such was our bargain. Well, yer riverence, it was a lovely evening when my master proposed to take poor Eily (for he never called her his wife) out on the river for a row. Not a ripple was on the surface, so we three started together. I had a gun, as I said, to kill fowl, at the bottom of the boat. My master brought his flute, which he played merrily as we skimmed along. There is a little island about four miles beyond Glynn, and here the master landed, desiring me to take Eily a further row. To this we assented, and away we went. When we were about 200 yards from the

island I took up the gun and began talking about
death. Oh, yer riverence, if ye'd heard her speak of it—
had ye heard her call down blessings on the master! I
raised the gun. 'What's that you're at; sure you'd
not hurt poor Eily, who prays for you every night;'
and she gave me the look of an angel. The fallen one
himself could not have harmed her. So I threw down
the gun and rowed back to the master, and told him I
couldn't, I wouldn't do it.

"Upon this the master cursed me, and called me a
coward, and threatened me if I didn't do it; and said
he'd do it himself, only he could not go to Ameriky as
I could, and he offered me more money down, and
swore he'd purtect me, and all that. Well, at last I
jumped into the boat again, and as soon as I got a few
yards out I up with the gun, and, without looking at
her, gave her a blow on the head with the gun stock
which stunned her; she screamed, and the master, who
was watching us on shore, began playing the flute to
drown her cries. I struck her two or three times, till
I thought she was dead, and then I lifted her and
threw her into the water. I then took up the oars
again, and was about to row for the shore, when she
arose to the surface and grasped the edge of the boat.
By this time I felt more like a tiger than a man, and
I smashed her hands all to pieces with the oar. She
let go her hold, and slowly sank. But as she died she
gave me one look—oh! such a look—it haunts me at
night—it pursues me in my pleasures. Even when I
drink to drown remembrance, I see that last glance of
poor Eily's. The master sent me away soon after.
But I could not travel away from her last look—I

even fancy I see it now. I do believe it smiles, since I've told the truth—the whole truth!" and here the wretch made a most solemn asseveration of the truth of his statement. He was examined and re-examined. He never wavered in a single particular. On the way to the gallows, he turned to the officer who guarded him, and declared that since he had confessed Eily had appeared to him no more, and on this fact he built his hope of being forgiven.

On the scaffold he acknowledged his guilt, and confirmed all he had previously stated. At the last moment the priest said to him—"You are about to enter into eternity. Are you guilty? Did Mr. S—— plan and assist you in the crime?"

"As I hope to be saved, he did!" and the next moment the culprit had ceased to live.

I have here endeavoured to sketch as correctly as I could the facts of a case which will ever be remembered by the inhabitants of Munster. Many versions have been put forth, but I feel confident that mine is an exact and unbiassed statement.

All the parties interested and engaged in this fearful affair have, I believe, passed away. "May they rest in peace!"

RECEIVING RENTS.

VOKES and myself were dining at the hotel in Tipperary, when we were joined by Mr. H——, one of the most intelligent members of the legal profession in Ireland, who, besides his other duties, performed those of several first-rate agencies in Kildare, Queen's County, and Tipperary. The addition of this pleasant companion to our company gave great satisfaction to my relative ; and, indeed, I shared the feeling, when, warmed by a glass or two of punch, our friend poured forth a string of most amusing anecdotes. After an hour thus agreeably employed, the magistrate turned round, and abruptly asked him—

" And what brings you here ?"

" I am come to collect the rents on the Kilbarry estate, for which I am the agent."

" Are you going to try the experiment when the country is in such a disturbed state ?. Sure, your life is not worth a day's purchase if you do."

" Oh, this is the third time I've done so, and here I am, safe and sound. On the first occasion, it is true, I ran a considerable risk ; but I've now no fear."

" How is that ?"

" Oh, it's a long story, though a curious one,

strangely illustrative of the Tipperary peasantry; but—"

" Oh, let's have it ?"

" Pray do," I chimed in.

" Well, I'll tell it you, for I think I can recollect all the circumstances.

" I was barely three-and-twenty years of age, and wholly unacquainted with this county, when I was nominated agent to the Kilbarry estate, a small but snug property, worth about 1000l. or 1200l. a year. When the first rent became due, I came down to Clonmel, accompanied by an assistant, and at once demanded the sums in arrear. I was coolly but determinedly met by a general refusal from every one of the tenants. It appears the lands had been lately sold; the farmers assured me that they looked upon the sale as illegal, and one and all declared their consequent determination not to pay one farthing. They also added this comforting assurance, namely, that though they did not wish to be uncivil, the sooner I returned to Dublin the sooner I should be in safety. My assistant, on this hint, at once fled, and on my appealing to a friend in the locality, he strongly advised me to do the same. Nothing could be done on the spot, that was clear. The man I had taken with me would alarm others; indeed, I could better serve my cause in Dublin than in Tipperary; by these and other arguments, I was persuaded to return to the Irish metropolis. Thence, a short correspondence ensued with the defaulters, but not one wavered. They again positively refused to pay, and dared me to enforce my claim. In the meantime, I found myself (what is called) *fixed* for the whole amount, and as I could ill afford the loss, I determined, whether it cost me my life or not, to make one more personal effort. Having thus made up my mind, I sought out Charles Macklin, a barrister, and a schoolfellow of mine. I knew he would do anything to serve me. After stating my case to him he for a few moments remained in silent doubt, and seemed mentally to canvass some idea. At length he turned round and abruptly exclaimed, 'Yes, you shall have it; it is the only way.'

" I looked puzzled.

"'Yes, I'll give you a letter to the only man in the whole county who can assist you. But if I give you this introduction, you had better be entirely guided by his advice.'

"'I will,' said I; 'but is your friend a magistrate?'

"'By no means,' said Macklin, smiling. 'I am about to present you to Bill Quiglan.'

"'What?' cried I, starting up with astonishment, 'Bill Quiglan, the supposed murderer, the most desperate man in the county?'

"'The same,' replied he, coolly sitting down and writing a short note, which he carefully sealed. 'The same; if he cannot assist you, none can. Keep, however, your own counsel, and see him, if possible, before it is known that you are in the county. Good luck to you—good bye.' He handed me the letter, and I took my leave.

" I went down by the then night mail, and, keeping close, made myself acquainted with the locality where my redoubted friend resided. I ordered a covered car and as the evening shades closed in, I started.

"In the middle of a wild bog stood the cottage I sought—a more exposed, a more desolate spot I never beheld. But I boldly knocked at the door, and, lifting the latch, I entered. The whole dwelling consisted of one room. Over the fireplace a well-kept long duck-gun was suspended, and a brace of pistols served as a further ornament between the bed and the chimney corner ; a pitchfork was thrown carelessly against the wall, and everything denoted warlike defence in case of attack. At the same time, although the habitation consisted of a single chamber, there was an air of neatness and comfort about it, far beyond the-average of luxury displayed by Irish cabins in general.

" Bill, who was a tall powerful man, decently dressed, and possessed of a fine countenance, rose on my entrance, put down his *dudeen,* and perceiving me to be a gentleman, bowed to me respectfully. He showed little or no symptoms of surprise—though evidently ill pleased with the visit.

" ' Good evening Mr. Quiglan.'

" ' Sure I'm generally called Bill Quiglan—at your service. Can I be of any use to you, sir ? '

" ' This will explain,' said I, handing him my letter of introduction. ' It is from Mr. Charles Macklin, now in Dublin.'

" ' Then, sir,' said he, hastily banishing the frown from his brow, ' then sir, you are welcome a thousand times. I trust his honor is well ? '

" ' Quite well—quite well. But you had better read his communication.'

"'I'll do that same.' Ho opened the letter and perused it with great attention, then suddenly turning round, he exclaimed : "And now, sir, what can I do for you ?'

"'I am come for the purpose of enforcing the payment of the rents on the Kilbarry estate. Mr. Macklin thought you could assist me ?'

"'And so I can.'

"'Well, what had I best do ?'

"'Arrest Tim Macarthy, the chief tenant!'

"'Macarthy ? He has several labourers ; he is well lodged, and I fear I can find no bailiff to undertake the job. Why he is the most lawless fellow of the lot.'

"'That's true for you : not a soul would dare to try it. That's the man—he should be seized.'

"'Then what am I to do ?'

"'Charles Macklin is your friend : it is sufficient—I'll seize him myself.'

"'What assistance will you require ?'

"'None: they'd be bold men, and bad ones too, who'd offer resistance to Bill Quiglan, of Ballybeg. Sure you have heard of me before—have you not—or else why do you thus come to me ?'

"'Well, Bill, it is true I have heard,' and here I began to speak in a somewhat nervous manner, 'I have heard that some years ago you had the misfortune to—that is—'

"'Out with it—don't stammer or mince the matter. You've heard I murdered Tim Dooler—sure it's no secret—all the county rang with it—and I must admit that the jury brought in a fair verdict when they pronounced me guilty. It's well for them I considered it so, or some of them would not be riding about their farms at this moment. I had no right, you see, to punish them for a just verdict.'

"'But if you were convicted how did you get off?'

"'Ah, then, you might have guessed it from the way in which I treat Counsellor Macklin's note. Didn't he find a flaw in the indictment, or some such thing, and by his exertions didn't he get me off clear and clean—so there was an end of *that* affair.'

"My looks plainly expressed my horror and astonishment. This he at once perceived.

"'You now know why I'd lay down my life for Charley Macklin—may Providence bless him! Faith, I'll be true to him as steel. And as you are his friend, I'll go through fire and water to serve him; so you needn't fear me. Though, faith, I believe you are about the only man in the county that does not. Sure, I'll seize him, and lodge him in Cashel gaol.'

"'I'm much obliged to you; but even that won't do. He must appear in Dublin, and I fear it will be impossible to convey him there.'

"'That's true for you; they'd never allow it. Bedad! the boys are true to the cause. It's not a stranger they'd allow to carry off one of themselves. Your only way will be to apply for a large detachment of soldiers and police, and march him off. Faith, they'll have a rough walk of it; and it's not so sure they'll get him to Dublin after all.

"'Right, Quiglan; but cannot you suggest any other mode?'

"'Hould your tongue for a minute, and let me think.'

"He pondered while taking three or four whiffs of his pipe, then suddenly turning round, he asked me—

"'Do you know the contents of the note you brought me?'

"'Not I.'

"'Then I'll tell it to you. He merely says 'H——, the bearer of this letter, is my best friend; treat him as you would treat myself, and serve him if you can.'

"'Upon my honour, I'm much obliged to him.'

"'And you know,' continued 'Big Bill,' 'that the counsellor saved my life, and therefore you must be aware I'd risk that life ten thousand times over to please him. He tells me to serve you as if you were himself. Faith, then, I'll not shrink from it, though the task is difficult. I'll seize him, and convey him to Dublin to-morrow night.'

"'A thousand thanks.'

"'That will do. You will, of course, pay all expenses, and give me 10l. for my trouble?'

"'Willingly.'

"'Well, then, give me the writ.'

"I produced several.

"'This one will do,' said Bill, selecting the writ against Macarthy; 'and now be off, and if any one stops you, tell him you are a friend of Bill Quiglan. Don't be late in Cashel; I'll be there before five. Good night;' and he closed his door as I drove off to Tipperary, wondering whether my new friend could really carry out his promises.

"I arrived on the next evening, about five o'clock, at the inn in Cashel, and learnt that a person had called

11

and ordered a car for himself and a friend to proceed to Clonmel at seven o'clock.

" 'Do you know who the person was ?'

"After a moment's hesitation, he replied, 'It was Bill Quiglan, sir; he has brought a prisoner, whom he wishes to convey to Clonmel, where the assizes are going forward.'

"I felt surprised, and almost feared treachery on hearing that he had thus publicly proclaimed our intended departure; but as it was now too late to retrace my steps, I made the best of it, and sat down to a hurried dinner. This was scarcely over when my bold companion was announced. He was now dressed most respectably, and assumed an air of gentility and confidence which I had not perceived on the previous evening.

" 'Well, sir, when you are done, we will, if you please, at once start. I wish to get into Clonmel as early as possible,' and he gave me a knowing wink unperceived by the waiter.

"I was going to say, ' Quiglan——.'

" 'Nabocklish. Run, Pat, and hurry the car. Sure we're to go round by the gaol to take Macarthy up.'

" ' Well,' thought I, ' this man is the most imprudent fellow I ever met with,' and I loudly expressed the idea as the waiter closed the door.

" 'Whist I these walls have ears.'

" ' Yes; but you don't understand. It's not——.'

" 'Hisht ! faith, do you take me for an omadawn. All's right; you'll see presently ;' and without allowing me again to speak, he descended with me, and jumped on the car. Within a quarter of an hour we were clear of the town, with Macarthy seated beside me well secured.

"In silent astonishment we drove along the road, with which I was thoroughly acquainted, and could not help fancying that I was betrayed; indeed, I had begun mentally to reproach my folly in having thus trusted myself in the power of such a villain, when suddenly Bill turned round and peremptorily ordered the car-driver to turn up a bye road.

"'Sure that's not the way to Clonmel?'

"'I know that; but turn up——.'

"'Faith, thin, I'll do no such thing. I was hired to go to Clonmel, and to Clonmel I'll go.'

"'You know me, Thady Ryan; you well know that I value a man's life just as much as I do a dog's. Do you see this—and here he produced a large horse-pistol, which he presented at the man's head. By the heavens above me——.'

"'Ah, then, Bill, sure you wouldn't murder me? You know I'm sworn to go to Clonmel.'

"'Do so, then. Jump down; I'll drive. You may now walk on and tell the boys; but, as I said before, may the curse of Cromwell light on me but I'll blow your brains out if you mount a horse, or hasten beyond a walk, to inform your friends that we've changed our destination.'

"The man sprang down, and scanned Bill from head to foot with a savage glance, evidently weighing the chances of an encounter. But Quiglan's looks were now most strangely altered; he no longer wore a bland smile. His brow was contracted, his teeth fixed firmly, and as he followed the movements of the other ruffian, con-

11—2

tinuing to keep the muzzle of the pistol pointed at him,
I never beheld so fierce an object in the course of my
life. The hesitation lasted less than a minute; in that
period the driver had slunk off, conscious of his danger.
Bill had seized the reins, and was making the horse
gallop in an opposite direction to that in which we
had originally started.

"We hastened on, in this way, for several miles;
no person was visible. The cross road we were following was evidently unfrequented. At length I perceived a horseman in the distance, and mentioned the
circumstance to Bill, who instantly handing me his
pistol, desired me to point it at the head of the
prisoner, and instantly to blow out his brains if he
endeavoured to escape. I complied with the first part
of his request; I much doubt, even in case of need,
whether I should have followed the second portion of
his directions.

"Presently the rider came up with us, his horse
evidently much distressed by the pace he had been
compelled to keep up. The man held a bundle in his
hands, and as he approached us, roared out to us to
stop.

"'Not a bit of it,'" growled Bill.

"Sure haven't I brought some clothes for Mr.
Macarthy, and I only want you to stop while I deliver
them.'

"'Not a taste of it, Tim Grady; and what's more,
if you look at my friend on the car, you'll see he has
the very pistol in his hand which sent your friend
and namesake Tim Doolan into another world, and
I've its own foster brother inside my waistcoat; and

what's more, if you attempt to spake to the prisoner, I'll make short work of it. You know Bill Quiglan well, and you know he never lies; so be off wid you, or, by my soul, I may be tempted to try the little argument I have ready cocked in my breast. Be off wid ye ; do ye hear ?'

"The man looked at him, then muttering something in Irish, turned back.

"'By dad, Tim, it's little I care for your threats. I'll come back, and you won't even dare to repeat the words you now utter, much more attack me. And now, sir, we must drive for our lives.'

"'Couldn't you stop and ease my wrists a little ; they hurt me very much,' chimed in the prisoner.

"'Then by the vestments I wont, so you need try no tricks on me. Sure, don't you well know there are ten or twelve of the boys coming after us, and Tim only outstripped them by virtue of his horse's speed. Faith, I fancy I can almost hear them now.' We went on at full speed, and a mile further on, turned into an open and broad road.

"'We're better off now,' said Bill ; 'but we're not safe yet.' Presently the noise of wheels was heard, and our bold driver shouted, 'It's all right now,' and stopped the car, and having taken back the pistol from me, began to help the prisoner down. At this moment the Kilkenny mail, *en route* for Dublin, came up, to intercept which, had evidently been Bill's object.

"'Stop! stop!' cried he, and having spoken to the guard, Macarthy and myself were soon comfortably placed inside, while Bill followed in the car about two miles further on the road, when, the coach delaying for a

few minutes at a rustic tavern, he commended his
vehicle to the care of the innkeeper, promising to
return for it in a few days, and jumped into the mail
with us, which fortunately had only our three selves
inside it.

" Bill was rather an amusing companion, and chatted
away in high spirits, and even Macarthy, seeing there
was no use in being sulky, joined in our conversation,
and more than once shared a glass, in perfect good
humour with his captor. This in England would
appear strange, but such conduct in Ireland is by no
means uncommon.

"Early in the morning we arrived in Dublin, and my
friend was duly lodged in prison. After a few days,
seeing there was no hope, he offered the amount of his
overdue rent. But by Bill's advice, I refused it, and
insisted on his appearing in Court unless all the others
paid likewise. After a short hesitation he assented to
this, and handed me the full amount of every claim, and
succeeded in getting his discharge. I joyfully handed
Bill double the sum I had promised him, and from
that moment to this, though I have frequently visited
the estate, and collected the rents of Kilbarry, I have
never been annoyed by incivility or default. While
as to Bill, I rather think his reckless boldness on
this occasion has made him more popular in the county
than ever. Of course I've changed some of the names;
but to the truth of the circumstances I have narrated,
I pledge myself.'

"'By George, you are a plucky fellow,' exclaimed
Vokes, delighted with the anecdote. 'I only wish
you were a magistrate in our county.'

"'What, to be shot at every night?'

"'Ah, now you are exaggerating. It's not so bad as that.'

"'Do you mean to say you were never fired at?'

"'Oh, as to that, it does sometimes happen : I was shot at last night within a mile of my own house. By the bye, that reminds me I must buy a new hat,' and he displayed his old one with a bullet-hole through it. I stared with astonishment, for my friend had actually supped with me immediately after the event, and never alluded to it.

"As I had had no startling hint respecting the danger I had myself personally run, I proposed to take a stroll, and then to return to Limerick. We did so. Mr. H—— slept at Tipperary, and the next day visited Bill, and Tim, and Macarthy, and the rest of his now friendly tenants.

"Certainly Ireland is a strange country."

THE CHARMED BULLETS.

As I came up in the steamboat from Kilkee with my
daring friend Vokes, I could not help blaming him, in
no measured terms, for the reckless manner in which
he was in the habit of running into every danger, and
took this opportunity of remonstrating with him, as I
had only just heard that two days before he had rode
unarmed, and unsupported, save by a single orderly, into
the middle of a faction fight, and seized a notorious character, although he full well knew that there were hundreds of persons engaged in that struggle who had privately and solemnly sworn to take his life whenever an
opportunity offered. And where indeed could such an
occasion so appositely present itself as in the midst of
a violent tumult, where no one could in particular be
identified as committing a murder, since all around
was noise, riot, and bloodshed? How foolhardy, then,
must be the man who thus, as it were, purposely and
knowingly braved a fearful doom.

"*Giggy mi gow!*"—(a favourite term of derision used
by my friend)—"Giggy mi gow! Sure aint I here safe
and unhurt, and why are you thus mourning and
croning over me as if I was a corpse at your feet?
Faith, your dull look and your lachrymose tone are
both too melancholy even for a well-conducted wake."

" But if you care so little about your own life, recollect you have a wife and children."

" Bother, Master Hal. Don't I tell you they wont
hurt me."

" But why ? What prevents them ?"

" Well, then, I don't know. But perhaps it may
be, because they think I have a charmed life."

" A charmed life ? What do you mean ?"

" Oh, it's very simple; I'll tell you. You must
know that soon after I was appointed a magistrate
I went without any fixed intent to a great cattle
fair near Adare ; here I found some thousands of
farmers and others assembled, and here I heard all the
usual coping and squabbling, the sure concomitants of
such a festival. Several people had been taken up for
picking pockets, and some for horse-stealing ; one man had
houghed two cows out of spite, while another had ridden
off clear with a horse he had been allowed to mount,
and had not yet been overtaken. The usual number of
broken heads had been patched up and bathed in whisky,
while one or two who had had their arms and legs
broken had been carried off to hospital—in a word it
was a regular Irish fair, and I felt, as a magistrate,
that before long my duties would become onerous.
I must tell you, however, that a short time before this
I had been shot at, whilst sitting at table, and though
the ball had passed between my body and my arm I
was not touched, and that on another occasion I had
an equally narrow escape. So the superstitious peasantry
began to talk about my having 'a charmed life,' and
all that sort of nonsense.

" I might, however, have been about two hours in the

fair when a young respectably dressed farmer came up
to me and challenged me to sell the mare I was riding.
Now it so happened that it was the very thing I wished
to do. So, after some apparent objections, I, with
seeming reluctance, assented. The farmer required a
short trial. This was but fair; so I got down, and he
was soon in my saddle. 'Walk, trot, or gallop him,'
said I, 'but do so along the road, and do not go beyond
the stone which stands about 150 yards off.' 'Agreed!'
replied the proposed purchaser, and away he went.
He first proceeded gently, then broke into a trot. At
this moment a policeman whispered in my ear—'Sure
your worship, that's Jerry, the most clever horse robber
in Ireland.' I was startled, and at once saw through
the trick, so I roared to the rascal to come back, but
such was clearly not his intention, for without turning
his head he set off at full speed. I called louder and
louder, and the crowd, who always favour a clever
thief, cheered him for his activity. I seized a long
horse-pistol from the policeman's holster, and roared out
that I'd shoot him if he did not stop. 'You'll shoot
your horse, Major,' cried a bystander, grinning. 'He's
too far off by half,' added another. 'Could you shoot
the moon?' screamed a would-be wit, and they all began
laughing.

"'Boys,' said I, 'I'll bring that fellow down. It's
true he's far beyond the usual shot, but I'll hit him.
I wont kill him, but I'll hit him in the heel,' and
instantly levelling the pistol I fired. In another
moment, to the astonishment—I may fairly say the
dismay—of the crowd, the fellow was heard to scream
out, and, with a fearful bound from the saddle, he fell

wounded on the road, while my horse galloped on without a rider.

"To depict the surprise of the people assembled would be impossible. The shot was at a range of 300 or 400 yards, made with an old police pistol and carelessly aimed. They could scarcely believe the evidence of their eyes. But when some of those who had run off to the spot, screamed out that 'Jerry was shot in the heel!' and when, on his being brought back, it was discovered that the ball had actually divided the tendon Achilles, their astonishment vented itself in loud exclamations—all declaring that it was a *charmed shot*—'that I was in league with certain nameless powers'—'that, faith, that same Major was something more than a man.' In fear they shrank from me, and during the whole day not a soul would approach me; and thus it was my claims to the possession of supernatural protection first arose. Poor Jerry had three months' imprisonment, but he never murmured. He only blamed his luck in having these bad dealings with the devil. Another act, somewhat similar, soon after confirmed my demoniac character, and after all it has so aided me, although I have loudly disclaimed it and much dislike it, that I laugh at any threat they make."

Arriving early at the cottage, and having nothing else to do, we together took a stroll in the country— followed in the distance by a couple of policemen, a most necessary precaution, which had I been consulted I should certainly have doubled.

After an hour's walk I felt thirsty, so we turned into the house of a small farmer, who professed to be a great friend of Vokes. Here I asked for a cup of milk, or buttermilk. But the worthy tiller of the land was far too hospitable to hear of this ; he insisted on my taking a piece of bread and cheese (for he was what is called a *comfortable* farmer) and a glass of cold whisky-and-water. After some objection I consented, and he went to the cupboard to take them out. Scarcely had he opened it, when Vokes suddenly called in the policemen, and desired them to seize the man. "Halpin, put handcuffs on that fellow, and take him across to Rathbane, while you, Reedy, search the closet, and bring all the contents with the prisoner."

I stared with undisguised astonishment. The poor agriculturist turned pale, but held out his hands to be manacled without uttering a word.

Sergeant Reedy now announced the contents of the cupboard—a piece of cheese and a loaf, half a bottle of whisky, a pack of cards, a prayer-book, and three pistol balls. Nothing more.

" That will do," replied Vokes. " Bring him along, and don't let him touch any of the things." I was dumbfounded. Why a civil and obliging peasant, on whom we had called by the merest accident, should be thus cruelly and savagely treated I could not for the life of me understand. I had often seen the Major do strange things, but this beat all. Thus to disgrace a kind and hospitable fellow, without any apparent cause, seemed the very height of tyranny, and I felt inclined, as I had been partly the cause of the man's seizure by visiting his cottage, to remonstrate with Vokes. But then, again, I knew that he was a just man, and that he never acted harshly unnecessarily. And I also well knew he disliked cross-questioning, so I determined not to say a word till we were once more alone. In the meantime, I vainly puzzled my brain to pick out—either from the conduct of the man, his appearance, or the articles found in his safe—what possible circumstance could thus have placed him in arrest.

We soon arrived, and Vokes instantly proceeded to interrogate the prisoner; but not until he had summoned his secretary to be present—a somewhat unusual formality. But this he so far explained, as to state that as the affair was one in which he himself was personally interested, he wished everything to be conducted as publicly as possible. So while the magistrate, his secretary, and myself sat at the table, the prisoner stood, apparently in some agitation, at a short distance, surrounded by policemen.

Vokes at once began.

" Your name is Hayes—Tim Hayes, I believe ?"

" It is, your worship."

" You are a tenant on the lands of Kilballycrow ?"

" I am."

" And now, my good friend, you need only answer such questions as you think proper, for I tell you fairly, if you say anything to criminate yourself it will be noted down. Do you understand ?"

" I do, your honour. Sure my foster-brother's an attorney."

" How long have you lived in your present farm ?"

" Five years."

" I believe you have no arms ?"

"None, Major. I'll swear I have not a weapon of any kind."

"I know that," replied the functionary, quickly; "but your cousin Carmody has a fine long pistol ?"

The prisoner turned pale; and rather stammered out; "I b'lieve he has—that is, I don't know."

"Yes, you do, Tim—yes, you do; for you've cast bullets for it."

"The saints be good to us. Is it that; you mane ?" cried the now trembling captive. "I never cast any."

"Didn't you cast the three we found in the cupboard ?"

"Not I, then. Sure I don't know how it was done; them was brought me by my cousin, and left there by accident."

"Search the prisoner !" ordered Vokes. His pockets were rifled, and a bullet-mould produced. The man actually groaned with terror.

"What do you say now ?"

"Faith, I forgot it. Carmody must have put it there."

"Of what are those bullets made ?"

"I don't know," groaned the poor wretch.

"Yes, you do. Reedy, split one of those balls and give it to me." This was done. "Exactly as I thought. They are of silver—silver, Master Hayes—pure silver; and consequently meant for me. I have long known that Carmody has sworn to shoot me; and I also know that he declared he'd get silver bullets to shoot me, as I possess a charmed life, and nothing else could destroy it. All this I knew; but I was not aware as I am now that you were selected to cast them."

The unhappy prisoner threw himself on his knees, and earnestly offered to confess all. "Sure he knew from the beginning that it would have a bad end ; he felt everything was known to the magistrate ; he'd betray his companions ; he'd do anything ; but he hoped he would not be punished, as he only did it because the bad lot fell on him at a game of cards."

"Take him down to my office in William-street, and I'll see about it ; all will depend upon how much you have to reveal, and how far your truth may be relied on."

"Oh, as to that——."

"Away with him," and the man still calling out for mercy, was hurried off.

"Didn't I tell you, Harry, I bore a charmed life ? What do you say now ? Believe me, the superstitious fear of his enemy is a better buckler for a soldier to rely upon, than the best arm he himself carries. Come, my boy, the ladies are waiting for us, and we must really be punctual, or, after all, I may perhaps lose 'my charm !' "

THE VASES.

I HAVE seen and recorded so many scenes displaying the presence of mind possessed by Mr. Vokes, that few who have known him, or read these pages, can doubt his perfect coolness in the hour of danger. I have touched, however, but very slightly on the extraordinary way in which he carried these qualties into private life. I will therefore now devote a few lines in illustration of this strange, and much to be envied faculty of mind. I will premise this short sketch by stating, that the police functionary was one of the best fathers that ever existed, and that even in the moments of his greatest excitement, even when rebellion and danger threatened around, and he was called on and worried by conflicting parties, he never uttered an unkind word to his family, either of the first, or second, generation. His love for his children could only be exceeded by that which he bore for his grandchildren; with them the stern magistrate would play as a child, and woo betide the member of his circle who dared to affront one of those little ones: "the darlings were young; contradiction would injure their health; sure they'll know sorrow soon enough; they must not be vexed now." Such were the principles laid down by our friend Vokes. Of his love, more particularly for one of these children, I am about to give a sketch.

Our worthy C.M.P. had been engaged all day in the county court-house ; some most important trials, in which Vokes was officially concerned, here taking place ; he was unable to leave the case even for a moment, and was detained some eight or ten hours. At length the verdict was pronounced, and the tired and worn-out magistrate returned to his home.

In the drawing-room he found his family assembled, awaiting his arrival, and none more so than his little grandson George, who, to tell the honest truth, was, I believe, the grandsire's pet, and who warmly reciprocated his attachment.

After a few moments' conversation on other matters, and after having been supplied with some necessary refreshments, two porcelain vases were pointed out to Vokes—two most exquisite specimens of Sèvres china —which had been sent to him as a great present from Dresden. In the pride of her heart, his wife had placed these highly-prized objects of *vertu* on the mantelpiece, and now pointed out their beauteous effect.

Every one admired them, and a friend who had accompanied the magistrate home, a man of some travel and taste, declared their value to be at least 50*l.*

The child, seeing the attention of every one directed to these tempting looking toys, desirous of possessing them, or jealous of the admiration they excited, had quietly and unseen climbed up, and in the next instant, in his endeavours to grasp the glittering china, dragged it down. With a loud crash it fell upon the hearth, and dashed into a thousand pieces.

All around uttered an involuntary cry, while the wretched little culprit stood in silent agony, gazing on the wreck which he had caused ; pale, trembling, his mouth wide open, his eyes transfixed, too frightened to cry ; he stood the very image of mute despair.

In an instant, quick as lightning could flash, Vokes had sprung forward, and seizing the fellow vase, dashed it on the fender beside its broken companion, crying out, " Georgy, darling, you see I can do that as well as you !" and then burst out laughing.

In a moment the child recovered its serenity, and ran up smiling to its grandpapa—" Darling Big Tom " (so he loved to be called,) " can do everything better than Georgy."

The little fellow by this act was probably saved from convulsions, and his kind relative considered that such an escape was cheaply purchased, even at the price of his beautiful ornaments. He again smiled, and assured that the boy was all right, played with him for a few minutes and then had him conveyed to bed ; while he went down to consult over certain documents with Sir Matthew Barrington, the clerk of the crown (his most intimate friend)—documents which properly or improperly treated might save or destroy the lives of several accused persons.

Like the elephant, who when enraged, frequently runs a sort of muck, destroying every man or brute he meets upon the way, yet carefully places aside and in safety the new-born baby he finds in his path, so Vokes, even in his moments of the greatest anger or agitation, might be at once calmed by the sight of one of his loved children.

A SLIGHT MISTAKE.

GEORGE L——— was an intimate friend of Vokes. Tho latter had laid him under some slight obligation, and George possessed a grateful heart. He used, therefore, vociferously to declare, he'd go through fire and water for the Major. On the other hand, my relative had a real friendship for the young man, who was decidedly not only one of the best riders and the best shots, but one of the jolliest fellows in the county of Limerick. Not a race—not a wake—not a pattern could take place but George was there; indeed, no orgie was complete without his presence, who could drink punch or troll a hunting song with any man between tho Suir and Shannon. I need not say that on some of these occasions our friend was the life and soul of the circle by whom he was surrounded. He was universally popular, and consequently sought out; he therefore sometimes might be found in company unworthy of him.

It was on an occasion of this kind that the following affair occurred.

George was spending his evening at a country town, near Bird's Hill, after a day's fishing at Killaloe. He was half asleep, dozing over his often-renewed pipe, when he heard the sound of several loud voices in the adjoining tap. Ever, and equally, ready for a "fray or a feast," George did not hesitate, but at once walked into the room where the apparent disputants were assembled ; but who at a glance might be discovered to be warm friends talking loudly and together, but by no means differing in opinion. As L—— walked in, the conversation ceased. The new comer prayed them to renew it. A few questions were put to him by one who seemed to take a lead in the conversation, and, on his pronouncing "all's right," the broken thread was renewed, and the subject, interrupted for a moment, again continued in half whispers. George, who was evidently taken for an English tourist, and therefore wholly unacquainted with the Irish language, seemed little noticed, while, as I said before, the animated discourse was again renewed in pure Irish.

George, however, well knew his native tongue, and attentively listened, while a deliberate and extensive cruel outrage was planned. But what struck him with more horror than the rest, was the proposal made by a little miserable cripple with a shock-red head, that if it was determined that " Major Vokes "—that " curse of the world"—was to be destroyed, the job should be left to him to accomplish. All the party assented to this. For, to tell the truth, few envied the little wretch the risk he would thus incur. He was therefore fully nominated as the murderer of that devil's child, Tom Vokes; and, the better to inaugurate the appointment, a fresh tumbler of punch was given to this wicked lump of deformity. Far from being frightened at the danger, the savage dwarf seemed rather to exult in the task.

George could scarcely contain himself; and while they then proceeded to plan and arrange an extensive and cruel murder, which it appears they had long settled on, he carefully concealed his emotion, and sat plotting how he could thwart their designs. It is true, he had intended to pass the night at Bird's Hill, but now he was all anxiety to meet Vokes and tell him what he had heard. He therefore quietly left the room, and obtained an outside car to convey him into Limerick; before, however, he started, he once more looked into the tap-room, but it was too late, the party had all broken up and left. George almost blamed himself for not having prevented it; but then how could a single man, and that man unarmed, effect this?

He now jumped on the car, and desired the driver to gallop into Limerick. He promised the fellow half-a-crown if he got there in an hour. Need I say, the old horse was whipped into his best pace?

G. L——had scarcely proceeded a mile, when he overtook a solitary individual. To his great joy he perceived it was the stunted ruffian who had agreed to murder his friend. He did not hesitate a moment, but stopping the vehicle, he jumped off and seized the fellow, who, without any resistance (for, indeed, against such a comparative Hercules such an attempt would have been madness) allowed himself quietly to be placed on the car and driven into Limerick.

As they approached Vokes's house, George watched him closely, expecting every instant that he would endeavour to make his escape. But the wretch, though apparently conscious of his danger, made no effort to get away. The chief magistrate was at his cottage, a circumstance which pleased our friend, as his rustic residence was used frequently by the Major as a semi-police-office. So to Rathbane he drove, in full triumph, with his captive.

We were sitting at supper when L—— arrived, who insisted, even before he would taste food or imbibe a single drop of the creature, on telling his tale of horror, which I confess filled me with terror indescribable. Not so Vokes. I suppose habit had indurated his feelings. He had become professionally calm. Let it be as it might, there he sat, without displaying the slightest emotion. George seemed rather nettled at the coldness with which his news had been received, and then, fancying that his tale might possibly be disbelieved, he vowed solemnly to the truth of what he had asserted.

"And where is the ruffian that is to murder me ?"

"I left him in charge of two of your men, with directions to shoot him if he attempted to escape."

Vokes rang the bell, and ordered him in.

George L——'s description was perfectly graphic. The circumscribed monster that stood before me fully realized the frightful description he had drawn of him.

"Is this the man ?" asked Vokes.

"It is," replied his friend.

"I thought as much," said the magistrate. "Take him away ; lock him in the loft above the back kitchen; and give the fellow something to eat. We may hang him ; but we must not starve him. I'll come out and examine him myself presently," and with that the assassin was led away.

Guess, however, George's horror, as he plainly perceived his friend the magistrate, unseen by any one else, give a knowing-wink and a half-smile at the bloodthirsty prisoner.

What this could mean was more than puzzling. L—— felt indignant, and determined on closely cross-questioning his friend the functionary. But the latter gave him no opportunity; he evaded his questions, parried his queries, and by dint of sheer hospitality and kindness compelled his guest to sit down and share his supper previous to giving those explanations, which he promised to afford most amply to him when the meal should be over.

The captor was of course compelled to submit to these conditions, and we again sat down to our long-interrupted evening repast. Why or wherefore I knew not, but my relative seemed fidgety and anxious, and evidently lingered over his supper. Of course all this was a mystery to me.

Just as we had concluded, a knock was heard at the door, and the chief magistrate loudly called to the person outside to enter. A horse-policeman (I think it was Sergeant Macgrath) came in covered with mud and dirt, as if he had ridden in at full speed, and going up to the Major he whispered a word in his ear.

In an instant all care was banished from our entertainer's brow. "Go and meet them, and bring them in here, as quick as you can."

"Yes, sir," said the sergeant, as he saluted, and then closed the door after him.

"And now for a tumbler of grog."

"Not so," remonstrated George; "you have promised to give me some explanations. I think I deserve them."

"Well, that's true for you. But I have my reasons. I faithfully promise you that in ten minutes all shall bo cleared up.

That period had scarcely elapsed, when another knock was heard, and on the door opening, again marched in the weather-beaten sergeant, followed by no less than four prisoners, strongly handcuffed, and escorted by a half-dozen of policemen, armed with carbines.

Vokes took the whole affair as a matter of course, and coolly turning to George, asked,

"Do you recognise these men?"

"By Heaven, I do. They are the four scoundrels I left two hours ago at Bird's Hill, plotting a murder," cried he, his eyes wide open from astonishment.

"Can you identify them?"

"That I most certainly can. But how they came here it is impossible to say. I only know I had no hand in it. I only arrested the other ruffian, the—"

"Hush!" quickly interrupted Vokes. "Not a word of that. It is enough. March them down, sergeant, to the county jail; let them be lodged separately. Off with them;" and away the wretches were marched.

George, now in real anger, turned upon him whom he had hitherto so highly respected. "Major Vokes, I would have gone to the death for you; but you have now offended me. You have treated my efforts with contempt.'

"By no means."

"How? Have you not received all my revelations with coolness and carelessness? Have you not smiled on the base villain who would have murdered you. It is true that you have captured the gang without my aid, and thus my services are of no use—"

"Georgy, my boy, don't talk like an angry child, and I'll tell you all. But you must keep my present explanations a strict secret. You have conferred a most lasting favour on me. You can now identify these ruffians whom I have long endeavoured to entrap, and thus save me from bringing forward my most valuable approver, whose loss would indeed be most fatal to the ends of justice; yet who, if once publicly known, must quit this country for ever within an hour after he gives evidence in court, or he would be too surely destroyed. You, however, as a free country gentleman, run no such risk, and thus through your means I preserve my most valuable agent."

"And who is this valued gem?"

"The well-looking young gentleman you were good enough to bring up to me; the little gentleman who wormed himself into the confidence of these ruffians by promising to destroy me. He has had his supper; he has doubtlessly drunk your health, and is now comfortably snoring within ten yards of us. I'd not have a hair of his clever head injured for his weight in gold."

"But how then came the police to take charge of him when I ordered them?"

"Then upon my honour they don't know who he is, more than you then did. Now mind and keep my secret, for you already know more of my tactics than any man in the county. We'll transport those would-be murderers at the next assizes; you shall have all the glory of it."

"And so I ought," growled George, "after making such a confounded fool of myself."

THE THREATENING LETTER.

I CAME down late to breakfast, and found my worthy
relative reading his letters ; one of these more particularly seemed to engage his attention. For several
minutes he sat pondering over it, and turned it over
and over again, closely examined the superscription
and the post-mark, and peered curiously at the writing.
Presently he rose, and after glancing at the edges of
the half-sheet, on which the communication was
written, went to the window and held up the paper
against the pane of glass, at the same time taking out
a magnifying-glass. He most minutely examined the
document, doubtlessly wishing to discover a water-mark
or other indication by which he might ascertain the
identity of the writer. His efforts seemed fruitless,
for with a slight "hem!" indicative of disappointment, he again folded up the epistle and put it in his
pocket, then joined with a smiling countenance and an
honest appetite the excellent meal his hospitality had
placed before us.

Breakfast over, he suddenly turned round to me.

"Harry, my boy, you seemed curious to know the
contents of the letter I examined so carefully just
now ?"

" It is perfectly true."

" Well, then, I'll satisfy your curiosity. Read it :
it is a perfect gem of its kind."

He threw me over the note, which, from the address,
I perceived came from some person belonging to an
inferior class, for the writing was of the worst description, whilst the missive itself was dirtied and crum-
pled—two favours evidently bestowed upon it previous
to its having been dropped into the post. From the
outside, then, I expected some " peasant literature "
to be found within, and tearing it open, I was already
moulding my mouth to a hearty laugh, when to my
horror and surprise I found the communication headed
by a rude sketch of a coffin. I now perused it seriously;
it ran thus—

"Let the fate of young Martin be a warning. His father, like
yourself, was a cruel magistrate, and didn't we kill his son? Didn't
we kill him as we left chapel, within ten yards of the door, and
though the poor boy went down on his knees and begged for his
life, and though he tried to cling for mercy to several who knew
him well, and though we knew the priest would set his face against
us for it—yet we then and there destroyed him; and he only a poor
innocent boy? how much more, then, shall we delight in killing
you—you murderous villain of the world. By the light that shines
—by the cross we love—by —— if you don't release Pat Toomey,
and leave off worrying and murdering the boys, you shall be a dead
man in three days. So order your coffin. By night, by day, by
twilight, we are on your track. Thirty boys, who never flinched,
have sworn your death. So Tom Vokes prepare for your certain and
cruel end. I have sworn it,

"PADDY MOONLIGHT."*

---

* I have turned the words into good English, as few of my readers,
I fear, could understand the strange terms used in the original. I
have also suppressed the real name of the victim, though every
Limerick man of a certain age will recognise it.

"What do you think of that?"

"By Heaven! it horrifies me. What do you mean to do?"

"Discover the foolish writer, if I can."

"And is that all? Do you call a threat like this _foolish?_ Why, it is horrible—barbarous—savage!"

"Giggy mi gow! Sure it's only foolish—nothing more! Don't I know all that it contains? Hav'n't I caught and convicted the murderers of that poor boy, one of the nicest lad's that ever lived? Don't I know that there are plenty of persons who have vowed to destroy me? There's not much news in that; and the only wonder is that they don't effect their purpose. But not by letters like this. It is useful as a warning, it may be useful as evidence, and, above all, it may lead, and I've no doubt it will, to the detection of the gang. So you see I'm quite justified in saying that the fellow was a fool for writing it. But don't let's talk any more about it—don't mention it to a soul, but go off to barracks with a light heart, while I go down to the police-office."

"Under the present circumstances you surely would not walk?"

"Bah! Go and attend your parade; don't mind me. I'll die in my bed yet;" and away went Vokes in high good-humour.

Two days elapsed, but the busy magistrate never referred to the subject; the family were fortunately ignorant of it, and my own business had driven the recollection of the anonymous letter out of my head; and if I ever did think of it, it was rather to do so with derision, for I now fully began to agree with my friend that it was a mere idle threat, when the following incident recalled it to my memory.

It was on the third evening following—say, about seven o'clock—the stars were shining clearly, and the frozen damp· cracked under each footstep, that Vokes was walking home to the cottage to partake of a late dinner. As the moon had not yet risen, the surrounding scenery was still partly buried in darkness ; but the starlight did its part, and objects in the immediate vicinity might easily be discerned.

He had arrived at the top of Upper William-street, where the roads fork into two wide branches. His route was to the right, but just as he was about to diverge, a young girl, apparently of about sixteen years of age, and, from the slight glimpse which could be caught through the opening of her cloak, (for she wore it in the Irish manner, thrown over her head and over her face like a cowl) rather well-looking, stepped forward, and in the most piteous and whining terms besought " the gentleman to come and see her poor grandmother, who was dying ;" and though Vokes showed her the total inutility of doing so, she still urged him in the most pathetic manner to accompany her. Now, if the truth must really be admitted, it is as well to confess that a pretty face was a wonderful argument with the worthy magistrate, who, after vainly endeavouring to shake off the girl, at length—for reasons I shall not attempt to fathom—consented to follow her to her cottage. So, wrapping his cloak more closely around him, and his pace unimpeded by any luggage, save by a roll of new music he was carrying home, he trotted off after his pretty young guide, who, at a speed which not a little astonished the gallant Major, set off towards the left-hand road.

My Limerick readers will remember a large tract of waste land which formerly existed, and indeed which still exists in a great measure, situated between the road to Tipperary and that by which the mail-coach used to travel to Dublin. It consisted of a large number of fields, on which only a cabin or two had then been built; near the Dublin side there was an old church-yard, long since fallen into disuse. Across this plain now hurried the girl, closely followed by the C.M.P.

They had crossed a couple of fields, when they came to a somewhat wide dyke. To Vokes's surprise, the active damsel jumped across it with ease, although my relative found some difficulty in following. They soon came to a second, across which the girl again sprang; but on this occasion—his suspicions aroused—the acute magistrate watched her movements more narrowly, and saw that, instead of being barefooted, as is usual with Irish females of the lower class, she wore a pair of strong brogues. Conviction at once entered the mind of Vokes, and he hastily jumped after her. They had not, however, proceeded ten paces, when he suddenly seized the fair damsel, and throwing off his cloak, presented the roll of music (the only weapon he had) at her head, and dashing off the covering which enveloped her, beheld, through the very imperfect light, a boy standing before him, who, on his part, fancying the music-roll was nothing less than a horse-pistol, began shouting for mercy.

" Silence, wretch ! or this instant is your last. Utter

but one cry—refuse to answer me a single question—
and I blow your brains out."

" Oh, mercy, mercy, Major !" .

" Who sent you out ?"

"The two Wegeralds."

" And where are they ?"

"Just beyond, in the berring-ground.   The Lord
be good to us !"

" You'll walk into Limerick before me."

" Oh, Gradi ! Gradi ! sure you wouldn't hang a poor
lad ?"

"That depends upon yourself.   If you go quietly on
in front of me, and don't look back : if you tell me
all the strict truth, I'll not hurt a hair of your head.
But if you attempt to give the alarm, or endeavour
to deceive me, you're just as dead as Julius Cæsar," and
again Vokes flourished his arm, holding the music roll.

The affrighted boy—too glad thus lightly to escape,
returned with the chief magistrate, who, on his
arrival, immediately sent out a party to arrest the
would-be murderers ; while he despatched the boy
again (disguised as a female) to watch at the corner
of the street, whom the prisoners would be sure to see
as they passed; thus shielding him from the danger
he would incur were it known he had betrayed
his friends, and thus deeply concealing the source
whence Vokes derived his criminal information.

All turned out as he had foreseen.   The prisoners,
disarmed and crest-fallen, stood before him.   This I
knew, for alarmed at his long absence I came down to
William-street office to meet him.

" Search these men !" cried he, turning to a policeman. The functionary did so. Some powder and balls were found in the pockets of one. In the other only a pocket-handkerchief and a scrap of writing-paper.

"Hand me that piece of paper!" The policeman did so, when Vokes, to my surprise, closely examined it—taking the greatest apparent interest in the investigation. Presently he pulled out of his pocket the threatening letter he had received three days before, and holding them both up to the candle, called my attention to the fact that they were identical, and showed some very peculiar water-marks.

"That will do," continued he, replacing the letter in his pocket. "That will do. Here, Sergeant, keep this scrap of evidence till the trial. I now commit them for having sent a threatening letter—one of the very heaviest crimes they could commit."

" These men will be transported—the example in this instance is worth the execution of a dozen murderers," said Vokes, as we walked up to the cottage afterwards. " These fearful missives are more dangerous, and more thoroughly alarm and demoralize the country, than even an assassination. If they are transported—which I am sure they will be—we shall have no more of these menacing epistles for some time."

During the following assizes, the worthy magistrate's prediction was amply fulfilled.

THE PIG MARKET.

I ENTERED the Police-office in Limerick for the purpose of asking my relative and friend, Major Vokes, to
join our pic-nic to Castle Connel, and as I had already
secured the attendance of his family, I little doubted
that the worthy functionary, who was ever ready to
make one of a jovial party, would assent. I found
him in the very midst of business. He was sitting in
a back parlour surrounded by policemen, while a
couple of wretched prisoners stood before him, accused
of some petty crime. As they were all talking in
Irish, it was impossible for me to discover the subject
of the present investigation ; but as I saw them led
away to undergo seven days' imprisonment, their crime
could not have been one of magnitude, and they left the
presence of the magistrate thanking him (as well as I
could understand them) for his leniency. How he could
manage to carry out the inquiry I was puzzled to
imagine, for the front room was crowded with barefooted females and well-clad men (such is the dress of
the lower orders of the Irish peasantry, and in which,
by-the-bye, they show little gallantry ; for while the
woman is bareheaded and barefooted, the man is comfortably clad in a pair of fustian breeches, good worsted

stockings, and a pair of strong shoes, and he always wears a hat, such as it is), who continued to shout and roar out their comments and opinions in spite of the policemen, who kept driving them out of the office. Babel must have boasted less confusion of tongues. As the prisoners I had seen tried were let out, a fashionably dressed gentleman (evidently a person of respectability) was ushered in. The magistrate looked up, but took no further notice. He offered him no chair. He addressed him in the same tone and in the same serious manner as that which he had made use of towards the peasants. There was none of the flunkeyism which we often see in the metropolitan courts of England. Major Vokes evidently looked upon an offender against the law as one to be adjudged, and, if guilty, punished. He knew no distinctions of rank.

The gentleman before him had committed some gross breach of the fishing laws, and he adjudged him to pay a heavy penalty, or the alternative of incarceration. The fine was paid, though the captain protested strongly against the manner in which, as a *gentleman*, he had been treated.

I now spoke to my friend, and asked him to join us ; to this he assented, and there being no more business to be done, he walked out of the office with me, his hat stuck jauntily on one side, and a heavy riding-whip under his arm.

" Come this way, Harry," said he, taking my arm; " I want to meet some one in the Pig Market."

" Your expectant friend must be a *bore*," I replied.

196 RECOLLECTIONS OF AN IRISH POLICE MAGISTRATE.

Vokes laughed heartily at my poor attempt at wit, and we lounged up to the top of William-street, where the unsavory market was then held.

To describe the scene is quite impossible. It would baffle the admitted powers of a Lever or a Carter Hall to do so. Suffice it to say, the place was redolent with the fumes of the very worst tobacco, smoked in the *dudeens* of women as well as men, commingled with the strong and certainly not pleasing perfume arising from our porcine friends, together with the piercing cries of the pigs, which were almost drowned by shouts in a language wholly unintelligible to me.

Major Vokes was in unusually high spirits. He asked the price of some of the animals before him. He chatted with one or two young men about some potatoes he had purchased. He had a joke for more than one pretty *colyeen*, and sent away the only policeman present on some trivial errand.

All this was very fine; but why he should walk up and down in such a place I could not make out, and, though I asked him the reason, he refused to satisfy me.

Presently he stopped, and called to a tall, fine-looking young man, who appeared to have nothing to do, since he had scarcely moved from the spot where I first saw him standing as we entered the market.

"Pat Conolly," said the Major, "why don't you kill me?"

"Is it me, yer honour?" demanded the other, turning rather pale. "Is it me would injure yer honour! Faix, then, I don't understand ye."

"Don't you? Did you not swear at the shebeen

house, near Patrick's Well, last Tuesday night, to shoot me to-day as I passed through the Pig Market? Now, my fine fellow, why don't you do it?"

"Oh, then, sure yer honour's glory they've been telling you a lie. Is it me would do it? Wasn't it last winter you gave the wife a sack of potatoes?"

"You had, perhaps, forgotten that circumstance when you came here this morning to destroy me?"

"Oh, thin! yer honour is joking."

"Am I!"

"Sure, thin, I'll swear by the holy—" and he raised his hand to his breast.

Major Vokes, to my surprise, give him a sharp cut across the arm, which at once brought it down in agony, and stepping up to him, he thrust his hand into the man's waistcoat, and drew forth an old pistol loaded up to the muzzle. The man fell on his knees, and began whining.

"Get out of that, you cowardly hound! I know you, and shall have my eye upon you; and when you return to-night to Cahirconlish, you may tell Tim Ryan if he attempts to fire into my windows, he shall be hanged, as sure as I'm Tom Vokes. Be off!" and he spurned him with his foot. The fellow rose, and ran away like a frightened hare.

"But do you not mean to punish him?" asked I.

"Oh, no. That would do little good. The effect of his tale, told to-night amongst a lawless society, will strike the whole party with more terror than if the fellow were hanged."

"Very likely! very likely! But will you do me a

favour !   Never ask me again to parade up and down in front of a fellow with a loaded pistol, ready and anxious to commit murder."

"Pooh! pooh! there's no danger.   Now we'll go and see about this pic-nic."

TRIED AFFECTION.

"I HAVE asked you, my dear Vokes, to call on me, in order to consult you on an affair of some importance— at least, as far as my family circle goes," said L. D.—to the chief magistrate, as that functionary entered his counting-house.

"Indeed! If I can be of any service pray command me."

"You remember Mary Toovey, whom you recom- mended me as a trustworthy girl to assist in looking after my children some six years ago?"

"I remember her well. Her father was an honest fellow in Adare. His daughter was brought up at P.'s Sunday-school."

"Most true ; and until within a very few days I always looked upon her as one of the best behaved young women I have ever met with."

"And you have had reason to change your opinion of her?"

"Unfortunately I have. You must know"—and here L. D—— dropped his voice. "Unfortunately, I say, I discovered that I had been systematically robbed of a series of small sums, and, watching closely afterwards,

I still perceived that these pilferings unhappily continued. It could only be some one under my roof that thus abstracted small sums; and as I have a stable-boy of somewhat loose habits, I at once suspected him, and accordingly I marked some pieces of silver and placed them with two or three one pound notes in my drawer, leaving my keys, as if by accident, on the the table.

"Having thus laid my plans to entrap the thief, I went out to dinner and returned too late to make any search that night.

"On the following morning I went to the place where I had deposited the cash, and here, to my great horror, I found that a bank note and three half-crowns were missing.

"Without telling them why I summoned them, I called up my servants, and having locked the door, stated to them what had occurred, and called on the pilferer to confess the crime, and thus earn pardon.

"None, however, admitted the alleged guilt, and I now, with their cheerful permission, proceeded to search them.

"Imagine, my dear Vokes, my horror, when, after vainly searching the servant man and some of the females, I turned to your *protegé*, and having ordered her to display the contents of her pockets, I discovered two of the half-crowns which I had marked, and could now distinctly swear to. I called upon Mary to explain this strange circumstance. I eagerly demanded to know how she had become possessed of them. But, alas! all in vain. She was dreadfully agitated, and was only relieved from a fit of fainting by a copious flood of tears which came to her relief. She is now downstairs in charge of a policeman. I wished if possible to avoid the pain of sending her, whom I have known for so many years, to prison, and therefore I wrote to ask you to call on me, and if possible, assist me in discovering the particulars of this distressing affair."

"Has she had any followers—male or female?"

"None."

"Has she ever absented herself from the house?"

"Never."

"Do your family know what has passed."

"No; they are all at Kilrush, with the exception of my eldest son, who assists me in business, and he went last evening to Waterford, and will not return before four o'clock. So, strange to say, not a soul is aware of the discovery I have made."

"Call in the girl—let us examine her together."

The poor culprit came in, more dead than alive. When she saw Vokes she covered her face with her hands and burst into a flood of tears. For several moments she was so convulsed that even the stern magistrate hesitated to address her. At length, after causing her to be placed on a chair, and having swallowed a glass of water, she became calm, when he thus spoke :—

"Mary Toovey, I am summoned here to interrogate you relative to a robbery which has taken place in this house; and as part of the money, marked for the purpose of detection, was found upon you, I have every reason to believe that you are guilty."

"I am! indeed I am. I am a wretched girl, sir,"

cried the prisoner, throwing herself on her knees before him.

"And yet, religiously and well brought up, I can scarcely believe that you could have acted so base, so ungrateful a part, as thus to rob your employers. I would rather have suspected any one in the house than you."

"Oh, sir, indeed, sir, it was I. I am a wicked, bad girl, and I confess the crime."

"Are you sure that no one instigated you—no one advised you to commit this robbery?"

"No, sir—no one. It was all my own doing."

"And still I think it is my duty to inquire further. I will, if possible, discover your accomplices."

"I have none—I have none. I alone am to blame."

The worthy merchant now chimed in: "Mary, I am told, by Michael the groom, that he saw you two nights ago talking with a strange man in the garden."

"It's false—it's false."

"Have you mentioned this to any one?" asked Vokes of L. D——

"To no one."

Vokes again turned to the girl. "Are you still determined to admit your guilt?"

She had now recovered her calmness, and answered firmly, "I am!"

"Do you know the consequences? Do you know that if found guilty you will receive a fearful punishment?"

"I do."

"And still to save youself you will not betray your accomplices?"

"I have none. I alone am guilty—I confess it."

"Take her away, sergeant. I must inquire further into this affair;" and trembling far less, seemingly relieved at having thus unburthened her conscience, the wretched girl was led away.

When she was gone, the Major turned round and addressed his friend.

"If you do not insist on it, I will not commit this girl till to-morrow. In the meantime we may discover her accomplices. It's very strange—very! But, by George, I can't believe Mary to be guilty."

"But her own admission—the money found on her?"

"All true; such proofs should be convincing; but still I am not satisfied. Do me a favour. Come you, and your son, to dine with me to-day, at six o'clock, and we'll talk it over; but mind, don't mention the circumstance to a single soul on earth—not even to your own son. Don't write it to your family; and if any one asks you for Mary, say she's gone to Adare to see her friends. Pray do this, and you will oblige me."

"Certainly you make a strange request; but I'll strictly attend to your directions, and be at your house, with my son George, at six. Perhaps it will be better; for my wife and daughter, and even George, who is generally very distant and haughty, is very partial to this girl. I can assure you, Major, we have treated her rather as our child than our servant, which makes her conduct the more detestable."

"True for you; but now, adieu. Remember—six, and silence. And off went the police functionary towards his office.

On arriving there, he called for Macdonald, a young policeman whom he often entrusted as a messenger.

" You took a note for me to young Mr. D——, some evenings ago, relative to lending him a hunter ?"

" Is it Mr. George you mean ?"

" I do."

" Well, sir, I delivered it to him, and he said there was no answer."

"I am aware of that. Where did you find Mr. George ?"

" In the billiard-room beyont—in George-street."

" And what was he about ?"

" Well, your worship, I can't rightly say; I didn't much observe. But I saw him drinking and smoking."

" Was he betting ?"

" Ah, then, Major, I can't say surely; but I think he was, for one of the young officers from the barracks called out and said, ' You've lost, George ;' and so I suppose he was, your worship."

" That will do," said Vokes, and then proceeded to try one or two cases of drunkenness and riot which were brought before him for judgment. Presently he got up, and putting on his hat, he strolled leisurely up George-street.

On arriving in front of Mr. S.'s shop—at once a place for refreshment, the supply of tobacco and punch, with a billiard-room attached—he turned in, and after partaking of a sandwich, he carelessly asked the female who was at that instant serving behind the counter, whether Mr. G. D—— had been in lately.

" Not since yesterday morning."

" What did he call for then ?"

"He came to get some cigars, as he was about to go out of town; and he left a pound-note with me to hand to Captain D——, that he had lost on the races."

"Have you got that pound-note?"

"No, sir," replied the girl, who seemed startled at the inquiry.

"Did he pay you for the cigars?"

"He did."

"How did he pay you?"

"With a half-crown piece."

"Have you got that half-crown?"

"I believe it's still in the tobacco till. I hope, Major, it's not a bad one; it may bring me into trouble." And fearful of being mixed up with the transaction, she examined the till with anxious care, and at length triumphantly pulled out the piece of money in question. "Here it is, sir; sure I didn't know it was bad, and I'm sure Mr. George didn't. Here it is." And she handed it to Vokes, who, after peering at it with great curiosity, put it into his pocket, and then throwing down two shillings and a sixpence, carelessly said—

"Don't you see, I suspect there's some bad money in Limerick, so I'll take away this piece. But don't tell a living soul what I've done, or faith I'll have you up for a witness."

This threat was quite sufficient to render the girl dumb. So Vokes, without further conversation, walked up to his cottage, where he was carrying out some improvements.

At six o'clock precisely, Mr. L. D—— and his son arrived in George-street, and shortly afterwards partook of a most excellent dinner, which I was lucky enough to share. No other guest was present, and all appeared in high good-humour, and drank their fair fill of claret before the punch apparatus was placed on the table. This done, Vokes desired the servant not again to disturb him till he rang the bell.

Well knowing the habits of the chief magistrate, I saw that something was coming.

"Mr. D——," said he, addressing his senior guest, "you have now my permission—nay, I may add, my request—to tell your son and my son-in-law here of the dreadful occurrence which has taken place in your family." ·

The worthy merchant did so, in the fairest manner.

During the recital George D—— appeared more agitated than I should have expected. He evidently was dreadfully shocked, and seemed to bear a true affection, more than an ordinary affection, for the poor girl, and as his father concluded he violently exclaimed,

" I am sure she is not guilty. I'll stake my life she is not."

" Can you then point to any other person as likely to have committed these robberies ?" asked Vokes.

" Me? me? certainly not. What should I know about it ?"

Oh, nothing, nothing; only you are wrong thus to acquit Mary without proof."

" But I have proof. Her established good character, the manner in which she has always proved her worth and respectability——"

"Are strong, I allow; but in face of her own admission, and the evidence against her, will avail her but little; she will be convicted."

"Oh, don't say so."

"Unless, indeed, you can give us any clue to the real thief."

Poor George seemed dreadfully agitated. He was evidently fond of the unhappy girl. He suddenly asked—

"Is there no way of getting her off; can you not aid her to escape; my father shall pay all expenses. But to convict poor Mary would for ever stain the character of our family."

"I can't see that, George," chimed in his father.

"Nor I," said Vokes; "but let us change the subject. I hear you lost at the late races?"

The young man, seemingly thinking of something else, merely uttered, "Did I?"

The father appeared astounded, for he had ever considered George to be far too rigid in his moral principles thus to have gambled on the turf.

"You did," went on Vokes; "Betsy, at Goggins, gave the pound note you left for Captain D——."

The detected sportsman was now all attention; his agitation was really frightful.

"Ah, you seem surprised at my knowledge. I'll tell you more. You bought some cigars at the same time, and paid for them with this half-crown, a half-crown strongly marked," added Vokes, as he partly produced it, but carefully shrouded it with his hand.

"What's that you say?" said L. D——.

"Nothing, nothing at all. But see, your son is not very well. He has probably over-excited himself. I'll take him into my dressing-room—administer some restorative essence, and he'll soon be well. Nay, you must not come, you will only do harm ; see, he waves you off. Come, George, you'll be better presently ; come along," and he led the poor sufferer off.

I need scarcely tell you that during the absence of his son and his friend L. D—— spoke but little. He adored his son, and thus to see him strangely attacked completely paralysed the old man. Five minutes elapsed—ten minutes elapsed—and the anxious parent would fain have sought his child ; but I gently detained him.

In about twenty minutes Vokes again appeared, followed by George ; who, though still pale, seemed to have recovered his strength, and in reply to his near relative's inquiries, assured him that "it was nothing. It had now quite passed away."

For about five minutes a gloom—a painful silence —hung over us all. This was abruptly broken by Vokes.

"George and I have discovered the pilferer, Mr. D——, and I will be guarantee that you are never so robbed again."

"Was it Mary Toovey ?"

"Decidedly not !"

"Who was it, then ?"

"That you will never know. It is sufficient to say he has been punished and you are safe for the future."

"But why, then, did the girl admit it ?"

"She best knows."

"I shall closely cross-question her when I go home."

"Then, indeed, you will not, for she is now several miles on her way to Dublin, where, well knowing her innocence, I have sent her to live with a sister of mine. You will see her no more!"

"This is very mysterious!"

"And so let it remain; make any fuss about it, and the punishment of your garrulity will fall heavily on you. Let me beseech you never again to allude to it; make what excuse you like for Mary's absence, but never hint at your first unjust suspicions."

"Unjust!"

"By heaven, they were! Harry, pass the hot water; we'll never allude to this subject again."

If L. D. did not *read* the case aright, he was indeed a happy man.

L. D. has been gathered to his fathers. His son George, who has settled in Dublin, married twelve months after his death a certain Mary Toovey—a girl who, I believe, would willingly have given her life for him.

THE

MYSTERIOUS DISAPPEARANCE.

———

VOKES was seated in his office in Limerick, surrounded by policemen and clamorous applicants for justice, giving his orders and receiving reports, when a most respectable female drove up on an outside car, and requested to speak privately to the "Major." In a few minutes the room was cleared, and the lady shown in. After a short hesitation, in some trepidation, she thus began—

"My name is——"

"I know it—Mary Malone, of the small farm near Patrick's Well."

"The same. I was not aware that you knew me; but oh, Major, I've brought you in bad news that you don't know. Sure my husband, Thady Malone—he's gone off and deserted me. He went last night."

"Not so; he went on Monday last. Never tell me a lie."

"Ah, thin, Major," cried the wretched woman— "ah, thin, it's myself that am so upset that I scarcely recollect the day."

"That's odd; for you wrote a note on Tuesday to

William Johnston, the wheelwright, announcing the fact, and sent it by Paddy Rhu."

"The Lord be good to us!" almost screamed the unhappy female. "You know everything. Sure it's true."

"And in that note you said you did not expect him back. Why did you think so?"

To make use of a common English term, poor Mary was struck all of a heap, and she vainly tried to look calm; but being a strong-minded woman, and somewhat annoyed at the system of espionage exercised on her movements, she now recovered her spirit, and with boldness met the inquiring glance of the magistrate.

"Well, now, I'll tell you—of course it's between ourselves—it cuts me up to confess it, but as you insist on it, faith, I'll tell the truth. I suspect he has gone off with a hussey of a soldier's wife, whose husband is quartered in the Castle Barracks."

"Indeed! What is her name? We'll have her arrested."

"Oh, thin, it's not myself that exactly knows it—though I think he called her 'Ann.' As to following her, sir, that's out of the question, for they went off in a ship the very next day to America."

"My good friend, you mistake. Not a vessel has sailed from this port to the United States for ten days."

"Oh, thin, I can't be sure—and, oh, I hope I may be! For with all his faults, I loved Thady dearly. If he don't come back, heaven only knows who's to console me or take charge of the farm."

" Wouldn't William Johnston do as much for you ?"

Mary Malone turned scarlet, but ere she had time to reply, Vokes again spoke.

"Was not your husband a great drunkard ?"

" He was, your honour."

" He sometimes got insensibly drunk ?"

" He did that same; but I loved him for all that."

"Did you ever quarrel ?"

" Oh, thin, why would we quarrel ?"

"Well, I only ask̩ed you because I had hoped he might have left you in a fit of passion.

"Ah, thin, perhaps it was so. We did sometimes have bits of difference."

" He accused you of preferring some one else ?"

" Faith he did ; but a bigger lump of a lie, by——" Then suddenly lowering her tone, " It was all a mistake, for I loved Thady dearly."

"I thought he sometimes beat you ?"

" Well, he might ; perhaps I deserved it. But I'll forgive him all if he'd only come back to me."

" You asked to see me ; you now say you do not wish me to pursue him. What, then, do you want ?"

"Oh, thin, Major, sure I wanted you to come out and just look in on me, and show the neighbours by kindness that I bear a good character. For, sure, there are some of them husseys who go the lengths to say that I'm glad that Thady's dead."

"Dead ?"

" No, I mean gone way. By dad, I'd pitch them and the Johnstons and all the world over Trow Hill to see my Thady return. Ah, now thin, Major, will ye come ?"

" I will. Remain you at home to-morrow, and I'll be with you in the course of the day, Mrs. Malone. We'll settle their gossip."

" Oh, thin, may heaven be gracious to ye ; ye are always kind. Sure, I brought in a small keg of butter of my own churning."

" I never take presents of any kind. So, now, away ; I'll be with you to-morrow ;" and away went the grass widow, apparently much pleased with the result of her visit.

No sooner was the distressed lady gone, than Michy, one of Vokes's best aids—if a rascally informer who had hung his own brother on his fraternal evidence, and betrayed a gang of some twenty ruffians, could be so designated—was called in to counsel. My little friend, who was Protæan in the forms he assumed, was dressed as a simple country boy; he had already been some time with Vokes before I entered, and had evidently given him important information.

Now there are stern moralists who may condemn this mode of obtaining evidence—this horrible way of arriving at facts through the means of a wretch, often unworthy of belief. Perhaps so to assist the efforts of any other man than my relative would have been dangerous, but the deep search *he* ever carried out to arrive at the real truth, the acuteness of his cross-examination, the stern certainty that if deceived he would at once withdraw his protection from the deluding party, which in effect would be little less than delivering him up to be punished by the friends of those whom he had betrayed, kept these otherwise dangerous emissaries in the most wholesome check. While detained by Vokes for pur-

poses of justice they were protected, clothed, and fed,
and if after a time they could be spared, they were
sent off to America with a good round sum in their
pockets. If they misbehaved, or indulged in falsehood, lynch-law would soon be executed on them.
No wonder, then, that their evidence, under wholesome
examination, might prove useful.

Of all those who had given evidence for the Crown,
Mickey was the only one retained as a necessary spy,
or, as we should more politely call it in the present
day, a detective. He was far too well trained and
taught to attempt any deception. Whatever he said
might be relied upon.

"And so, Mickey, you can recollect the words that
were posted up on the smithy beyond Rathbeale, last
Saturday night?"

"I can," replied the other, looking at me most sus-
piciously.

"It's only my relative—go on."

"Well, sir, I gave a shilling to Paddy Rooney to
drive his car for him, and by the same token he was
so drunk he couldn't drive it himself; so I bought
two noggins of whisky, and I guv him one, yere
honour ; and then I laid him down, and having put
on his top coat—for it was raining awfully—and having
put on his Jersey hat, I lays him in the car, and made
a pillow of sods of turf for his head—for, faix! he
seemed uncommon inclined to choke—and away I
druv. On the way, who should I overtake but Bill
Brophy, of Ballymondus."

"'God save ye!' says he. 'Sure you'll give me a
lift, Paddy Rooney, like an honest boy?'

" ' I will,' says I, stopping the car.

" ' Fait l' says he, ' you ain't Paddy Rooney.' And he was a going to turn away.

" ' Stay, Bill,' says I. ' Ain't I all the same ? Sure there's Pat Rooney drunk in the car, and ain't I driving him home ? So jump up.' And with that up he jumps.

" ' Bill Brophy,' says I, ' what makes you away so far from your county—and where are you going ?'

" ' Faith, then,' says he, ' the climate's become rather warm down there, ever since somebody houghed the Englishman's cattle. So I came down here, and I'm going to meet some of the lads at the smithy beyant, if your blood pony—bad luck to him—will only draw us there.'

" ' Oh then, there's no fear of that.'

I now interrupted Vokes, and as I had come purposely to fetch him, urged him to hasten his prolix informant.

" It wouldn't do," whispered he, " if I didn't let him tell his tale his own way. I'd never get at the truth ;" and then, turning to the informer, he merely said, " Go on."

" Well, your honour, I soon pumped out of Bill— whose lips are like sieves, through which everything runs—that a party were about to meet to form some plans ; but what they were he was not quite sure.

" ' Nabocklish !' says he, ' you are a true boy, I believe, since you know me and my father, though I don't recollect you ; and if there's a loose share in the fun, you shall have it.'

" ' Thank ye,' says I.

" Well, we came to the smithy, and there there was
a large party, with lots of potheen.   But as I see'd
Ryan among them, who might recognise me, I wouldn't
go in, but sat outside.

" Presently I heard them singing and talking, and
the smoke of tobaccy came out like the smelling of a
rose ; but then when I sniffed this, and the scent of
the raal potheen, it was as much as I could do to
resist.   But I had promised to wait for Brophy, so I
thought it safest to remain quiet.   In the song they
sung they mentioned all the affairs they had been in ;
and John Leary boasted 'twas he as settled Fitzroy.
But they all bragged of so many deeds of the kind, I
didn't believe them."

" But the song—was it funny ?"

" Very ; it was all about murdering the gentry, and
getting the land to themselves ; and they always wound
up with some chorus, saying how they'd serve your
honour."

" Do you recollect ?   You said just now you did."

" I do."

" Repeat it, then."

" Well, Major, I'm not a good singer ; but the end
of each verse ran thus :—

> There's Hoskins is going, and Going is gone,
> George Lake and Tom Vokes are the next to come on.

What do you think of that, Major ?"

" Oh, if that's all you learnt, it was scarcely worth
the trip.   Lines—almost the same—were posted on the
inn door where I slept at Kilmellock, and even on the
Chapel door, a month ago."

" Ah, but I didn't tell you how I wormed out about Mrs. Malone from Bill Brophy."

" And you are sure Johnston knows nothing of it ?"

" Quite ; he's a real respectable man, and don't care a trawneen for the woman."

" Well, be off; I'll see to all this."

" But Brophy, your honour ?"

" I'll have him taken within an hour, as you happen to fear him ; but believe me, he'll never suspect you of giving evidence. So now, go out the back way ; I'm going with my friend for an evening's fishing on the falls of Doonas." And away we went.

The next day Vokes, attended by an uncouth servant in livery, drove down to Mrs. Malone's. She received him with kindness, and warmly expressed her gratitude. She placed before him a plenteous luncheon, of which the good magistrate largely partook. His horse had been put up, and the servant now amused himself by strolling through the farm-yard, which closely adjoined the house. He seemed to saunter about carelessly ; but any one who had closely watched his eyes would have seen them wander around with piercing intelligence.

Vokes, on his part, was no less busy. What these close, though unperceived investigations meant, we shall see hereafter. Nothing could exceed the civility of the functionary towards his entertainer, and he took down copious notes from her statement relative to the sudden disappearance of her husband. He shortly, however, took leave of Mrs. Malone, who promised to be in Limerick on the following day, to have her statement made out in writing and placed before the bench

218 RECOLLECTIONS OF AN IRISH POLICE MAGISTRATE.

of magistrates, for the purpose of recovering, if possible, her errant partner.

Vokes and his servant, who was no less a personage than Mickey, drove back to Limerick, but few words passed between them.

"I think, Mickey, you are right. But if so, where is the corpse?"

"I can't say, but I think I know. The dunghill has been opened and closed, but not enough to let in a body; it's that puzzles me. There's something too, I think, down the half-dry well. I'm sure there's something quite white at the bottom of it. But I'll go out again if you wish it, Major?"

"No—it is enough. Did you observe, as I did, that the copper has been lit and the inside scoured since?"

"I did; but——"

"Never mind—that's enough. Did you pick up anything?"

"I did; this knife. It was hid behind the pig-stye."

"Ah, it has been recently sharpened and used. You say that Bill saw a great smoke, and that there was a bad smell came from the malt-house."

"That's the truth."

"Well, then, be ready to march with Serjeant Reedy at daybreak, and get beyond Malone's cottage without being seen, and mind the instant the woman leaves get into the premises, and search every part. I'll give directions to the Serjeant. So now jump off. Don't be seen with me going into town. I think we are on the right scent."

Some hours afterwards I went with Vokes to the

theatre, where, to my great amusement, Vokes was received with three groans by the people in the gallery, while I was loudly cheered. I looked at my friend, who laughed heartily and bowed to them, and when I timidly asked—I wonder why they cheer me. Sure it's because you are a stranger and in uniform. They'd cheer a certain old gentleman himself if he wore gold epaulettes. A voice, however, at this instant called on "*Dirty Betty Carmody*" (a most respectable serjeant in the militia, and the leader in the orchestra) *to play up !* and having compelled him by vociferation to sound Garryowen, they began screeching, hallooing, and beating time, till the wretched old theatre nearly tumbled about our ears. An Irish theatre some thirty years ago was, indeed, a strange arena, over which the "gods" themselves most arbitrarily presided.

A revenir.

Next day, soon after noon, the interesting Dido, so cruelly deserted, drove up to the police-office, and for a few moments Vokes treated her in a most courteous manner.

Presently a message was brought in, and his whole manner changed.

"Send in Smith and Macgrath." The altered tone in which the magistrate spoke, appeared to surprise Mrs. Malone.

They entered. "Arrest that woman!"

"Me? me, Major? What do you mean?"

"I arrest you as the murderess of Thady Malone, your late husband."

"What!" screamed the astonished female; "you cannot mean it. It is impossible. I loved him dearly, and I am as innocent as you are; I swear by——"

" Don't perjure yourself. I've proofs."

" That's out of the question," cried the prisoner, brightening up, for she had been deadly pale and awfully agitated, on the first accusation being made. This, however, was no proof against her. Any other woman would have been equally taken aback at such a dreadful—such an unlooked-for—accusation. " Sure he's gone, and far away by this time."

" You murdered him, Mary Malone."

" Where is your proof?"

" Bring in your parcel, Sergeant Reedy," who immediately opened it, and out rolled, to the horror of all around, a human head. It was bleached, and looked more like the head of a calf than of a human being.

The woman could not repress a scream.

" Is that your late husband's head?"

" I don't know—no—no. I'm sure it is not."

" Sergeant, you knew Thady Malone; is that him?"

" It is, sir; I will swear to it."

" Where did you find it?"

" In the dunghill, in his farm-yard, close to the house. I had two witnesses with me."

The wretched culprit sank in a chair; then starting up, she exclaimed, " But why say I had art or part in it? may not some one else have put it there?" and she looked round triumphantly.

" Send the next constable in;" he bore a basket.

" Sure it's an arm and a leg I found in the old well, though how it came so white I can't tell."

"Do you recollect Bill Brophy bringing your husband home on Monday afternoon very drunk, and that you plied him with liquor?"

The murderess—for by this time it was tolerably apparent to all that she was so—shuddered.

"Faith, then," said Vokes, "I'm about to commit you to gaol for the murder of your husband, and to show you that I don't wish to entrap you, although it's unusual, I'll tell you all I know. I shall probably have more before your trial, but in the meantime I tell you so much, in order that you may make a good defence if you can, and I only hope, Mrs. Malone, that as I've known you long, you may escape the dreadful doom, which, if guilty, you will not only deserve but suffer."

"I have reason to believe that, being in love with another man, although that man rejected your advances you determined on getting rid of your husband."

"Ah! then, that's not true." •

"Silence and listen, or I'll say no more. On Monday evening last Bill Brophy of Ballymeadows brought Malone home to the cottage in a state of intoxication; you plied him, as I have already told you, with liquor till he was senseless; Brophy then left the house, but not the neighbourhood. He watched through a crevice in the door."

The prisoner sighed deeply.

"No sooner did you think yourself unseen, than, taking out a knife you had previously sharpened, and which I have here, you cut poor Thady's throat, taking care to catch the blood as far as possible in a flat dining dish. This done—the man destroyed—you went into

the washing-linney,* and here you lighted the copper
fire—the boiler had evidently been prepared, for it was
filled with water and the fuel ready. You then returned
to the kitchen, and with the hatchet—which you afterwards buried, and the knife I have got—cut up the poor
fellow, and then boiled him piecemeal; look at the
head and those limbs, and you will see that I am right."

A groan of horror went round; all appeared shocked
except the prisoner, who maintained her calm demeanour.

"At this dreadful work you remained till long past
daylight, when Brophy went away."

"Brophy's a perjured villain!" cried Mrs. Malone.

"I remarked myself the newly cleaned copper; there
are some four drops of blood near the fireplace, and I
pocketed two buttons, torn from the poor man's coat,
while you left the room.   In the mean time an active
agent looked over the premises and remarked that the
dunghill had lately been disturbed.   He also found the
knife and other trifles he will produce at the trial.   In a
word, Mrs. Malone, you murdered your husband whose
head now lies before you, and boiled his mutilated
remains.   Don't deny it, or you'll offend heaven; don't
admit it, or it will serve to convict you at the assizes.
So take her away, serjeant, and may heaven have more
mercy on her than she had on my once honest tenant
Thady Malone."

Proved and convicted on the very clearest evidence,
Mrs. Malone was hanged shortly after the following
assizes.

* Linney is generally applied in Ireland to any shed attached to
the dwelling-house.

THE DEAD CAPTURE.

Vokes had some business in Ennis; so, without making any fuss, he ordered out his favourite nag, and wholly unattended, started for that town early in the morning, desiring, for obvious reasons, that his absence should not be notified to any one who might happen to call.

"But what shall I say to them?" asked his footman as he was quitting the hall—"what shall I say?"

"Say I'm not visible."

"But why shall I say you are not visible?"

Vokes, who was bothered by thus being cross-questioned, and annoyed by the pertinacity of the servitor, who had only lately entered his service, turned round sharply, and said—

"Say? I'm engaged—ill—dying—dead, if you like. But don't bother me." And springing into his saddle, he dashed down George-street, and was far on his journey before the rest of the family were stirring.

Accustomed, however, to his frequent absence from the breakfast table, the family sat down to that meal without making any inquiry, and the business of the day went on as usual.

At about noon, a peasant, who it afterwards appeared

came from the county of Clare, called, and asked to see "the master."

"It is impossible."

"Why? Sure I want to have spache of his honour?"

"Well, then, I tell you you can't."

"And why not?" persisted the other.

"He's ill."

"Oh, then, never mind that. Faith, I'm sure if he's alive he'd see me. Haven't I come all the way from Cratloe Wood—a good ten miles—and faith, I'm not to be sent back without setting eyes upon him."

"I tell you you can't see him."

"Sure I'm Thady Watson; he knows me well."

"If you were his Holiness the Pope, you couldn't see him."

"Sure I must. Now let me only have spache of him for a bit. In holy truth, then, I *wont* go away till I have——"

"Once for all, be off, for I tell you the thing's impossible!"

"Impossible! And why?"

The servant was a bit of a wag. He was angry and annoyed with the continuous pleading of the fellow. Besides which, if the truth must be told, he wanted to get back to the kitchen, where his warm, comfortable dinner stood cooling, and so determined at once to come to a conclusion. He quietly replied—

"The reason is very clear—he's dead!" And slamming the door to in the astonished peasant's face, he burst out laughing, and ran downstairs.

The surprised countryman stood silent on the steps

of the entrance, and with the usual cunning of a low Irishman, began to canvass in his own mind the probability of the news he had just heard being true or otherwise; and then, with a complacent grunt—uttered as if a good thought had struck him—he ran across the street, and hence took a full survey of the house. Here he saw every blind down (the morning sun resting on the windows), and this bore out the correctness of the footman's statement—a statement which was still more fully confirmed when he saw two policemen turned away from the door; and, last of all, Mr. Denmead, the undertaker (who happened to have been sent for by Mrs. Vokes—he being a carpenter—to make some trifling repairs) enter the house.

With a look of mystic importance and delight, the Clare-man went off and fetched his horse and car, and without waiting to transact the business he had come about, set off in haste to announce the joyful news throughout a county which had long dreaded the power of the terrible Major.

When the footman, some half an hour later, related to his fellow-servants the witty answer he had given, he was astonished to find they did not share the joke; far from it, they loudly blamed him, and foretold the serious scrape he had got himself into. John began to feel uncomfortable; but as it was now too late to undo his folly, he wisely made the best of it, and went on cleaning his master's plate.

Vokes in the meantime carried out the measures he came over to propose, and then dined at the house of a friend. It was dark when he started to return; but to this he did not object, as he was by no means

15

anxious to be recognised ; for the same reason he declined to be attended. The only precaution he took was slightly to vary the route he had followed in the morning.

As he got a few miles out of Ennis, he beheld several large bonfires lighted on the hills, and he almost began to regret that he had left Limerick, as these illuminations were always used as signals for outbreak, or to telegraph some important news.

Not far from the wood of Cratloe one of these fires blazed, and although it was somewhat hazardous to do so, our bold magistrate determined on visiting the spot and learning the origin of it. So he jumped off his horse, and concealing the pistol which he carried in the holster that he now cast from him, he covered his chin with his muffler, put the hat *straight* on his head, which he usually wore jauntily on one side, and changing his appearance and accent as far as possible, rode slowly up the ascent, whistling the " British Grenadiers."

On his arrival he found an enormous fire, around which fifty or sixty people were assembled, smoking, drinking, and chatting.

" Good evening to you, my friends," cried the Major, assuming to his own satisfaction the pronunciation and manner of an Englishman. "How do you do, my friends ?"

The surprised peasantry started up, but seeing a single horseman, they again resumed their places, the neighbouring blacksmith calling out, " Faith, what are ye after ? What do you want ?"

" Oh, nothing—nothing at all ! I only rode here to

say I had lost my way in this confounded country, and
wished to ask you which way I should go ?"

"And where are you going?"

"To the city of Limerick. I think you call it
Garryowen in Irish."

The people burst out laughing at this specimen of a
Cockney, and the word *omadthawn* (idiot) might bo
heard issuing out of more than one mouth, as they exchanged observations in Irish.

"Thin it's yer way ye're asking?"

"Well, that's all, I believe. I really should like to
find it. I'd give a shilling to any fine fellow who
would tell me the way I should go ?"

This new Cockneyism (as the Irish people call it)
produced a fresh laugh, and seeing that the man was
perfectly innocent, and a stranger, they asked the fool
to partake of some of their cheer. He did so, and
seemingly allowed the liquor to open his mouth, for
now on his side he began to ask questions.

"Tell me, my very excellent friends, why have you
lit up this very nice fire on the top of this bleak
mountain ?"

"It's to convey the news."

"What news ?"

"Don't you know it? Faith, thin, ye're the only
man in Clare that don't. Sure, Tom Vokes the prosecutor's dead."

Vokes could not conceal a start.

"You may well be surprised, and so were we when
we heard it, for he was alive and well yesterday.
Here's his health."

The magistrate mentally joined in the toast.

"And a speedy passage to the bottomless pit," bellowed the farrier, with a savage burst of delight.

Vokes did *not* join in this.

"Sure, he hanged my brother for shooting an exciseman."

"And didn't he transport my cousin Pat for a simple burglary ?"

"Oh, he was a savage, a raal right down savage. Bad luck to him !" chimed in a third.

"And haven't I been out these nine months on account of the burning of ould Macnaulty and his daughter. Haven't I been hunted up and down the county like a wild beast, and after all I was not the principal—I only strangled the ould fellow to prevent his telling. Ye all know it was Fred Dwyer as stabbed the girl, and robbed her, and fired the house ; and there now for ye, he's down comfortable like, at his uncle's, beyant Ennistown, and aren't I here in terror of my life ? Bedad, I'd like to stick a knife in his heart, the blackguard, before they bury him."

"Ah, there, Teddy Lynch, hould your tongue ; you talk too much," said a female of the party.

"You're right, Biddy agrath. He'll talk himself into a hempen collar, some day, if he don't look sharp."

Vokes had now learnt all. The man of all others he wished to seize, stood within three paces of him ; the fellow who had so long eluded his pursuit was now within his grasp.

Not liking the turn the conversation had taken, the C. M. P. gave notice of his approaching departure, not in a hurried manner, but in a cool, slow way, drawling out his words to the great amusement of his hearers, who looked upon the Londoner's accent as a subject of fair game, without even for an instant suspecting that their conversation, which had been carried on in pure Irish, could even have been guessed at by the Cockney before them.

Several persons now offered their directions relative to the best road for the stranger to follow, while Teddy Lynch, more eager than any other, doubtlessly desiring to earn the promised shilling, pressed forward and proffered his advice, declaring he knew every yard of the country.

Vokes at once addressed him. "My good fellow, you are pleased to say you know this wild country well. Now I'm all alone and unarmed, and I never was here before, and I don't much like travelling in strange parts, you see, after dark; so what will you take to come and guide me?"

"Me—is it me?"

"Go with him," shouted two or three, "for the fun of it."

"If you'll come, I'll give you a pound-note."

"*Tare a nouns*, it's a good offer; but you'll let me off as soon as we get to Banrathy Bridge, for I have reasons for not wishing to enter any town just now."

"It's a bargain, my good friend," replied the magistrate, and away they went, the peasant walking beside the Major's horse. In this manner they proceeded, little conversation being exchanged, till they arrived at Banrathy Bridge, when Lynch turning round, declared that he had fulfilled his task, and demanded the reward.

230 RECOLLECTIONS OF AN IRISH POLICE MAGISTRATE.

"And you shall have it," roared Vokes as he jumped off his horse—"you shall have it," cried he, seizing the surprised peasant by the collar. "Attempt to escape, and your brains shall be scattered over this bridge," added he, drawing out his pistol and presenting it at the fellow's head. "Hey, police! police! Come here quickly. Nay, it's no use struggling, Tim Lynch, for I am Tom Vokes."

The murderer looked at him, and seemed at a glance to read the truth of his assertion. His altered manner and a few words of Irish he had mingled in his address too surely told the assassin that he was in the hands of his most dreaded enemy. He no longer struggled. He submitted to his fate. The dead had, as he believed, come to life in order to seize him—how then could he struggle! Terror-struck and paralysed, he allowed his captor to drag him over the bridge, at the foot of which stood a small police barrack. Here the force, aroused by the calls of their superior, were just hurrying from their beds, when Vokes entered, dragging in his formidable prisoner. He only remained to see the fellow handcuffed and confined. He wrote a short note to the nearest magistrate, who lived within a few yards. Then mounting his horse, he galloped cheerfully off, to trace the origin of the report which had seemingly removed him from this world.

After some trouble he came at the real truth, and in consideration of the important. capture to which it had unwittingly led, the footman was forgiven.

Tim Lynch was hanged at the next assizes held at Ennis, to the great joy and comparative security of the whole county of Clare.

A SPORTING ADVENTURE.

Mr. L—— was one of the most active and zealous magistrates in the county of Limerick. He came forward on every occasion, and did his utmost to quell the disturbances which in 1821 convulsed the district, and were the precursors of those outrages which for many years subsequently disgraced the South of Ireland. Ever ready to afford his services, and equally prepared when called upon to risk his life, the worthy magistrate led far from a comfortable or a peaceable existence. On one occasion, about the time I speak of, he was solicited to attend with some yeomanry and a large body of regulars the fair at Rathkeale. Here the ordinary festivities took place—that is to say, after the usual horse-coping and bargaining, the usual dancing took place, and when this was done, the usual drinking was indulged in, crowned, as it always was, by the most fearful riots between opposing factions, in the course of which several persons were killed, in spite of all the exertions made to keep those savage antagonists (who had probably met here by mutual agreement "to fight it out") quiet and orderly. The unhappy result of the conflict, and the interference of the troops, was that the soldiery in turn (compelled to

do so in their own defence) fired on the people, and so
ended the affair. The latter quickly quitted the field,
leaving the place in quiet possession of the powers of
the law.

Three or four dead bodies lay upon the ground;
some of the military were wounded. The people
uttered wild threats in tones which reached the ears of
the exasperated troops.

The magistrate desired (at least so I have ever heard
it asserted) a grave to be dug on the spot, and into
this he threw the bodies of those men who had fallen
in fighting with the King's troops. He then ordered
some quicklime to be thrown over them, and the hole
filled up. This was done, and shortly afterwards the
forces left Rathkeale and returned to their quarters.

Upon what grounds they based their belief, I know
not; but certain it is, that ever afterwards the peasantry
boldly asserted that the men who had been shot were
buried alive ! that they had turned round in their last
resting-place, and that they might have been recovered
had it not been for the operation of the quicklime !

Such a wicked and false report having been indus-
triously spread, it can scarcely be wondered at that
Mr. L—— was held up as an object of horror, and his
life placed in hourly jeopardy.

The old man, however, passed away, and left a son
to represent him, one of the pleasantest and best
young men in the county, celebrated for his convivial
powers, his reckless daring, and his great superiority
in every athletic exercise : he was at once the best
rider, the best shot, the best runner, and the best
thrower of a sledge-hammer in the county of Limerick.

G. L—— was more than once fired at, but never wounded. By his fleetness on some occasions, and his great bodily strength on others, he had frequently escaped from the hands of ruffians who sought to injure him. As we have stated before, George had even been denounced in the songs of the people—his death was foretold. But our stalwart friend laughed alike at personal attacks and anonymous threats, and continued his jovial and sporting career in spite of the *"bad boys"* who, though disliking him, feared to approach him.

One afternoon I was seated with Vokes, when our friend rushed in. From his dress he had evidently been out shooting; and such proved to be the fact. He had tried snipe-shooting in Cappagh Bog, and for some time enjoyed good sport; unfortunately, however, he had been induced, by thirst, to enter a cottage and ask for a drink of water. This was cheerfully accorded to him, and the potatoes just boiled for their family meal freely offered by the two women, who were alone in the cabin, to George with a friendly invitation to partake of them. Fancying that he would please them by accepting their proffered hospitality, and well knowing that a refusal to eat under an Irish roof is considered a decided slight in that country, the sportsman freely swallowed one or two, and in return gave them the birds he had just shot, and a glass of whisky, which he drew from his leathern pouch.

He now rose to quit; but to his surprise he found the door closely barred on the outside, and on turning round, after several ineffectual efforts to break open

the entrance, he discovered that during that time, at
least half a dozen peasants had entered at the back
way, and one of them was in the act of bearing off his
gun, which he had laid aside while eating. He sprang
at the man who had thus robbed him, and seized him
by the throat; but the fellow at once passed the
weapon to a comrade, who made off with it. He
vainly endeavoured to struggle with the party, who,
having thus possessed themselves of the arm they
coveted, took to flight, and left him again alone with
the two women, who had not ceased to cry and lament
during the whole scene, which had not, however, occupied five minutes.

"Och, thin, the Lord be merciful to us, Master
George—it's well it's no worse !"

"You know me then ? "

"Troth, I do. My father was herd to your father
—God rest the old gentleman, though they tell wicked
stories of him ; and faix, I'm a thinking it was on that
account they spared your life. But take my advice,
yer honour; don't come to the Bog again. They are now
pleased at getting your gun, and don't care to harm
ye. Sure, they mayn't always be so agreeable, and
you might get an ugly puck—not to say a death-stroke
—so don't come, Master George ; and, faith, if ye're
wise, ye won't say much about it."

Long ere the well-meaning women had done speaking
the young man had left the cottage, and now sought
Vokes for advice.

"Well, what do you wish me to do?" asked the C. M. P.

"I want you to try and recover my gun."

"Do you know that if I took any steps to find out and arrest these men, it might lead to bad results."

" Is the county then in such a dreadful state ?"

"In truth it is," replied Vokes, who now quitted the room, and was absent for about ten minutes.

" Your father-in-law is in a queer humour," chimed in L——.

"He is so," I replied, "but he is so strange in his ways that I never question him. You have now told him your tale. You had better say no more. He'll not forget it ; and notwithstanding all he says, depend upon it he'll try and recover your gun if an opportunity offers itself."

"I have no doubt you are right. I'll say no more about it."

Presently Vokes came in, and having succeeded in persuading our victimized friend to stay to dinner, he branched off into all the light talk of the day, carefully avoiding any allusion to George's loss.

About eight o'clock Sir R. F—— came in, a relative of Vokes, and his medical adviser. F—— challenged the magistrate to play at piquet, and they sat down to that scientific game, while L—— and I amused ourselves by chatting over our respective feats in the hunting-field.

It was about ten o'clock when Vokes was called out of the room. He seemed to expect the summons, which could be nothing very extraordinary, as he remained to finish the game ere he arose to attend to the call.

He shortly returned, and walked straight up to George.

" You would know your gun again ?"

" Decidedly.'

" You could swear to it ?"

" I could."

Vokes went to the door and opened it. Sergeant Toomy entered ; he carried a fowling-piece in his hand. L——'s eyes actually danced with delight.

" Is that it ?"

" It is. But how did you get it ?"

" That is my business. Give back the piece to the police-sergeant. It will be returned to you after the trial."

" What trial ?"

" The trial of the four men, and their accomplices the two women, in Cappagh Bog."

" Indeed ; but can you catch them ?"

The door opened, and four fine-looking peasants entered and two women, in custody of a small party of police.

" Are these the men who assaulted you, and took your gun ?"

" They are."

" And these the women, who (unseen by you) sent off a boy to fetch them ?"

" They are the women ; but I don't believe——"

" Silence ! the crime of seizing arms, more especially with force, from the person, is an offence of the most serious nature. Desire Mr. Woodbourne to make out a committal, and march them up to the county jail. And now, F——, let us finish the rubber of piquet these fellows interrupted."

The wonderfully quiet manner in which Vokes first gleaned information, and then made use of it ; the calm and dispassionate mode in which he treated those brought before him, the strange way in which he seemed to possess a certain knowledge of everything that was passing; had a powerful effect on all around him.

On the evening in question, though highly gratified in having recovered his lost treasure, I am certain that our friend left the doorstep in George-street, convinced that the peasantry were right when they said " Tom Vokes had dealings with ——"

THE HANGMAN.

ALTHOUGH I had given a brother subaltern two days'
duty in order to shirk the disagreeable sight of a
criminal being hanged, for to my great annoyance—
though not to my surprise, it being an event of frequent
occurrence in Ireland—I found myself detailed for the
"execution party," or, to express it in less technical
terms, I was ordered out in charge of some twenty-five
dragoons, to be present at the execution of a culprit—
a degrading service to which the cavalry are continually
liable in the sister country, and as I said before, a
duty to which I so strenuously objected, that my
military chief allowed me to transfer it to a brother
officer—he bargaining that I should take his orderlies
for two days, and thus release him to the joys of the
hunting field.

But though I thus eschewed the horrors of seeing
a poor wretch put to death, I must admit that I had
a morbid desire to behold the victim ere he suffered,
and to examine the fearful apparatus which was to
put an end to his existence.

I therefore asked Vokes to take me into the new
gaol to see the condemned felon, to which, after a

slight sneer at my inconsistency, he assented, and we walked up together.

On our arrival we were shown into the cell where the unhappy wretch sat awaiting the summons which was to call him forth to expiate the crime he had committed.

A couple of turnkeys were in attendance on the man, who sat in seeming calmness on a stool, freely conversing with the persons around him. He had confessed his crime, and had probably been absolved by his clergy, for he seemed in tolerably good spirits and fully prepared to meet his fate. He spoke coolly about the murder he had committed, and appeared more anxious for his poor children than himself. He had taken leave of his wife and family: he had, as he considered, made his peace with Heaven, and he now resignedly awaited the last struggle which was to wrench him from life to eternity. He was a tall athletic young man, some five-and-twenty years of age, dressed from head to foot in white flannel, and perfectly ready to converse about himself, but equally determined not to betray the companions of his crime, nor the fearful links which probably bound him to carry out the organized will of others. Even now, were he to afford a clue by which one of those secret societies, those brotherhoods of blood, might be discovered—even now, at the last moment, he might hope for a respite, for the judge was still near. But no! The wretch who had steeped his hands in the lifeblood of his fellow-creature, who had rendered a once happy hearth desolate, and sent forth the widow and orphan unprotected—even this wretch, I say, felt a false sense of honour—an obligation to shield his accomplices ; and while he recklessly committed a crime of the deepest dye before the eye of his offended *Maker*, he still refused to break an oath which he had sworn at the bidding of his terrible copartners in guilt.

Well assured of this, I felt less sympathy for the man before me than I should otherwise have done, and hurried out of the cell—feeling that the presence of such a being was highly distasteful, and far from being that object of commiseration I had fully expected to find in him.

As we re-entered the yard, Vokes asked the head gaoler whether the prisoner's clothes had been destroyed. The official bowed assent, and we passed on. I could not resist my desire of asking the chief magistrate why this was done.

" I'll tell you," said he. " It has proved most efficacious in repressing crime."

" Burning a man's apparel a measure calculated to check crime ! Pshaw ! you are joking."

" Not so. Did you not see that the prisoner was dressed in white flannel—his own habiliments having been made away with, probably burnt. It was to ascertain this fact that I walked up here with you."

" Upon my honour, your ways are most strange. Pray explain yourself. I really should like to know the connexion between the destruction of a coat and breeches and the suppression of murder."

" I will gratify you. You must know, then, that when this county first earned its fatal celebrity, every means were adopted to put down the lawless bands which then paraded through our fields in open daylight. Special commissions had no effect. Prompt executions were of no avail. Guilt still enjoyed her supremacy. And when an execution took place, it was rather a scene of triumph for the condemned man than the severe and wholesome lesson it was intended to impart. Cheers greeted the monster as he ascended the scaffold, and when he was cut down his body was carried away to be interred with drunken pomp. The latter portion of this was, however, easily put a stop to. The bodies were ordered to be buried within the precincts of the gaol : and, indeed, on some occasions, they were given over to the surgeons for dissection, to the great horror of their relatives. This gave a temporary check to crime ; but after awhile, it was clear that they became callous on this head, and even these salutary measures ceased to alarm them.

"About this time I became an officer of Government, and I mentally vowed to find out what consolation they had introduced to meet the terrible stroke aimed at them, in thus depriving them of the dead bodies of those they loved.

"After considerable trouble — for they jealously guarded their secret—I found out that immediately on each execution taking place, the friends of the culprit came to the prison-gate and claimed his clothes, which, as the governor of the gaol thought they had an undoubted right to them, were duly delivered ; and loaded with these, they set off to some neighbour's cabin—generally speaking, in some distant and secluded spot — and here, having arranged the garments in a proper form, they went through the whole mockery of WAKING THEM ! Here the whisky flowed,

16

and the tobacco-smoke formed a canopy of cloud ; here they danced round the apparel of the deceased ; here they poured forth blessings on the soul of the man who had been hanged, and called down curses, mingled with oaths of vengeance, on his murderers—thus designating all who had in any way assisted in bringing the assassin to justice. Drunk, furious, and ungovernable, these creatures, consisting of men, women, and children, screamed round the supposed corpse, and long ere they were sober, attended the clothes in mock burial to some hole which had been dug in the garden to receive them."

"Well, how could you stop them ?"

"In the most simple manner. On the morning of his execution, each condemned· felon, male or female, was stripped of his or her usual habiliments, and plain costumes, made of white flannel, placed on them. Thus clad, they appeared before the crowd, to their great horror and astonishment, which was not a little increased when, on application at the gate, they were told that the clothes of ——, the person just hanged, had been burnt that morning by order of the justices. Ridiculous as this remedy may appear to you, it alarmed all the superstitious fears of the peasantry, and afforded a more effectual check to crime than any other measure I have hitherto been lucky enough to originate."

This explanation, I must confess, surprised me much at the time it was given ; but I subsequently found that it was perfectly correct, for I personally observed, when more closely investigating the character of the Irish peasantry, that the sorrow for death melts away

before the triumph of a "grand wake"—a long remembered glory, quoted ever afterwards in the family
of a poor man, with the same pride which bestows a
magnificent funeral on a member of a superior class—
a tribute of vain respect paid by the living to the dead
in the sister country—a tribute which can do little good
to the latter, while it has often proved ruinous to the
unhappy survivors.

We now entered the small square room immediately
beneath the drop, where a band of officials were seated,
awaiting their turn of duty in the approaching melancholy ceremony.

From the corner of this apartment a winding staircase leads to the platform above, where the gallows is
erected. To this staircase I was hurrying, when I felt
myself suddenly *lassoed* (if the term may be allowed).
I was caught tightly round the throat by a rope which
had a slip-knot, now drawn tightly close, while I beheld at the other end of it the most fearful-looking
little monster that I ever met with. There he stood
grinning at me, the living picture of Hans of Iceland.
Not above four feet high, blear-eyed, strongly wrinkled
from age—active as a cat—there he stood tugging away
at me, or rather firmly holding me—for, truth to confess, the tightning of the cord partly arose from my own
plunges to escape—while the men around us joined in
the horrid laughter which exposed to my view the
wide mouth and the thirty-two pearl-white fangs of
this fearful nondescript. Overcome by a feeling of
danger, I drew my sword, and I verily do believe that
the next instant would have seen me pass it through
the diminutive ruffian's body, had not Vokes, checking

16—2

his mirth, roared out, "For shame, man! put up your sword; it's only little Micky, the hangman."

"Gradi, gradi!"* cried the facetious monster, holding out his hand in the most unmistakeable manner. "Gradi, yer honour!"

Had I had gold in my pocket, instead of small silver, I think I should have bestowed it all with alacrity on the disgusting fellow, so anxious was I to get out of his clutches; as it was, I threw him a few shillings, and asked a turnkey standing near to take off my "hempen collar," for I shrank from the touch of little Micky; and half ashamed of my unseemly violence, I clambered up the steps, which in another half hour would feel the last tread of the condemned felon.

The apparatus that I came to see was of the simplest kind. The portico on which it was reared was surrounded by a high wall, so only those could be seen who mounted the actual platform, some five feet above us; so I had time to look at the terrible engine, without being perceived by the populace, who had already collected in large numbers.

The small spot on which we now stood closely resembled a battery, and I believe this idea was not absent from the mind of him who selected it as a place of execution, since any attack on the authorities, or attempt to rescue the prisoner, the slightest suspicion of such an event occurring, and the whole party could shelter themselves behind the breastwork, and retire down the staircase or not, as they might deem best.

Vokes told me a strange superstition—namely, the conviction in the popular mind, that when a man and

* Charity,

woman are executed together—which in these times
was not a very rare occurrence—if they happened in
swinging about to turn their backs to each other, it
betokened their guilt : a token from Providence which
none could dare to doubt.

As the time for the awful ceremony approached, we
got away; and I confess I was glad to again find
myself at home.

But here my annoyances did not end. About two
hours later, I received an order to escort the hangman
back to Ennis, which was anything but pleasant, as it
was quite sure we should be pelted with stones the
whole way; but as I had already shirked the public
performance of Mr. Micky, I did not see how I could
get out of the scrape. I stated my case to Vokes, and
added the sore grievance of my being forced to give up
a most pleasant dinner-party in order to shield, during
some eight or ten hours, a being whom I disliked and
loathed.

Vokes laughed at my chagrin, but promised to re-
lieve me from my unpleasant predicament. He put
on his hat and went across to the general (Sir C. D.);
in a few moments he returned, and with a smile handed
me a scrap of paper—a copy of an order sent to the
barracks : " Thirty men of the 32nd, in charge of a
subaltern officer, will proceed to Ennis this evening, at
five o'clock p.m., on escort duty. The men to be supplied with the usual rounds of ball-cartridge." I at
once saw that I was free, and after thanking my relative, asked him how he managed it.

" Well, then, can't you see? Sure the horses might
get injured by the stones which are sure to be thrown

at them by the angry crowd; and as the cart in which
Micky travels only goes *foot-pace*, he requires infantry,
not cavalry, to protect him properly."

I quite agreed with the magistrate, and silently
drank his health, as I sat at M——'s pleasant dinner-
table.

Though trifling, the incident showed that Vokes was
ever ready to meet and overcome circumstances.

The escort party were much annoyed; some of the
men were hurt; all were irritated by the manner in
which they were treated and abused. The officer, who
had great difficulty in preventing his men from firing,
assured me he would not pass such another night—one
so unprofitable, so tiresome, and at the same time so
degrading—to obtain a step in rank.

PEASANT PRIDE.

"There are decidedly many traits of our Spanish origin still existent amongst the Irish peasantry," urged Vokes. "In the superior ranks these strongly marked characteristics, however, are, it is true, lost. But I account for this difference of feeling in a very simple way. The landowners and gentry of Ireland have ever sought alliances with English families. Add to which, the many grants conferred on your countrymen, my dear Harry, by Cromwell, King William, and others, and you will at once trace the dilution of these attributes. Nay, do not look annoyed; I do not mean by the word in question any weakening of their strength, but the natural change which such a com-mingling must bring."

"It is not of the upper orders I would speak. I was trying to come at the distinctive points of a thorough-bred son of the soil."

"Well, then, as I said before, I look upon their origin to have been *Spanish*. Does not the very designation *Hibernian* convey it. Is the expression itself more than a mere corruption of the old Latin name of Iberia ? Are the prominent points of their disposition not decidedly Iberian? Are they not revengeful, lazy, and proud? Will they not assassinate in cold blood for hire?"

"This is indeed a dark picture."

"Every picture may be viewed in different lights. Are they not equally warm-hearted, generous, hospitable, and brave, attached to their ancestors, and wedded to the spot on which they were born? Are they not naturally witty, handsome, and affectionate?"

"Your sketch is somewhat conflicting."

"Not more so than the character of those I would portray. A Protestant clergyman was cruelly murdered on the public road some months ago, while travelling with his family in an open car, on one of the most well-frequented roads in the county of Tipperary. The men were taken up, and proved to be strangers to the locality. For fifteen shillings each they had travelled from their own home, situated some thirty miles distant, and without any motive, beyond that of securing the bribe, shot the unhappy victim. On tracing their movements and acts subsequent to the assassination, I found that one of them only had wasted the "price of blood" on drink; a second bore it home, and handed it over untouched to his bedridden parent; a third gave ten shillings of it to his sweetheart; while the fourth (for that was their numerical force), probably shocked at what he had done, paid nearly the whole sum for masses in favour of his father's soul. Here surely we recognise the fearful carelessness with which these people treat human life. The Irishman substitutes the more manly weapons, the gun and the pistol, for the poisoned bowl and the dagger, but they are no less ready than the Spaniard to destroy a fellow-being, if paid for so doing."

" I hope this is an isolated case ? "

" By no means ; it is rather, as the American legend was, " *unus e pluribus.*" But let us pass that over, and see whether the native of Erin is not as proud as the most bigoted child of Spain. Why, if you will scrutinize them closely, you will find that there is not a tenant holding a quarter of an acre of land on any gentleman's property in Munster that does not speak of his wretched holding—his mud cabin—as an hereditary estate, and will fiercely put that man to death who dares to attempt to evict him from it, or as he more pompously observes—"the man that would cruelly drive him from beneath the roof of his ancestors." It is from this simple cause that all our most sanguinary struggles have arisen. In England, your small cottages often change their inhabitants. If a large proprietor finds that a small dwelling interferes with the view from his mansion, he orders it to be pulled down. If a tenant refuses to pay rent, he is at once turned out. Heaven help you, my dear fellow, if you tried such an experiment in this county. Your life would not be worth a day's purchase. While as to pride, every cottager believes himself to be the descendant of some great chief, and his eyes lighten up with triumph when he by chance hears of the deeds of a Desmond or a Brian Borholun. They are as proud as any hidalgo in his Most Catholic Majesty's dominions."

" But you said they were lazy ? "

" To see them working on their own little gardens, or to see them cutting turf in the bog for their winter's supply, would almost persuade you that they are the most laborious people upon earth. But as to working for wages, they will always shirk it when they can. I will recount to you an anecdote illustrative of this fact.

"Some years ago, an officer in the 4th Dragoon Guards, who was quartered in Ireland, felt so much for the labouring classes in this county, compelled to work all day long for sevenpence per diem, that he mentally resolved to assist the over-worked peasantry, if ever he had the power to do so. This opportunity shortly afterwards presented itself. A relative unexpectedly died, and left him 10,000*l.*. Full of his favourite project, our friend E—— instantly sold out of the army and came over to Ireland then and there to do good to himself, and to raise the degraded condition of the labourer and mechanic in that country. Filled with this noble, and, at the same time, profitable idea, he at once embarked for Cork.

" In this fine county he soon found an establishment where he could employ fifty or sixty hands, and which, even supposing he gave the workers in it double wages, would still afford him a broad margin of profit.

He then hired a very pretty little farm, and here his calculation was even still more flattering; so he at once took into his employ some two hundred persons, engaging to pay them one hundred per cent. more than they were in the habit of receiving. This was a glorious windfall for the Corkians, and as E—— hoped, a no less fortunate idea for himself.

"During the first month matters went on most prosperously; the mill yielded its full quantum, and the ledger showed, notwithstanding the high wages paid, a most profitable return. Paddy worked hard for his increased pay, and my friend's agriculture was quoted as unequalled.

"After about three months the attendance of the persons engaged was not quite so regular. Many of the hands in the mill were compelled by sickness to absent themselves, while the ploughers, and sowers, and tillers had so many engagements elsewhere, and met with so many accidents, that not one half of them ever answered at roll-call.

"This was disheartening, especially as spring was coming on. But E—— had a sanguine hope that matters would soon mend. But, alas! they grew worse and worse. The philanthropic speculator's affairs got into confusion. His half-worked mill, his half-farmed acres, plunged him into trouble, and in little less than a year the name of E—— appeared in the *Bankrupts' Gazette*. Poor fellow! He left this country disappointed in vanity and feeling, ruined in prospects and in purse, and still worse, carrying with him the assurance of his faithful Irish superintendent, that 'faith, his honour could expect nothing better in a free country.'

" 'Why so?' echoed the ex-dragoon.

" 'Ah, then, did you think we were all fools? Did you think that when a man could live on sevenpence a day he'd work more than three days in the week? or imagine a fellow would toil six in a mill when he could make enough in three to keep him? No, no; we're not such omadthawns as that!'

"E—— returned to England, where he made a second fortune, a better and a wiser man."

I laughed heartily at the anecdote, which indeed I

have since heard confirmed from the lips of E——
himself, who is now a celebrated physician in London.

At this moment, the police magistrate was called
away, and I thought no more of the subject. Nor
indeed did it ever occur to me again, till I met my
relative several years afterwards in London, when he
handed to me a copy of an Irish newspaper, and with a
glance of triumph exclaimed, " Read that trial of a
man in our county, and I think you will allow that I
was right in my description given of the peasantry.
Ryan Pack, for many years the scourge of the county
of Limerick, has been taken up, and his trial shows
how a man may be *hired* to shed blood in the south
of Ireland, as well as the pride which lurks in the
breast of even a convicted assassin."

I took the journal and read it. The case had been
tried before an especial assize. I do not recollect the
minute details, nor would it be necessary, even if I
did, to record them *in extenso.*

The leading features which affected the statements
of Vokes, I think ran thus :—

A certain Ryan Pack, against whom several
charges of murder had been sworn, had long eluded
the vigilance of the Limerick and Tipperary police.
In vain they looked after him. He seemed Proteus-
like to change his form whenever they approached him,
and when they set off, in full conviction of catching
him on one side of the county, his actual presence on
the other was fatally announced by some terrific
murder in that direction. On one occasion, it is said,
two policemen slept in the same cabin with him, un-
aware of his proximity, and on another, a policeman

drove into a village riding on the shafts of a turf-cart, in the centre of which Mr. Pack was carefully packed. The ruffian was here, there, and everywhere. He laughed at the rewards offered for his apprehension, and surrounded by crowds, tore down the printed bills describing his person. Bold, reckless, and cruel, he was at once the idol and the terror of the multitude. I have reason to believe that it was through the untiring exertions and intelligence of Mr. John Stephen Dwyer, a magistrate for the two counties, that Ryan Pack was at length captured and placed in durance vile. And now began the many difficulties which arose in bringing the wretch to justice in a country where no one would willingly come forward to bear testimony against him.

Among other proofs which fell into the hands of the lawyers, was a scrap of paper—evidently a page torn out of a sort of diary which the prisoner (he being a scholar) appeared to have kept with great regularity. In addition to the one I here quote, others were found which proved that Pack was most particular and strict in his religious duties and attendances; and indeed his conduct in prison proved the sincerity of this feeling—for no man was ever more attentive to the good advice of his clergy, or more ready to satisfy the inquiries of justice when desired to do so by his priest. To return, however, to the memorandum in question. It ran thus :—

"1838—April. To a cursitshute 1
1840—Feb. To a cursitshute 1
1842—May. To a cursitshute 1
1846—Jan. To a cursitshute . . . . 1."

And other similar entries—altogether sixteen in number.

The meaning of these items baffled even the acute penetration of the Crown lawyers, and was only solved at last by the magistrate I have mentioned, who thus made them into English :—

"1846—Jan. to a cursed shot . . . £1."

i.e., Ryan Pack had received one pound for shooting a fellow-being, though he well knew at the time that the deed was accursed. Mr. Dwyer is said to have arrived at this solution by observing that the dates of each entry exactly tallied with a corresponding date on which a cruel murder had been committed. The correctness of the deduction was confirmed afterwards by the murderer himself.*

"There now," said Vokes, "can any system of assassination, save that which disgraces Spain, bear comparison with that which seems indigenous to Ireland ?"

"Well, I must admit your premises so far; but there does not appear to be much pride shown in becoming a hired spiller of blood."

"Wait awhile; go on; read through the case, and

---

* The late trial of Walsh in Limerick proves that the same mode of getting rid of an enemy still exists, and that assassins are always to be found who for a trifle will kill the most virtuous individual. It has been very broadly asserted that Beckham and Walsh—admitted, I believe, by the latter—received only fifteen shillings between them for destroying Mr. Fitzgerald, one of the most amiable and inoffensive men in Ireland. But as the whole case will be laid before the public in a few weeks, when the now supposed bloodthirsty employers are to be tried, it would be unfair in me to say more.

then you will see that my estimate of an Irish peasant's ideas are not far wrong."

In reading through the details of the trial, in the course of which the counsel for the Crown closely examined the prisoner, in order to exhibit the state of feeling throughout the district, I found him asking several witnesses whether they would shoot a man for a bribe, and in two instances out of three, to the horror of the Court, they admitted they would, and seemed to glory in their recklessness.

At length the jury pronounced a verdict of Guilty, and Ryan Pack heard without emotion the sentence of death passed on him.

In the following number of the newspaper, with that morbid punctuality so welcome to journal readers, the sayings and doings of the wretched criminal were described in the most minute manner, from the hour of his conviction to that of his death. A party of county gentlemen had visited the culprit, and had, out of a strange curiosity, asked him—

" Would you have shot any one of us for a pound-note ?"

" I would."

" What! even if we had never offended you ?"

" Faith, that was not my business."

" Would you have shot Mr. W——?"—(naming a popular magistrate). " Would you have shot him for one pound ?"

" Decidedly !"

" Why, he is a Catholic."

" The more sure of going to heaven."

" Would you have shot *this* gentleman ?" asked

one, pointing towards Mr. Dwyer, who just then entered. "You would have shot *him* with pleasure, I'm thinking."

"Not so," said Ryan Pack, quickly. "I never should have thought of trying it—not I : for though he's sharp and rather severe, he's just and fair to those whom he fancies wronged, and right good to the poor. I wouldn't have shot him—indeed, I could if I had liked it; but, as I told you, I wouldn't. And now I'd like to be left alone."

"I only came," put in Mr. Dwyer, "because you sent for me."

"Faith, it's true for ye. I knew that you would not come out of mere curiosity to look at a dying man like a wild beast. I don't mean to offend you, gentlemen ; but as you are here, you may as well hear what I have to say. I sent for you, sir," said he, addressing Dwyer, "to tell you that I forgive you for causing my apprehension, and also that I consider that you conducted the whole affair in a just and upright way, and to acknowledge that my sentence is just."

"I am glad to hear you say so, Ryan. If you have anything on your mind at once unburthen it, and I'll do all I can to console you."

"Oh, as far as that goes, I have confessed to my clergy, and made my peace with Heaven. But one thing does afflict me and grieve me in the moment of death."

"And what is it ? Can I alleviate your sorrow ?"

"Impossible ! Besides, his reverence says my feeling is wicked."

"What is it ?"

"Well, then, I'll tell ye. It is that I, who have always held my head high, and lived as a respectable boy, should now be hung for shooting a low feather-merchant, when I had opportunities every day of killing a magistrate, or a grand juror, or the first land-holders in the county, and so dying decently for a genteel crime, instead of thus sneaking out of the world for destroying a low feather-seller. Mr. Dwyer, this it is that grieves me."

In the next newspaper the execution of Ryan Puck was described. He died calmly, and without fear or apparent remorse.

" Well, Henry, was that not pride ?" asked Vokes.

"I admit that it was, and therefore for the future will ever believe in the Spanish qualities of an Irish peasant."

THE ABDUCTION.

Some forty years ago, there existed in Ireland a race of young men called *Bucheens,* or *Squireens,* the idle sons of gentlemen of estate, who, possessing little or no means whatsoever, sought by impudence and wit to earn their daily meal, at least until such time as a stroke of fortune might happily enable them to find a five-pound note in their pocket—an event which seldom occurred, unless through the medium of a commission in the army or a fortunate marriage. The young men of the present day born and bred in the sister isle, are glad to become clerks in public or private offices, or to accept any post which may give them an independence. But this was not the case in the first quarter of the present century. A gentleman's son despised commerce of every sort. He shunned the first merchant's office with the same proud disdain with which he treated the lowest shopkeeper's. Money-grubbing was beneath his dignity ; the drudgery of an office he contemned. He preferred lounging about the streets in half-starved idleness ; riding occasionally a borrowed horse, or shooting, at the risk of being taken up as a poacher, with a gun and a licence belonging to a neighbour. He swaggered in pride, and boasted in ignorance. He looked down on painstaking respectability, and impatiently awaited the day when his father should thrust him forth in a pair of leather breeches, bestriding a broken-down hunter, and armed with a purse containing some four or five sovereigns. Like a modern Gil Blas in search of adventures, the world before him, he carelessly took the first path that presented itself, and with a light heart and a brave spirit the "young master" set out to make his fortune, trusting that the proud "O" or the ancient "Mac" which introduced his family name to the world, would gain for him a useful friendship or a profitable love.

Need I say that we had our full share of these precocious youths in the county and city of Limerick ? Ever ready to win the hand of a dowered maiden, ever ready, if necessary, to fight for it, the Bucheens who lounged up and down George-street were a most formidable body. They had all to gain, nothing to lose ; who, then, would enter into strife with them ? Their sons little know, in 1862, what wild lads their fathers were before them.

These young gentlemen generally contented themselves by strutting about, and occasionally playing off practical jokes ; but the following anecdote shows that they did not always confine themselves to innocent freaks.

One of the prettiest girls in the neighbourhood was the daughter of a gentleman farmer, alike celebrated for his large fortune and the jealous care with which he watched his adored child, she had only just completed her fifteenth birthday, and on that auspicious occasion

the doating father had so far relaxed his usual strict-
ness that he had given a ball, and invited to it
many of the young gentlemen, sons of the magistrates
and grand jurors, who lived around him. These plea-
sure-seeking lads gladly accepted the proffered civility,
anxious at the same time to dance with the lovely
heiress (for she was an only child), and make up for
the stern exclusiveness of their parents, who refused
to visit one whom they styled a mere yeoman.

Young —— saw the sweet and interesting creature,
the heroine of the fête, and danced with her. To see
her was to love her, and poor —— at once became
desperately enamoured with her; love at first sight
never wounded so deeply. The stricken youngster
came home an altered man. He could neither eat,
drink, nor sleep. He no longer followed the hounds,
as he had hitherto done, sometimes on horseback, sometimes on foot; the oyster-cellars were forsaken; the
racket-court abandoned; the wretched victim could do
nothing but talk of his enchantress during the day and
dream of her at night. It is true that he had attempted to broach the subject to his parents, who at
once united in a dire threat to turn him out of the castle,
if he dared again to speak of the "low creature." His
mother, who was the niece of a nobleman, fainted away
when she heard her son speak highly of a "yeoman's
daughter." Thus stood matters in his own house.

Young —— was no less unfortunate in his attempts
to win the hand of the lovely girl with the consent of
her father. Far from considering the proposal as an
honour, the irritated sire desired the Bucheen to leave
his house, and threatened him with personal castiga-

tion if ever he caught him again within his ring fence.

The young lady gave no encouragement to the deeply-enamoured Squireen, whose passion seemed only to increase with obstacles, and at length became a settled madness.

Determined to possess the object of his hopes at any price, and seeing that all ordinary means failed, the reckless youth determined on carrying her off—a mode of gaining a wife, *bon gré, mal gré*, but too often adopted in the South of Ireland. For this purpose he secured the assistance of some of his friends and some unprincipled retainers, and one day, when Miss —— was riding home, attended by a single servant, who it is believed was in league with the abductors, they pounced on her and carried her off.

Within a few hours it was ascertained, though not without considerable trouble, that young —— had carried off his prize to a solitary farmhouse, standing in the midst of an extensive bog, some twenty miles from her father's residence.

The bereaved parent was naturally angered at the outrage, and in his first fit of passion vowed to destroy the cruel abductor; but on calm reflection, on consultation with his best friends, he became convinced of the futility of any personal exertion on his part—any single attempt to recover his lost treasure. He therefore rode into Limerick, and swore informations before the bench of magistrates then sitting. These gentlemen at once ordered out a considerable force, consisting of military and police, with strict injunctions to proceed to the farm-house in the bog, and bring back the imprisoned girl.

The anxious father saw all the preparations made, and was about to ride home and obtain some further information as to the exact locality, when a note was thrust into his hand by a little ragged urchin, who no sooner saw it in the yeoman's possession, than he fled quickly, and was soon beyond the reach of pursuit. Mr. —— opened the note; it ran thus :—

"SIR,—It is true that I have carried off your daughter, and brought her here. It is true that I adore her, and intend to marry her. If she is wise she will consent; for I will prove myself a good and affectionate husband. If you are not silly, you will advise her to do so, and thus ally yourself with one of the oldest blood-stocks in Munster. I say this in a friendly manner—desiring peace. If she refuses, by all I hold sacred, I will marry her by force. I am no boy—and she will repent it. So now take your choice. If you send an answer by a little boy (and I can see all who approach within a mile) I will show it to her. So I advise you give her good counsel in it. If, on the contrary, you attempt to recover her by force, by ——, you shall repent it. If you bring any of the soldiery or the Peelers near me you will for ever rue it. I am determined—I am sworn. And the very first man that approaches this house I will destroy, and then, as I know that the struggle is useless, I will instantly shoot your daughter, and then blow out my own brains; for as I hope for Eternity, I cannot, will not, live without her. If you try force, you, not I, will be the murderer of your daughter in the sight of heaven !

"HUGH ——."

The wretched man staggered as if he had been shot. He well knew the desperate character of his daughter's abductor; he fully believed that he would carry out, to its full extent, the threat contained in the young man's letter. What could he do? His love for his child overcame his desire for vengeance, and he went back and earnestly begged of the magistrates to postpone their attack. This, with great reluctance, they consented to do, but only extended their forbearance for four-and-twenty hours.

The next step which naturally suggested itself to the affrighted parent was to call on Vokes, who at once took up the case, on the strict condition that he should not be interfered with. .This was agreed to, and he at once began his measures.

"Write," said Vokes, "write a reply."

"What shall I say?"

The Major dictated an answer; it ran thus:—

"Until to-morrow, I pledge myself not to molest you; this will give me time for reflection. It will give you the same advantage. If a spark of honour still lurks in your breast, you will not injure my child.

"JOHN ——."

"But how shall I transmit it?"

"Give it me; I'll have it placed in the fellow's hands. I'll send it by my milking-maid; they will allow her to approach. So be easy on this subject."

"You think, then, he'll deliver my daughter up?"

"Decidedly not."

"What, then, do you think? As you value my

peace of mind, tell me candidly. I beseech you to open your breast to me?"

"Well, then, to tell you the truth, I think that when he finds you are determined on recapturing her, he will marry her."

"Marry her?—marry her? Oh, do not say so; pray do not!"

"It is my opinion. To-night he will send for a priest, real or mock, and go through the ceremony of espousing her. To-morrow he will throw open the doors and offer her back, if you will take her."

"Oh, this is too horrible. Can nothing be done? I'll give any money, I'll risk any danger, but let me have my darling back again. Oh, Major Vokes, I know your wonderful powers—do exert them on my behalf."

"Well, I really feel for your situation, and will do all that I can."

The bereaved yeoman after a few more words left the chief magistrate, and by the desire of that functionary returned to his now desolate home.

Soon after this, Vokes quietly strolled down to his office, and ordered two of his men to steal separately and unseen into the neighbourhood of the farm-house in the bog, in plain clothes, and then to hide themselves in some of the outbuildings till a signal should be given them, when they were instantly, if possible, to make a forcible entry; but on no account to allow themselves to be detected before that period. They need not start on the expedition till after dark, and were to take notice of anything that occurred, and let him know. He would be in a small cabin about two miles from the spot, and would there await intelligence from them.

All went on well. No suspicions were aroused, and Vokes and his men took up their respective stations, hidden from sight by the darkness of a winter's night.

At about eight o'clock, a low tap at the cottage door, where Vokes was seated alone, aroused him from a short nap he was taking, and having opened it himself, for he had no follower with him, having sent out the proprietor of the hut in order to avoid observation, he ushered in a man in a large horseman's cloak, escorted by a policeman, who withdrew to a far corner, and allowed the magistrate to examine the stranger.

" Why am I brought here ? "

" I'll tell you that," replied the Major, "after having learnt how you fell into the hands of the policeman yonder."

" I came from the farm in the bog. I was sent on a message by the young master, and I'd like to know by what right I have been seized and dragged here, and who are you, who dare to sanction such an outrage on one who has never offended."

" There you mistake, James Mackinespie. You killed Lame Murphy at the fair of Cashel." The man started, and evidently looked round with an idea of escaping.

" And as to myself, I am Tom Vokes."

" The Lord be good to me," cried the now trembling wretch. " The Lord be good to me ; I'm a lost man."

" Not so. Be true to me, and you shall be free before daylight. I'm not looking for you just now."

" May Providence preserve you, Major dear. Sure

I'd give my life for you. Oh, then, spare me, yer honour ; you'll find me true to ye."

" On what message were you sent, and to whom ?"

" To the clergyman, sure."

"And what for ?"

" The divil a one of me knows, then."

" How could you, then, tell him what was wanted ?"

" Ah, then, sir, if you must know——"

" I *will* know," roared Vokes, " or I send you off to Limerick at once."

" Well, then, yer honour, don't do that. Sure the master gave me this bit of a note."

The magistrate snatched it from him, and · tore it open.

" REVD. SIR,—Will you come here as soon as possible, and bring your canonicals and your book of prayer with you ? The bearer (whom you may trust in every way) will guide you. Pray make haste.

" Yours,

" HUGH ——."

" Umph ; the fellow wishes to make my reverend friend believe that it is to shrive some dying penitent. Faith, he's a cute lad, but I'll balk his plans."

" Well, sir, may I go now ? "

" Yes ; to his reverence. I'll accompany you. So come along. Constable, you may return to your post." And away trotted the C. M. P. and the messenger to the clergyman's.

Arrived here, none knew what passed, but the upshot was, that Vokes and the sacred minister shortly after left the house, and directed their steps towards the farm in the bog. The worthy functionary was closely muffled up in Mackinespie's ample cloak.

"Don't look round," said Vokes, as they approached the building, "when I follow you in; they'll take me f r the messenger they despatched."

"True ; but I hardly like the part I have to play. It is scarcely in keeping with my holy calling. I should not lend myself to a deceit."

"Not even to rescue an innocent girl from the clutches of a scoundrel, who must eternally ruin her unless we can now manage to circumvent him ?"

"And the danger ? "

"Oh, there is none to you, and as to me, I laugh at it. Believe me, sir, in thus acting, you do a good and noble deed."

"I hope so," whispered the other, as he knocked at the door.

"Don't forget to make some scruples at first, and then consent."

"I hate deceit !"

"Who's there ?" roared a voice, and a head appeared through the window. "Ah, I perceive it is your Reverence and James ; I could scarcely see you, it was so dark. I'll come down and let you in."

"Now, then, I succeed or die," slowly muttered Vokes.

The next moment they entered. The clergyman went upstairs with young ——. The supposed servant remained behind to fasten the door; how far he did so, the sequel will prove.

After a very short parley, it appeared that the priest consented to perform the ceremony. Two large tapers

were accordingly lighted, and his Reverence put on
his canonicals, and pulled out his book, while the
Bucheen sought the room in which he had imprisoned
his wretched captive, and dragged her out to be married.

In vain she besought him to desist; in vain she
knelt before him. He pulled her hastily and violently along, and seizing her in his powerful grasp, he
placed her before the table on which the volume lay
open; the clergyman stood behind it, and an old bel-
dame rocked herself in a chair, waiting to hear that
ceremony performed, to which she was to act as a
witness.

"Go on!" roared the excited youth. "Go on!"

"We must have a second person to attest the marriage," quietly replied the priest.

"Right, right; I forgot that. Here, Mackinespie,
come here—quick—I want you. Don't wait for anything; come up!" and hearing his supposed follower's
step approaching, he turned to the table.

Another instant, and the almost fainting girl gave a
loud scream, and attempted to dart away. Young
—— turned round. A pistol was presented at his
head, and a firm hand held him by the collar; a loud
whistle, and two men (policemen in plain clothes),
armed with carbine and cutlass, rushed in. In his
terror and surprise the lady escaped from his grasp,
and fled for succour to the priest, who now boldly
joined the intruders, and loudly denounced the wretched
abductor.

The sketch requires little more addition. Long before daylight the honest yeoman's car conveyed the
now happy girl back to her overjoyed parent. The

young man, by the consent of all parties, was sent off to Dublin. The affair was hushed up, and the feelings of all parties thus spared.

Miss —— (after her father's death) went out to India, and married an officer of rank. But she never returned to the county of Limerick, where she had no family ties.

The young Squireen, it is said, entered the Company's military service, and received promotion for some exceedingly gallant actions.

Who can say whether the abductor and abducted may not be the gay and happy couple who, surrounded by several beautiful children, disembarked at Southampton last year, having left Calcutta six weeks before?

Vokes is gone, and so are the parents of the young man. None now can solve the mystery.

270

A DAY IN LIMERICK.

LIMERICK, formerly one of the most beautiful and salubrious cities in Ireland, once the throne of gaiety and delight, can, alas! be no longer quoted as such. Her glories, her charms, exist no longer. Her once brilliant garrison appear to have carried away with them all the proud members of the "right old stock" who made this desirable spot their residence; while, worse than all, her "lovely lasses," the pride of Erin, the envy of the world, have equally disappeared, and their once fairy path in George-street is now usurped and troden by modern upstarts, commercial boors, and dowdy females, while the silvery tones, the bewitching smiles, and perfect forms of her lovely daughters are now replaced by the hooded huxter, and the peripatetic dealer in second-rate *lace*. The names of those who once honoured the Club-house by being members of it, are now superseded by those who could never have anticipated the honour of entering it. In two lines we may describe it by thus paraphrasing a passage in the prologue to Cato—

" A city struggling with the storms of fate,
And gently fallen with a fallen state."

Yes, such is Limerick in 1862. She is now perhaps

the quietest and dullest place throughout the whole of the sister isle. That she may still rank as a well-situated port, that profitable exportation and importa-tion may still be carried on here, I do not for a moment doubt, and that many respectable individuals make fortunes within her boundaries I am free to admit; but he who has known her in her halcyon days will mourn over the seeming blight which has come over her, and breathe a sigh as he vainly tries to discover a trace of those who once kept up her glorious hospitalities.

I am not, however, about to plunge into a lament over her sad change, nor am I capable or desirous of tracing the cause of her decadence; suffice it to say, that she is so changed that I cannot help thinking that the stirring incidents of a day passed in this gay city some thirty-three years ago, cannot be wholly uninteresting to those who now inhabit or feel an interest in her.

In the year 1829 I was seated at breakfast in the large coffee-room of Moriarty's (now Cruise's) Hotel; Vokes had just dropped in, and was chatting with me and discussing the news of the day, when we were joined by Tom Steele*—honest Tom Steele, as his

---

* The unfortunate end of Steele has been too widely chronicled to require repetition. Should there be any one unacquainted with his melancholy fate, it is sufficient to say that, after struggling with neglect and poverty for many years, he was unfortunately in-duced to attempt suicide; and, with this intention, threw himself off Waterloo Bridge. He was, however, rescued from a watery grave, and conveyed to Peele's Coffee-house, where he only lingered a few days. Death thus closed the career of this once celebrated character. He died amidst comparative strangers. But the unre-

countrymen called him, or as he styled himself, the Grand *Pacificator* of Ireland—a title, poor fellow, he endeavoured to earn by using on all occasions, when addressing the lower orders, the most violent lan- guage—language the most naturally suited to arouse this inflammatory people. Tom Steele stood con- siderably above six feet high; he stooped, however, more than any man I ever saw. His slouching gait and swinging arms were most ungainly, while his coarse, sunburnt hands, his shabby habiliments, and his scorbutic face, which might *falsely* have been supposed to have proceeded from drinking, together with a large bunch of soiled green ribbons attached to the breast of his coat, and a pseudo-regimental cap stuck on his head, might well prejudice a stranger against him ; but when once he opened his mouth, his voice was so extraordinarily mellifluous, his smile was so sweet, his manner was so soft and winning, that these feelings of predislike melted before his superior

---

mitting care and attention of those who surrounded his last couch, was gratefully proclaimed by poor Tom in his last moments. Alas ! however ; the painful picture does not end here. For though his remains were borne over to Ireland, and laid (by his own desire) in the cemetery of Glasnevin, within a few yards of those of his adored chief, they have not been allowed to rest there. If we may credit the accounts of a late number of the *Irish Times*, and indeed the facts have been officially admitted, his corpse has been removed from the vault in which he was originally laid, and taken to an- other. The guardians of the burial-ground declare this to have been done because the tomb had become "damp and fallen into decay." The correspondent of the newspaper asserts, that this act of cruel sacrilege was committed because the vault had been recently sold to the present Lord Mayor of Dublin. If the latter statement be correct, it reflects great discredit upon all parties concerned in it.

address—while his extraordinary intelligence, his great knowledge, and, above all, his sincere honesty of purpose, for which, indeed, he had sacrificed his happiness, fortune, station, and we might almost add his religion, so commanded the admiration of all, that Tom, in poverty and trouble, was still respected and liked by his equals, and adored by the peasantry, over whom he had an influence little short of that of the Great Agitator (or as Steele termed him, the Great Liberator,) himself.

Our patriot friend approached us, and handed to me the manuscript of a very clever, though wild article, he had written for me to be inserted in a periodical (*The Limerick Chronicle*) which I had started in that city, and which, by-the-bye, was edited by that very clever member of the Church who lost his high position in consequence of running away with Mrs. P—— C——.

Tom took a cup of coffee with us, and amused us by relating some anecdotes, which he did in a most racy style, though he modulated his voice (as was often the case) to so low a tone that *I* lost much of the wit mingled in their recital.

Presently, the great Dan himself entered, He was to leave some directions with his lieutenant, and at the same time receive the hearty thanks of his follower for having got him out of some pecuniary difficulties on the previous evening. These thanks the great man put off with an affectionate smile, and only expressed a hope that Tom would not get into any more scrapes —a wish, alas! most difficult of accomplishment, since the Pacificator cared for no life but that of struggle— no food, but that of excitement.

18

O'Connell now came across to Vokes, and shook him heartily by the hand, and exhibited by his manner and words not only his sincere friendship for the magistrate as an individual, but his high appreciation of his talents and his services as a public officer. I believe most firmly—I have, indeed, strong proofs—that he held my father-in-law in the very highest rank of his estimation; and none could better judge, since in public matters they were generally opposed.

Ottley now came in, and announced that the carriage was at the door in which he was to travel with his political chief to Dublin. Tom Steele handed O'Connell into his carriage, and then went off to attend a Mass at the Chapell, to be performed for the soul of the late Roman Catholic Bishop of Killaloe, an old friend and ally of his.

When he had left us, I went across with Vokes to his office, where he presented two of his constables with 5l. each, as a reward for their activity in capturing the murderers of Major Hare. I inquired the circumstances. It appeared that the gallant officer, who had served for several years in the Light Dragoons in India, had lately returned to Europe and taken a very nice estate in the county of Limerick, named "Fort Henry." Here, from his justice and kindness, he would doubtlessly have become popular; but unfortunately it became known that he had a large collection of swords and fire-arms within his mansion. This was a booty, of all others, the most coveted by the Whiteboys, and so they determined on seizing them. One night, when the Major had retired to his bed—little suspecting an approaching danger—he was aroused by a loud and violent demand made on him by the leader of a band of insurgents, who vociferously demanded that all the weapons in the house should be delivered up to him. The Major, a man of decided courage, at once refused their request, and most peremptorily desired the fellows—who were dressed in the well-known costume of Whiteboys—instantly to retire. To this, a shot fired at him, and from which he narrowly escaped, was the reply he received. So, arming his servants, he at once proceeded to barricade the windows and doors of the house. But, unhappily, it was too late. The ruffians had burst open the principal entrance, and were now rushing towards the apartment in which poor Hare and his wife slept.

He in vain endeavoured to oppose them. He was at once massacred in the most savage manner. His wife escaped by a mere miracle, and the murderers having rifled the house, retired from the scene of their bloodthirsty exploits, carrying with them all the arms they could find.

After the most strenuous efforts, and under the direction of the active magistrate, the two policemen before us had managed to get a clue whereby they were enabled to trace the culprits; this once gained, they pursued them with unremitting vigilance, and at last managed to seize the ringleader. This effected, many of the others were easily detected, and the most prominent actors in the bloody scene having been captured and legally convicted, were taken out under a strong escort, and executed close to the spot where the outrage had been committed. This unusual measure had been resorted to in the hope of deterring others; but it had

not the desired effect. The Whiteboys still traversed
the county in search of arms. Vokes, however, by his
untiring exertions, at last succeeded in putting them
down; and by his recommendation the present reward
was bestowed on his two Peelers.

The next person to be brought in was one of the
most respectable small farmers in the county. He was
accused of committing a robbery. His friends had
besought Vokes to hear the case in private, as the
publicity would be most disgraceful. The Major, however, turned a deaf ear to their entreaties. His prin-
ciple was, that there was but one law alike for rich
and poor, nobles and peasants; and in accordance with
this fair maxim he ordered the offender to be brought
down into the public office. But when, a few moments
later, a beautiful young woman fell on her knees before him, and assured him in agonizing terms that she
was the wife of the culprit, and that three young babes
would be ruined and disgraced by the exposure; that
even if the case were proved, it would be found that
he had been wickedly led into it in a moment of in-
ebriation; but, above all, that he supported by his own
personal exertions his aged parents—the heart of the
chief magistrate, ever awake to a tale of woe, was
touched, and the young man was privately examined.
What passed I know not; but within half an hour the
supposed culprit was discharged, and his accusation
blotted from the charge-book. He had become so implicated that a less lenient judge than my relative
might have committed him to prison, and perhaps have
destroyed for ever his prospects. But as he had been
rather morally than actually guilty, Vokes had let

him off with a wholesome admonition. The reclaimed young man subsequently became a poor-law officer, and never forgot the lesson of mercy, which from himself he now extended to others around him.

As Vokes had business in the country, I mounted my hack and cantered off to the Newcastle racecourse, hard by, where a match for a large sum was to be contended for. A racer belonging to an officer of the garrison was backed to beat a celebrated hunter, the winner of several similar feats. The military nag was to be ridden by Capt. H. M., the best sporting rider in the county, a gentleman highly and generally esteemed, but a Protestant; the other belonged to Mr. S., a dashing young fellow, careless whether he broke his neck or no, and a decided favourite with all the Catholic party. At this time religious feud ran high, and just as the gallant captain was mounting, he was warned that an effort would be made to throw his horse down on his attempting to leap the third wall, which had been agreed to be four feet high, built of loose stones. The gallant captain (or Widow, as I believe he was usually called), with the true spirit of his countrymen, spurned the notice, and jumping up, away they went. Over the first fence they passed well—nothing impeded their progress; but as the captain gained a little on his opponent the crowd rushed forward, and as Mr. S. came up to the wall, actually pulled it down to let him go over without jumping. And now all eyes were fixed on the result of the last leap; it was too late to interfere, and the spectators looked on in anxious dismay. As they approached it, a shout was heard on the other side—the wicked wretches were already there—

a cheer—a struggle was heard, as they rode up neck and neck—a groan burst involuntarily from many a lip as they together sprang over the bulwark which shut them out from view. For a moment the most fearful doubts were entertained, and we followed them at full speed. But here, all our cares and fears were at once dissipated; there stood both gentlemen besides their animals; Major Vokes was conversing with them, while at about one hundred yards distance stood a body of police, and in their hands a dozen of stout peasants. The whole scene was at once explained. The magistrate, who was aware of all passing, had received information of the intended outrage; without noise or fuss, he had marched a proper force to the spot and arrested the villains who were already awaiting to destroy their victim. Fortunately, however, no harm was done, no overt act was committed, so having shown them they could not break the laws with impunity, the Major at once discharged them, having already established in their hearts a wholsome dread of his prescience and his power.

On my return to the city I found a military band playing in the Crescent, while over the adjacent pavement I saw a galaxy of beauty promenading—a bright bouquet of loveliness, never since surpassed. The beautiful Miss F——s, daughter of a noble house; the Miss B.s, of Clare (nieces of a gentleman afterwards savagely murdered), lovely beyond description; the dashing and admired Miss S. D., the daughter of our general; the pretty Miss S.; pert little Betsy, and fascinating Julia, together with a dozen other girls who could elsewhere have passed for first-rate beauties, and a select knot of some heavenly looking young married women, made up the female characters of the delightful and striking picture ; while a host of dashing young officers and sporting young men from the country paid them well-deserved attentions.

Presently I heard that there was a disturbance taking place at the other end of George-street, so I hastened thither to see what was the matter. The whole town appeared to have assembled here, and loudly screamed forth their anger and annoyance ; while magistrates and policemen hurried backwards and forwards, and every one seemed excited, though few really knew what it was about.

I soon learnt the particulars. It appeared that a society or band of gentlemen, styling themselves "Brunswickers," had assembled to discuss their extreme political views at Swinburn's Hotel—now no longer in existence—and that during the time they were thus debating, some ill-judged member had foolishly indulged in bitter invectives against the liberal party, and spoken harshly of O'Connell. This had been carried out to the party in question, and Tom Steele, as their self-elected leader, had mounted on an empty cart, and was in the act of pouring out the most inflammatory address in terms somewhat treasonable to the Government and the King, mingled with words of the most dire abuse against the whole body of Irish Orangemen, when Capt. J. (the then mayor), followed by only four of his attendants, rushed up and seized the orator, and bore him off. To force him through the crowd to the court-house would have been impossible, so the plucky ex-captain of dragoons contented himself with lodging him safely at Moriarty's Hotel till the arrival of Vokes and his police, or if necessary a military force—for that functionary was in command of the city forces as well as those of the county. This was most fortunate, for I do sincerely believe that the rash act of the daring civic functionary might have ended seriously had not my relative arrived on the spot, and for the second time since the morning poured oil on the raging waters. How the thing was managed I know not, but within an hour afterwards Tom was again haranguing the delighted crowd, in a far less excited tone than he had hitherto used, while throughout his whole speech he never once alluded to his capture. The people had got their pet back again, they cheered loudly, and asked no questions.

At five we had a most excellent dinner, that early hour being fixed upon as one of our garrison theatrical representations were to take place at the theatre. Our corps was most numerous, consisting of some thirty or forty officers, quartered in and about Limerick. Indeed, some came (Lord A. Hill amongst the number) all the way from Cork to share our festivities. Captain Scanlon was my brother manager. Our actresses were professional ladies from Dublin.

During our meal we were disturbed by the entrance of Mr. L——. He came in in great trepidation. Vokes had informed him, in a confidential letter, that a conspiracy had been formed to assassinate him. But as he had a clue to the whole affair, the threatened gentleman need not be alarmed; he was well cared for. My friend the Major was annoyed at the communication being made public, as he declared that such exposures led to fresh crimes, and often defeated the ends of justice.*

My timid friend got rid of, I at once started for the theatre, and certainly I never saw a more brilliant sight. Not having to play in the first piece, I amused myself by looking over the theatre and doing the honours to the company as they arrived. I must confess I felt proud of my position. I was certainly at the head of one of the most elegant specimens of theatrical entertainment I had ever witnessed.

The pit and boxes, beautifully painted and decorated by an officer of the Springers (62nd Foot); the

---

* This does not appear to be the case at the present time, as every threatening letter is published in the newspapers. A few days before the publication of this work at least a dozen appeared in the journals, particularly one stated to have been communicated *by the Government* to Mr. Coates, a gentleman, a land-agent, highly respected in Ireland ; while it was added in the same paragraph, that the authorities had given directions that Mr. Coates should be accompanied and looked after by police, wherever he went, whenever he stirred out. This was followed by the following paragraph, given in the *Irish Times*, of the 26th August, 1862. We give it to show the great change in the system which has taken place within the last twenty years.

"THE ALLEGED WARNING TO MR. COATES.—As already stated in the *Irish Times*, a rumour has been current that Mr. Abraham Coates, of Ballycarbry, agent over the Cliften estates, a few days since received intimation from the Government that his life was in danger, a plot having been formed to take his life. It is further asserted by a local print that the room in Gowran Castle in which Mr. Coates was to sleep on the night of the apprehended attack was marked, arrangements having been made for opening the sash outside ! It is also said the attempt was happily frustrated by the activity of Mr. W. Rowney, S.I., who supplied the information in time to the authorities, which was the means of saving Mr. Coates's life. It is certainly a strange phase of the affair, with such a clue, that the guilty parties were not at once arrested and made amenable to the law."

benches covered with crimson cloth throughout; the drop-scene produced by Captain M—— ; a full military band in the orchestra; a blaze of wax-lights illuminating the lovely girls as they sprang to their places, assisted by well-dressed officers (for uniforms in those days were *really* becoming), while their mature and aristocratic chaperons followed them, led in by men such as Heff and Giles, and others, whose type are, alas! fast passing away. Such a sight was decidedly cheering, and at once called forth the encomiums of the elderly ladies, and the bright smiles which exposed the lovely teeth of the younger portion of the audience.

To describe the performance itself would be a work of supererogation; suffice to say, that it went off most pleasantly, and we all retired well pleased with the result of our exertions, and with smiles started off for the house of one of our best actors, Ralph J——, one of the most strange characters in all Ireland, where we had been invited to supper.

Here we were shown into a small room with an uncarpeted floor. Oaken chairs were placed around a deal table—whether meant as more expressive of a hospitable *board* than any other, I am wholly unable to say.

At one end a large tub of live oysters was placed; at the other, the same fish stewed; on one side was a dish of toasted cheese, on the other a plate of red herrings. In the centre stood, supported by trestles, a small cask of whisky; while on dumb-waiters were to be found hot and cold water, lemons, sugar, enormous tumblers, punch-ladles, and several coopers of delicious claret. A blind piper sat in the corner; one of the Limerick huntsmen waited on us in his scarlet dress, and on every conclusion of an air by the piper, favoured us with a *view halloa !*

Ralph was the best singer, and decidedly one of the most amusing companions that ever was known in Limerick, or indeed I may, I believe, truly say, anywhere else. There was no situation in life that he had not filled, and from choice he always deserted the county when the sporting amusements closed, in order to serve through every phase in life. In every class he had learnt something, he had gleaned some honey, which he brought home to his hive of anecdote, and above all he had learnt how to collect around him the brightest and best spirits of the neighbourhood. Need I, then, add how truly I enjoyed myself, and how reluctantly I was forced to admit that I saw the rays of morning stealing through the shutters? Warmed with good liquor, charmed with good music and racy story—half intoxicated in toasting the healths of my lovely though absent friends—I unwillingly arose from my seat, and once more sought my couch, again to gloat over in mental review the charms of a *then* day in Limerick.

DANGEROUS AFFINITY.

ONE of the most exciting spots, not only to the eye, but to every thrilling sense of a piscatorial sportsman in Ireland, is the "Salmon Leap" at Castle Connell, some eight miles from the City of Limerick. Here the noble Shannon, bordered on either side by ornamental parks, rapidly dashes through its rocky bed, at the rate of eight or ten miles an hour, throwing up its silver spray amidst the sunbeams overhead, which tint them with the sparkling beauties of the most brilliant gems. Fine old trees dip their leaves in the bounding stream, and shed their umbrage over the salmon which here abound. Here, seated at one end of a shallow canoe, fishing-rod in hand, the anxious angler stands at one end of his long punt, intent alone on the pursuit of his game ; while the professional boatman, armed with a pole and paddle, continually uses his every skill and exertion, to guide and steady the frail vessel, which only for a moment left to its own course, would be dashed to pieces on the rocks, or drawn beneath the foaming waters. Thus, then, there is that fair share of danger in the amusement which alone gives zest to sport, which demands that constant care and activity that may fairly be styled the salt of sporting life.*

It was to Castle Connell, then, that I now turned my footsteps, or rather those of my horse, who trotted cheerfully along, enjoying the occasional sharp nip inflicted by the cool breeze of an early day in spring. My tackle had been sent on, also a basket of provisions, as I had promised to visit the old ruins of the castle, battered down by Ireton (I believe) during the Irish invasion, the outward walls of which still, however, tower in solemn grandeur, laughing alike at the blasts of winter and the summer storm, forming one of the most picturesque objects which embellish this truly beautiful spot. Yes, amid these stately ruins, if permitted by the baronet's steward to do so, I was to share my pigeon pie with Lord G——, the most polished and fascinating man of his day, and the no less admired Kate F——, the adored of all adorers—the most perfect specimen of a lovely Irishwoman even that highly favoured nation could boast of having produced. I also made arrangements to dine at a friend's in the neighbourhood and sleep in Castle Connell, as I had made up my mind to attend a horse fair to be held at Bird's Hill next day.

All these plans I carried out to my own entire satisfaction. I had pic-nicked with my noble friend and his charming companion. I had dug up an old ring in the ruins, which I then believed to have once been the property of an Irish chief, but which subsequently

* It was on this spot that the Honourable Mrs. Massey, a few years ago, was drowned, with her servant and boatman, while crossing the river for the purpose of dining with her relative, Sir Hugh D. Massey, of Doonas.

I discovered to be the fraction of an old worn out cart harness. I had sat, or rather stood up, in my canoe for nearly three hours, and with great difficulty (and I must add, with the assistance of my boatman also) hooked, gaffed, and landed, two fine salmon. I had taken a late dinner with my country friend, and now had returned to my little modest hostel. I had grasped my night candle with the intention of retiring to bed, when I was startled by the sound of the ap- proaching steps of a horse. These ceased at the door of my hotel, and presently I heard some one enter.

The next moment, in marched my worthy father-in- law.

"Good gracious!" cried I; "what could have in- duced you to ride down here alone at such an hour?"

"I wanted to see you."

"Indeed! But why come down unaccompanied?"

"I was safer alone. There's a nasty, long lane, with a dead wall fencing, in Lord Clare's park. If they knew I was coming, even with an escort, our numbers couldn't save us. They could easily destroy us; and so I sent a patrol out, on the Clare road, to mislead them, and then rode down here by myself to see you."

"But why?"

"I'll tell you. You must not go to Bird's Hill fair to-morrow."

"Indeed! May I ask the reason?"

"Because, if you do, you'll probably be shot."

"And why?"

"Ah, now, why are you so opaque?"

"I never injured any one. I never interfere in religion, or politics. Why, then, should they shoot me?"

"Simply because you are my son-in-law."

"Bless me! that's very disagreeable; I never thought of that."

"And now, my dear Henry, let me give you another little bit of advice. You are really very foolish. I saw you through this open window all the way as I came through the village. You really should shut the shutters."

"Again, may I ask why?"

"Simply on account of the danger of being shot as you sit in your chair."

"You must be joking. Why should the quiet inha bitants of this peaceable hamlet wish to destroy me?"

"Merely for the simple reason that I afforded you just now."

"Upon my life!" muttered I; "I never before had any idea of the pleasing privileges attached to the honour of being wedded to the daughter of a police magistrate."

"What do you mean?"

"Not that I regret; on the contrary, I glory in being the happy husband of your lovely and excellent daugh-ter. But, upon my honour, I have not the slightest wish to claim a pistol-ball as her dower!"

"*Nabochlish a vich!* Every bullet has its billet, and we shall yet die snugly in our beds. But I must be off again."

"What, alone?"

"Decidedly."

"Decidedly *not*," said I. "I accompany you back, or you don't stir."

The magistrate remonstrated, but in vain; and away we went together—the bargain being duly made between us. The terms were these : on condition that I gave up the fair at Bird's Hill, Vokes was good enough to allow me to escort him home. Perhaps for the benefit of both parties, the agreement was carried out.

THE SHERIFF'S SEIZURE.

Vokes and I were travelling between Nenagh and Maryborough, when who should step into the night mail but Mr. ——, the sub-sheriff of Queen's County, a gentleman for whom the Major had a very high respect, one who, though young, had on more than one occasion caused the law to be respected during the short period he had been in office. The usual greetings over, my relative asked him, as a matter of conversation, what he was doing in that part of the country.

"I've just escaped from a somewhat perilous position."

"Indeed; were you attacked?"

"Far from it; it was a danger of my own seeking —a danger I incurred through ignorance on my part, and ill-timed zeal on the part of my assistant, who has just been carried off to hospital."

"Oh, pray tell us all about it," said I; "do tell us. It will wile away the night hours." Vokes backed up my request, and our official friend at once assented, and thus began :—

"You may have heard of Captain H——, usually styled 'the Recluse of the Mountain.' If you have ever read the celebrated memoirs of Sir J. B.——, you

19

will be able to judge of this strange being from an anecdote which that well-known writer relates of him."

We pleaded ignorance of the allusion, and asked the present narrator to supply it. He thus gave it :—

"Captain H——, disgusted with society, or for other reasons, chose, some years ago, to retire from the busy world and take up his residence on the summit of a very high mountain which divides the Queen's County from that of Tipperary. Here he had a snug, but isolated, residence built. And here,

"The world forgetting, by the world forgot,"

he amused himself with agriculture and the sports of the field, seldom or never straying beyond the limits of his mountain throne.

"A near relative of the popular Irish author, it appears, had a strange desire to shoot grouse on the aerial estate of the recluse, and with this object wrote to him, requesting permission to do so. As might reasonably have been expected, no reply was vouchsafed to his missive ; so one fine morning, without further ceremony, the proposed sportsman ascended the almost inaccessible height, and began to pepper away amongst the birds. The report of his fowling-piece aroused the "man of the mountain," who, in dire anger, jumped out of bed, and in a few minutes confronted the intruder.

"The greater number of our sex would have felt alarmed by the appearance of the misanthrope. He was above six feet two in height, and very powerful in proportion. His eyes glared wildly, and his right fist was clasped in passion—his left hand carried a gun —his whole appearance denoted violent anger.

"'What are you doing here, sir?' roared he in stentorian tones. 'What are you doing here?'

"'I came to enjoy a day's sport.'

"'And who the deuce gave you leave to do so?'

· "'I came without.'

"'How dare you poach on my property? I'll teach you better manners. Ah! there is your dog making .a point. By Heaven! if you don't instantly call him off, I'll shoot him!'

"'If you do so, I'll shoot you!'

"'Will you, indeed? Then here goes!' and he instantly pointed his gun, and the next moment the poor animal (a valuable one) rolled over severely wounded.

"'I never break my word,' calmly retorted the sportsman, and in another moment he had lodged a full charge of shot in the left arm and in the side of Capt. H——.

"Wounded and in pain, the now infuriated recluse sprang upon his antagonist, and a hand-to-hand conflict took place, during which the proprietor of the dog got a most severe mauling; indeed, I cannot now remember whether they did not both use their second barrels, and I believe with painful effect on the captain. But be that as it may, the lord of the rocky soil, maimed as he was, seized the plucky poacher in his arms and bore him down to Durrow, a village three miles off, and there left Mr. B. in charge of the local magistrate. Such is the sketch given by Sir J. B——, if my memory does not fail me.

"And was no notice taken of it?" asked I.

"None. In that part of the country it was looked upon as a fair (though strange) duel, and the unlucky grouse-shooter, instead of being pitied, was only congratulated on his miraculous escape from the most dreaded character in the whole county."

"He must, indeed, have been fear-inspiring."

"Aye, and if I am rightly informed, he has proved his prowess even since the event I have spoken of, by beating off, single-handed, ten or a dozen Whiteboys who came to seek for arms, and after killing one, and wounding several of them, he, alone and unaided, dragged into the nearest town the chief of the band, a man celebrated for his athletic powers, and lodged the fellow in the county gaol, although nothing would afterwards induce him to take the trouble of appearing against him."

"I have heard of the occurrence," chimed in Vokes; "but what has this to do with your present visit?"

"Everything! It unfortunately happened that the very first execution put into my hands was one against the 'Recluse of the Mountain.' As is usual in treating with a gentleman, I wrote to him in the first instance, and informed him of the unpleasant duty that had been thrust on me. He took no notice of my letter. I then made application for payment in a more peremptory tone. He now answered, and set me at defiance: 'He had not got the money; and if he had he would not pay it—he equally laughed at the law herself and her base myrmidons.' One only course remained open to me; I at once determined on personally serving him with the document, and, if possible, seizing his goods, for, to tell you the truth, I had no anxiety whatever to meddle with his person.

" On a former occasion, when danger had threatened us, my Irish assistant had run away and left me ; so on the present I picked out a sturdy old English pensioner named Hoskins, whose bull-dog courage nothing could overcome.

"Accompanied by my aid, I quietly, and without mentioning my intention to anyone, came down to this neighbourhood, and having slept at the house of a friend, I left at daybreak under some fanciful excuse, and with Hoskins trudged up the mountain.

"Although we arrived early at our destination, the bird had already flown. The house was perfectly empty ; but we were amply consoled for this circumstance by seeing some twenty or thirty fine cows grazing on the land around the cottage ; these would indeed repay us for our trouble, and satisfy the claim we came to enforce. Our only chagrin was that we had not brought proper drivers with us in order at once to remove them, and we were actually debating whether we should not return and obtain this necessary assistance previous to making our seizure, when several countrymen approached us. These men we thought might easily be tempted to turn drovers for the nonce—a proceeding which would not only save time, but money ; so we at once addressed ourselves to them. To our consternation we discovered that these mountaineers did not speak a word of English, and, alas ! we were equally ignorant of Irish ; so we tried as well as we could to make them understand our wishes by signs. They also plunged into personal hieroglyphics, but neither side could convey their meaning to the other, while both seemed irritated at the supposed stupidity of the opposite party. An old woman was dragged forward, but her attempt at our language was decidedly Gaelic ; an old man present, I believe, from the few words he uttered, could speak English tolerably well, but he was stone deaf; and though he could occasionally convey to us his meaning, in spite of a fearful stammer, he could not hear a single word we said. So we somewhat cavalierly dismissed him to the shades below.

" Matters now began to grow serious ; we had tasted no food, and like all hungry men, felt cross. The peasants roared and bawled at us, making signs first at the cows and then at themselves, which we interpreted to mean that they desired to take charge of the animals for us, and to this proposition we nodded an assent. But still they did not appear content, and as their number was now considerable, I thought it better to proceed to business at once, and so told Hoskins. He quite agreed with me, and stepped across to make the first seizure. In conformity with the rule, he first produced his authority, and then proceeded to lay hold of one of the cows. No sooner had he done this, than he was levelled by a blow from a stout bludgeon, while a general cheer of approbation, and a contraction of the circle which surrounded me, showed me that I must now be prepared for the worst. I felt in my pocket for a small pistol I always carried about me, and had just made up my mind to sell my life dearly, when I heard a loud shouting in the distance, and saw a towering figure on horse-

back galloping at full speed towards me, roaring to
the peasants in Irish, at least so I supposed, to desist.
There was a lull for a moment, and he dashed in
amongst us, and jumped from his horse.

"'Who the devil are you, sir?' was his courteous
way of questioning me.

"'I am the sub-sheriff of this county.'

"'What did you come here to do?'

"'To execute the law! Here is my authority.'

"No sooner did the excited bystanders see the document, than they again pressed forward; the captain, for
now I felt certain it was he, waved them back with
some difficulty.

"'And what did you hope to do?'

"'I have already seized all the cattle around, and
only await proper drivers to convey them away. In
the execution of his duty, my assistant has been struck
and injured by these uncouth savages. But they shall
pay dearly for it.'

"'Fool that you are! It is lucky they don't understand you. It is you that are acting illegally. Know
to your cost that not one of those animals belongs to
me. Though they graze here, they are *bonâ fide* the
property of these men. You must instantly give them
up.'

"'I shall not do so willingly, even though it cost me
my life, till you give me security for your debt.'

"'Well,' returned the recluse, 'you are brave even
to rashness, almost to fool-hardihood. But I admire
courage; it's the only thing I worship. A man of
your spirit must not be wantonly sacrificed. Come,'
said he, dragging me in; 'come in, and I'll try and

satisfy you.' He then turned to the excited bystanders, and apparently begged of them to be patient
for a few minutes.

" In the meantime he led me into what he styled his
parlour, I should have described it as his armoury,
where weapons of every kind were neatly displayed,
intermingled with every sort of fishing-rod, saddle,
bridle, and cudgel, that I believe ever had been in-
vented.

" ' And now, sir, what do you want ?'

" ' Money.'

" ' I have none. But as I never broke my word in
my life, will you take my promissory notes for
the amount payable in four, eight, and twelve
months ?'

" ' I will,' unhesitatingly replied I. ' I thus make
myself personally responsible for the debt ; but from
what I've seen of you, I have no fear of your mislead-
ing me.'

" ' I never deceived the man that trusted me in my
life. As an official, you may perhaps happen to have
some stamps about you ?'

" ' I have.'

' " Give them to me !' He filled them up, and returned them. ' Will they do ?'

" ' Perfectly. Good-bye ;' and I rose to depart.

" ' Not so,' cried the captain, laughing ; ' only leave
this room without me, show yourself alone, and you
are a dead man.'

" I started at the announcement.

" ' I'll soon settle this,' added he, and he went out
with me and addressed the people, while I endeavoured

to express to them that I had no claims on their cattle. The men seemed somewhat disappointed at losing their chance of skinning me, and turned sullenly away. I pointed out to my *now* good friend (for indeed he had proved himself such) the prostrate form of my assistant. He instantly ordered two of the fellows to lift him up, and carry him down the mountain; all, however, refused. In an instant, the captain's eyes flashed fire, and the man he addressed fell stunned beneath the weight of his heavy hand. The other instantly sprang towards the injured Englishman, and, with the help of a comrade, lifted him up, and, in company with the captain and myself, bore him down to the village.

"I would fain have spared H—— the trouble of accompanying me, but he assured me it was absolutely necessary.

"When he parted from me he extended his hand, and taking my comparatively diminutive member in his powerful grasp, he thus addressed me :—' Good-bye, sheriff; you are a plucky little fellow—your courage saved you; but never try such an experiment again. If tired of life at any time, and you desire to avoid self-destruction, return to this mountain and make yourself known. You will cease to exist in five minutes. I have saved you once. I have not influence to save you a second time, so pray to the Lord never again to see, ' the Recluse of the Mountain.'

" He then left me, and I remained at the inn (having seen poor Hoskins well stowed away in the hospital) till this carriage, in which I propose to travel to Dublin, passed. I have fortunately found pleasant companions, and thank you for listening to my long tale."

We soon arrived, and got out.   But afterwards, when quartered in the Irish capital, I met the worthy sub-sheriff, who assured me that the bills he had taken from the "Hermit Captain" had each been duly honoured and paid to the moment.

FINAL WORD ON IRELAND.

OF all the revolutions which have taken place within the memory of man, none can exceed the bloodless revolution which within the last quarter of a century has changed the social condition of Ireland —the habits of her people. The same fertile soil, the same splendid scenery, the same natural advantages of lake, river, and forest, still, and must ever exist, but her people are no longer the people of whose reckless bravery, and improvident hospitality we read in works written some thirty years ago. They are no longer the impulsive, witty, hard-drinking, rollicking boys of Charles Lever's pages. By slow, but sure degrees, they have undergone a change like that of the chrysalis grub, as it shakes off its ignoble form and soars a brilliant butterfly. By this comparison, however, I do not intend to convey the idea of the vast superiority in every respect which the modern Irishman may now boast over his progenitor; for although in many instances his character has much improved, there are certain points which in thus rendering him more prudent, more sober, and more frugal, have altogether cooled that warmth of

heart which once formed the amiable weakness of
Erin's children.

Our sketches may perhaps seem designed as an exagge-
rated illustration of the bloodthirsty propensities which
once led the Irish peasantry into crime, and disgraced
by its atrocity this lovely island, and, indeed, they rather
pourtray these than affect to be a personal memoir. But
we beg to assure our readers that we have in many
instances, particularly in those of Major Going, Blood,
Hoskins, and a host of others, avoided bringing into pro-
minence many of the most savage murders which took
place at the period when this little work is supposed
to chronicle the stirring incidents which occurred in
the South of Ireland.

A check was decidedly put on these fear-inspiring
acts, the organization of crime was almost entirely destroyed, the links of horror were broken, in no small
degree by T. P. Vokes, aided by the intelligent co-ope-
ration of his brother magistrates, acting unanimously
on a system laid down and carried out during a series of
years by the chief magistrate of police. I have therefore thought it but fair, now, when crime again raises
her head, and assassination immolates her victims in
broad daylight, to recount some of those means which
at a former period threw a protecting shield over the
landowner, and carried terror to the bosom of the
murder-seeking tenant.

The fearful deeds which were then enacted most
generally arose from differences in religious creed or
political action. The Catholic, still under penalties
which bound him down by unfair fetters, and deprived
him of all right to worship his Creator in his own way,

was an ever ready subject of discontent; while the manifest difference between the laws introduced to propitiate the English, and to grind down the Irish (at least so they were taught by interested demagogues), still further irritated the then impetuous peasantry of Ireland.

In the days I speak of, the kind-hearted landed gentry of the sister country knew no bounds to their hospitality and expenditure. It is true that they seldom received any rent, but they seldom asked for it. Meat was reared on their lands. Every article of life was prepared on their estate. Whisky was distilled in their mountain fastnesses, and woe betide the lawyer or the bailiff, even when supported by the posse of the sheriff, or a troop of dragoons, who dared to attack the lord of the soil. The castle doors were closed. Every tenant mounted guard, and the besiegers were fain to return as they came; though the commanders—both military and civil—often returned to dine with the "jolly defaulter," who loved them as guests beneath his roof—who laughed them to scorn as besiegers before his walls. Yes, such were the manners of the olden time—the halcyon days of Ireland. The county member could always give you twenty good horses, and a dozen postboys, to draw you from his seat, to the seat of Government. But he could seldom lend you 5l. to pay for your place inside the mail coach. A cask of claret, or of whisky, has often been tapped on the dinner table, when the neighbouring grocer refused to give tick for a bottle of ginger wine. *Troja fuit*—Ireland *was!*

But how different *now* is the state of the sister isle. Causes and effects have completely changed her. Her peasantry and her landholders have equally shared in this wonderful transformation—a transformation so general that I will defy any one now to find a single member of the old stock left. FATHER MATHEW compelled, by his eloquent reasoning, the lower classes to become sober. The ENCUMBERED ESTATE ACT compelled by its enactments the gentry to be prudent. And in both cases, as in every newly-inducted fashion, the disciples have decidedly gone far beyond the most sanguine anticipations of the original intention.

Wit and jollity were banished from amidst the lower classes by the moral preacher. Hospitality and generosity have fled before the Act of Parliament.

The consequences of this strange and sudden revolution should, and will, decidedly bring prosperity to the Green Island. The higher orders, who have not had their estates sold in spite of their wish, reside, generally speaking, on their lands, and do much good by their presence. The commercial community are decidedly extending their adventures; and many, many men may be now seen moving in Dublin society, or ruling the monetary transactions of the Irish capital by their great wealth, who entered that city some five-and-twenty years previously little better than paupers. Building houses, and purchasing lands, forming banks, and carrying out stockbroking operations, railway contracts, and cattle dealing—have all, and every one, created capital, and transformed many very poor men into merchant princes—humble shopkeepers into frequenters of the Viceregal Court.

Nor has the change been less marked amidst the labouring population of the country. A difference of religious creed is no longer a bar to friendship. The Catholic and the Protestant now boast equal laws and privileges. The priesthood of the former church, now highly educated in colleges, feel that they have a stake in the country, and an interest, human and divine, in preserving peace amongst all Christians. The consequence is obvious. Religious assassination, once so prevalent, is now unheard of, while daily assimilating laws (assimilating with those of Great Britain) and relief from heavy taxation, have drawn out that bitter sting which parties opposed in politics, once loved to inflict on each other.

The dirty mud cabin is quietly giving way to the small whitewashed farm. The dunghill has been removed from the front door, to the rear. The smoke goes up a well-formed chimney, and the pigs and poultry are gradually being banished from the inside of the house. The daily meal amongst the labouring classes is still potatoes—nothing but potatoes—but they are eaten with calm content, and crowned by the luxury of a pipe. The tiller of the soil is allowed a proper period thus to partake with his family of his homely food, and at night he now returns to his more comfortable cottage, rather than create a riot in the neighbouring *shabeen,* or plot murders, and indulge in irritating argument beside the smithy's brilliant fire as in former years.

The money of the small farmer, once spent on whisky, or shared amongst convivial comrades, is now hoarded up, and it would indeed be a useless task in the present day to attempt to coax a well-to-do agriculturist out of his cash. He lives frugally—he drinks

water—he works hard, and he now places in a bank
(an establishment he formerly abhorred) the hard
earnings which have rewarded his toil.

Such is Ireland in 1862. A happy state, that she is
likely yearly to improve, unless she once more gives
way to crime. Unfortunately, however, the most
cruel and wanton murders have lately stained her soil.
Unmanly threats have been used, and the firm basis
of social comfort between landlord and tenant shaken
by agrarian outrage.

Experienced and well-trained magistrates were never
more earnestly required than they are at this instant.
The efficiency (or otherwise) of the present police
system should be inquired into. Nearly 13,000 in
number, largely officered, presided over by some 200
or 300 stipendiary magistrates, with salaries varying
from 300*l.* to 500*l.* a-year, with a staff of clerks in
Dublin Castle, and a large barrack, with an adjutant,
officers, and a military chief, in the Phœnix Park—
surely this force should be sufficient to put down
murder and outrage. Ireland, thus filled with an
especial body, in addition to her vast army, should be
kept in such a peaceful state, that crime, affrighted
by the fears of detection and punishment, would fly
from Ireland for ever. I have therefore published the
foregoing sketches of one, the recollection of whose
untiring and efficient zeal may yet stir up the emu-
lation of the present police force, and in that hope I
have thrown them loosely off, without regard to literary
fame. One or two of them have already appeared in a
popular periodical ; but with these exceptions, they are
before the public for the first time, and touch rather

upon the less-canvassed incidents which occurred in the South of Ireland, than the more glaring ones made public by every newspaper in the United Kingdom— a roll of bloody deeds more fitting for the pages of a new edition of the "Newgate Calendar," than those of a mere railway volume.

THE END.

www.ingramcontent.com/pod-product-compliance
Lightning Source LLC
Chambersburg PA
CBHW031358270326
41929CB00010BA/1232